WRITING TECHNOLOGY:

STUDIES ON THE MATERIALITY OF LITERACY

WRITING TECHNOLOGY:

STUDIES ON THE
MATERIALITY OF LITERACY

CHRISTINA HAAS
THE PENNSYLVANIA STATE UNIVERSITY

 LAWRENCE ERLBAUM ASSOCIATES, PUBLISHERS

1996   Mahwah, New Jersey

Lawrence Erlbaum Associates, Inc., Publishers
10 Industrial Avenue
Mahwah, New Jersey 07430

Library of Congress Cataloging-in-Publication Data

Haas, Christina.
Writing technology : studies on the materiality of literacy /
Christina Haas.
p.   cm.
Includes bibliographical references and index.
ISBN 0-8058-1306-3 (cloth). — ISBN 0-8058-1994-0 (paper)
1. Writing—Social aspects.   2. Writing—Psychological aspects.
3. Authorship.   4. Word processing—Social aspects.   5. Word
processing—psychological aspects.   I. Title.
Z40.H325   1996
652—dc20   95-10138
                                                                CIP

Books published by Lawrence Erlbaum Associates are printed on
acid-free paper, and their bindings are chosen for strength and durability.

Printed in the United States of America
10 9 8 7 6 5 4 3 2 1

This book is dedicated to my father

Franklin Charles Haas

and to the memory of

Richard C. Deus

1915-1982

CONTENTS

PREFACE

For over a decade, academic and practitioner journals in electronics, business, language studies, as well as the popular press, have been proclaiming the arrival of the "computer revolution" and making far-reaching claims about the impact of computers on modern Western culture. Although the actual technology identified as a revolutionary force may have changed—from word processing in the late 1970s to electronic mail (e-mail) and hypertext in the 1980s to the InterNet as "information highway" in the 1990s—in most cases it is a technology of words, a technology that changes how written language is produced, processed, transported, and used. Implicit in many arguments about the revolutionary power of computers is the assumption that communication, language, and words are intimately tied to culture—that computers' transformation of communication means a transformation, or a revolutionizing, of culture. Although the term "revolution" may be hyperbolic, anyone whose own patterns of reading and writing have been "electronicized" over the last decade can attest to the sense of change in the character or even quality of written communication as the material circumstances of writing changed: As carbon paper gave way to photocopy machines; correction fluid and retyping gave way to word processors; memos and hallway gossip gave way (at least partially) to e-mail and bulletin boards; and searching (often in vain) through seldom-used library stacks gave way to on-line databases and the InterNet.

But moving from a vague sense that writing is profoundly different with different material and technological tools to an understanding of how such tools can and will change writing, writers, written forms, and writing's functions is not a simple matter. Further, the question of whether, and how, changes in individuals' writing experiences with new technologies translate into large-scale, cultural "revolutions" remains unresolved. The challenge of accounting for the relationship between writing—as both a cognitive process and a cultural practice to the material technologies that support and constrain it is great. I call it "The Technology Question," and I treat this question in more detail in chapter 1.

There are a number of difficulties inherent in addressing the Technology Question—that is, attempting to account for the symbiotic relationship between writing and technology. These difficulties arise for a number of reasons, not the least of which is that writing and technology are each, in their own right, highly elaborate and rapidly changing systems. Much remains to be understood about the complex set of activities called writing, including the ways that writing systems are developed and used; how individuals master, albeit incompletely, the writing systems of their cultures and how social patterns support or constrain the mastery and use of various writing systems. However, most literacy scholars would acknowledge that writing is a cognitively and culturally advanced, highly sophisticated, and complex human act. Culturally, writing takes myriad forms in modern societies, functioning in vital but vastly different ways in the spheres of economics and business, education, family and community. Over the past two decades, scholars of writing have articulated some of these cultural forms and social functions of writing and of written texts (e.g., Bazerman, 1988; Fish, 1980; Heath, 1983; Radway, 1984; Scribner, 1984).

At the same time, other scholars have documented the complexity of the writing process itself (e.g., Flower & Hayes, 1981a, 1981b; Bereiter & Scardamalia, 1987; Geisler, 1994), establishing that even the most straightforward of textual genres requires of the writer a store of relevant content and process knowledge; an ability to sustain not only the planning of the text but the complex physical and cognitive execution of text production; and the rhetorical wherewithal to consciously consider and act on relevant features of the discourse situation. More sophisticated textual genres, such as written argument, add to both the cognitive and the social complexity of writing. Further, when writers work together, as often happens in real-world writing beyond the classroom, the difficulties and complications of creating and using written texts are multiplied.

To say that questions of technology further complicate writing is, in one sense, accurate. Certainly an array of new computer-based literacy tools are available for writers today (e.g., word processors, hypertext authoring software, on-line information systems, e–mail, talk programs, etc.). Each of these highly advanced technologies augments in particular ways written texts and the social and cognitive processes by which they are produced.

But to see technology as something that is added to writing in certain situations is to misunderstand the essential relationship between writing and technology, and this misunderstanding adds to the difficulty of addressing the Technology Question. Technology and writing are not distinct phenomena; that is, writing has never been and cannot be separate from technology. Whether it is the stylus of the ancients, the pen and ink of the medieval scribe, a toddler's fat crayons, or a new Powerbook, technology makes writing possible. To go further, writing *is* technology, for without the crayon or the stylus or the Powerbook, writing simply is not writing. Technology has always been implicated in writing: In a very real way, verbal behavior without technological tools is not, and cannot be, writing.

Such a statement—that writing is impossible without the tools of writing—seems too obvious to need much explication. Yet it is precisely because technology is such an integral part of writing that it is often overlooked. As is often the case, what is ubiquitous becomes transparent: Writers do not notice most of the technologies they employ, simply because those technologies are always there, the technologies work, and their use has become habitual. Writers also tend not to notice the pen with which they jot notes—that is, unless it is out of ink, or unless a pencil was intended instead. Readers do not "see" the typeface of a text unless it is unusual or poor. Today, the personal computer is so much a part of writing that writers do not think about how it works, how it looks, or where it comes from: Its use has become habitual, and the technology itself—like pens, paper, typewriters, and maybe even clay tablets—has become virtually transparent.

This transparency is all to the good for writers: Writing would be inefficient and almost prohibitively difficult if writers had to constantly and consciously attend to their writing tools. Imagine using a pencil in which the lead broke every fourth or fifth word, or imagine learning a new word processing program each time you sat down to create a document. Writers value their technologies precisely because, through use, these technologies become transparent.

Much of what is written about technology—in both the popular and the scholarly presses—is built upon this notion of transparency: The tendency is to look through computer technology to the economic, practical, political, or pedagogical goals that the technology might serve. ("Technological transparency" is examined in more detail in chapters 2 and 8 of this volume.) This pragmatic approach is sensible enough—after all, there is a lot of work to do in the world—but looking through technology is not likely to lead to a grounded understanding of the technology itself, and the role of changing technologies in literate behavior. Further, expectations about the purposes that computers can and will serve are best based on a thorough understanding of the nature of technology generally, as well as of particular computer systems. In short, the images seen by looking *through* technology may be distorted without looking *at* the technology itself in a systematic way.

Similarly, it is precisely because writing and technology are so closely tied that technology questions are often overlooked within literacy studies, despite the fact that technological questions consume an inordinate amount of attention in the culture at large. As is discuss in chapter 3 (this volume), most theoretical accounts of writing treat technology in a cursory way, or ignore it altogether. In so doing, theories of writing implicitly claim that writing is writing is writing, regardless of the technologies used. No one would claim that writing with a stick in the sand is the same act as writing on a modern word processor, yet theories of writing, in ignoring the Technology Question, are making just such a claim, albeit implicitly.

For scholars, transparency, like common sense, is, or should be, suspect. Just as the commonsense idea often masks complex ideological beliefs, so the transparency of technology obscures the profound connection between writing and the technologies that support it. Throughout this volume, I try to work against the notion of the transparency of writing technologies. I argue that the technology itself is vitally important and that one should look at, as well as through, the technologies of writing, if one is to fully understand, and ultimately wisely use, the technologies of writing.

Closely related to the transparency issue is the question of how *technology* is defined. It may be obvious to readers at this point that by *technology* I mean something more than a machine on a desk. The primary focus of this book is technologies of literacy, particularly computers. However, a computer is best understood—as is any technology—as a complex of objects, actions, people, motives, and uses. A technology is not an object, but rather a vital system that is bound to the world of time and space; that is, a technology is always inextricably tied both to a particular moment in human history and to the practical action of the human life world in which it is embedded.

This book examines how writing and technology constitute one another. The title, *Writing Technology*, is intended to be read in both senses—as the noun technology modified by the adjective writing, and as an active verb (*writing*) and its object (*technology*). The goal here is to systematically examine the relationship between writing and technology in some detail. The subject of this book is how technology supports writing, but discussion is not limited to the particular instance (i.e., computers) in which the two concepts are convention-ally thought to intersect. Rather, I suggest that technology and writing are inextricably linked—indeed, that imagining writing without technology is both practically impossible and theoretically nonsensical. However, in claiming that technology and writing are inextricably linked, I avoid a simple technological determinism by examining the histories of technology (see chapters 6 and 8 of this volume.)

Part 1 examines the larger theoretical, historical, and disciplinary contexts of writing technology. Specifically, chapter 1, "The Technology Question," argues that writing is inherently technological and examines the relationship between writing and its material tools. Material tools, and technological changes in those tools, have the potential to transform the act of writing; the behavior of writers; the form and structures of written textual genres; and the uses, functions, and significance of writing within cultures. Given the complexities both of writing, which is at once an individual act and a cultural practice, and of the material-cultural systems of technology, it remains far from clear how, when, and in what manner the technological transformation of writing will come about. Further, chapter 1 discusses how the theoretical work of Lev Vygotsky can help articulate the role of material tools in the process and practice of writing. Such an articulation is vital for understanding, explaining, and ultimately using the power of technology.

The need for a multidisciplinary study of technology and literacy, the impediments that stand in the way of such a study, and possible theoretical grounds for it are discussed in chapter 2. The insights of literacy scholars—about the nature, history, and uses of writing—will be invaluable, both in explaining and shaping the new forms of writing that will be an important part of Technology Studies. However, cultural myths about technology and a lack of theoretical grounding provide serious impediments to the conduct of inquiry about technology and literacy. At the end of chapter 2, I examine a range of theories—including cognitive theory, classical rhetorical theory, postmodern theory, and theories of embodied practice—and suggest their usefulness in exploring the relationship between writing and its technologies.

In the studies contained in the remainder of the book, I make two major claims about the relationship between writing and technology: Cultural tools and cognitive activity constitute one another in a symbiotic relationship, and this symbiotic relationship is based in the embodied actions of human beings. Because these claims attempt to link questions of mind to questions of culture, a range of methodologies are employed in order to move the focus of examination along a continuum of detailed studies of individuals to larger cultural studies of power and ideology. These methodologies included the analysis of think-aloud protocols (chapter 4); detailed examination of writers' behavior in videotaped writing sessions (chapter 5); textual analysis of written artifacts produced with pen and paper and with computers (chapter 4); quasiexperimental methods and statistical analysis (chapter 3); interviews of computer writers (chapters 3 and 5); feature analysis of computer systems (chapter 3); rhetorical analysis of influential texts about technology (chapter 7); and a longitudinal participant-observer study (chapter 6).

The studies presented in Part 2 of this volume examine the effects of cultural tools on the thinking processes of adult writers. In chapter 3, I find important differences in readers' performance when they read from paper, from standard computer screen, and from advanced computer systems. I trace these differences to a set of factors, including size of the text, legibility and responsiveness of the writing system, and tangibility of tool and text. Chapter 4 examines the ways that computer-based word processing tools impact on writers' planning processes. I see the results of the study presented in this chapter—which show that different writing technologies can support very different mental processes—as a strong counter to the notion of technological transparency. The physical interactions of writers with their texts is the focus of chapter 5, which details how materially different conditions can lead to different mental representations of text. I call writers' representations or understandings of their own documents "a sense of the text;" this text sense is intrinsically tied to material tools and the physical interactions those tools support or require.

Part 3 examines how cultural tools and their uses and meanings are constructed. Chapter 6 examines the development of computer literacy tools and traces the evolution of one educational computing system over time, arguing that system design is shaped by the theories, activities, and power relations of its developers. Chapter 7 is a detailed rhetorical analysis of the underlying assumptions about technology that guide research, theorizing, and teaching writing within English Studies. These assumptions about technology in effect determine how literacy technologies are constructed and, consequently, how they are used.

The two chapters that comprise Part 4 (chapters 8 and 9) provide the book's conclusion. Chapter 8, "Historicizing Technology," argues that the much-touted computer revolution is not a done deal, and, in fact, that computers' transformation of human communication may have hardly begun. If there is anything to learn from the history of literacy, it is that the changes in writing that technologies facilitate will not be simple, easy to predict, rapid, or unitary. Therefore, I argue, an historical grounding for technology studies must go beyond the construction of historical analogies. The final chapter, "Theorizing Technology" (9), addresses this question: How is it possible that material technologies, implements, and artifacts can alter and shape the mental processes by which writing occurs? I argue in this final chapter that seeing writing as an embodied practice, a practice based in culture, in mind, and in body, can help to answer the Technology Question. Indeed, the notion of *embodiment* can provide a necessary corrective to accounts of writing that emphasize the cultural at the expense of the cognitive, or that focus on writing as only an act of mind. Questions of technology always and inescapably return to the material, embodied reality of literate practice. Further, because technologies are at once tools for individual use and culturally constructed systems, the study of technology can provide a fertile site in which to examine the larger issue of the relationship between culture and cognition.

ACKNOWLEDGEMENTS

As often happens when one finds work one loves, the distinction between my personal debts and my intellectual ones is blurred. Many, many people showed their affection for me through their support of this work, and many others supported the work by sustaining me. My family of origin continues to be a bulwark of strength and solace, and I could not have completed this work without their love. My daughters—Luisa and Augusta Funk—are studies in strength, determination, and force of will, and there were many days when I looked to them for example. They also provided hugs at critical times. I also thank Dawn Bark, as well as Sandra Gordon and her staff, for the unwavering support they have provided to my family; their efforts continue to allow me to manage a life of work and family on a day-to-day basis.

My friends have contributed to this work through their support and interest. I am particularly endebted to Cheryl Geisler, Jennie Nelson, Robin Becker, Rosa Eberly, Steve Kruse, Hilary Masters, and Nancy Penrose for their friendship. The very notion of this book was probably Cheryl's as much as it was mine, and many, many conversations with her—over conference hotel breakfasts or stolen in those rare moments when our (combined) four children were somehow not needing attention—helped me develop some of the concepts here. I thank Jennie Nelson for her abiding presence through most of my adult life; she is an exemplar of both strength and sense. Robin Becker somehow believed in me and the value of this work before she knew much about either of us. Alfred Haas and Steve Kruse provided technical support through their prompt electronic responses to my nuts-and-bolts technological queries. They also provided needed doses of humor when things got tough. Hilary Masters lent an ear and a shoulder over many a cup of strong coffee. Although she began this work as my student, Ann George has become my friend. She is a stellar rhetorician and an ideal collaborator, and I look forward to watching her star rise.

The Research and Graduate Studies Office of the College of Liberal Arts at Penn State provided support through the grant that allowed for the completion of this manuscript. In addition, many colleagues read chapters or parts of chapters and provided valuable input: Marie Secor, Don Bialostosky, Cheryl

Geisler, Jennie Nelson, Rosa Eberly, Dave Kaufer, Stuart Greene, Steve Witte, Rich Enos, John Logie, and Janet Zepernick. Marty Nystrand, Chris Neuwirth, Glynda Hull, and Bob Kozma read very early drafts and their encouragement was extremely important to me. My department head, Robert Secor, has been generous and supportive, and my colleagues in rhetoric at Penn State—Davida Charney, Jeff Walker, Marie Secor, Rich Doyle, Jack Selzer, Don Bialostosky, Jennifer Jackson, John Harwood, Ron Maxwell—have taught me much. The assistance of Jodie Auman, Ann George, and Patricia Gibboney was invaluable in the preparation of the manuscript. My students have also been my teachers, particularly the students in my graduate seminar in Rhetoric and Technology in the spring of 1994. Many students in my Advanced Technical Writing classes over the last few years have also indulged my enthusiasm for this work and have provided their own "tales of computer writing."

Much of this work had its origins when I was at Carnegie Mellon, and it was supported there by a grant from FIPSE to Christine Neuwirth, John R. Hayes, and myself. Chris and Dick collaborated with me on earlier pieces and their contributions to my thinking are clear in these pages. Although my association with the Information Technology Center at Carnegie Mellon ended several years ago, I remain indebted to a number of colleagues from the ITC for their knowledge, support, and friendship: Sandra Bond, Dan Boyarski, Maria Wadlow, Fred Hansen, Nathanial Borenstein, Jim Morris, Andy Palay, and Mark Lorence. In addition, Sandra Bond, Nathaniel Borenstein, Dan Boyarski, James Gosling, Fred Hansen, Chris Koenigsberg, Bruce Lucas, Jim Morris, Andy Palay, Bruce Sherwood, and Bob Sidebotham consented to long hours of interviews about the Andrew project. Fred Hansen was also a valuable early collaborator on some of the studies of computer reading.

Finally, my debts to my teachers are enormous, and are written on every page of this book. I especially want to thank Louie Attebery, Rich Haswell, Dave Kaufer, Rich Enos, Richard Young, Dick Hayes, Linda Flower, Mike Rose, and (the other) Chris Neuwirth.

WRITING IN THE MATERIAL WORLD

CHAPTER
1

THE TECHNOLOGY QUESTION

The relationship between writing and the material world is both inextricable and profound. Indeed, writing is language made material. Through writing, the physical, time-and-space world of tools and artifacts is joined to the symbolic world of language. The materiality of writing is both the central fact of literacy and its central puzzle. This materiality is the central fact of literacy because writing gains its power—as a cognitive process, as a cultural practice, and even as a metaphor—by linking these two powerful systems: the material realm of time and space with the quintessentially human act of language. The materiality of literacy is also a central puzzle, and I call this puzzle "The Technology Question:" What does it mean for language to become material? That is, what is the effect of writing and other material literacy technologies on human thinking and human culture? By naming this question one of technology, I underscore what I see as the inexplicable relationship between technology and materiality: Writing is made material through the use of technologies, and writing is technological in the sense and to the extent that it is material. Human beings have used and continue to use technologies (e.g., sticks on sand, pen and ink on parchment, #2 pencil on legal pad, cursor on monitor) to bring language to material life. Writing technologies are material not only in and of themselves, but also because they allow for the creation of the material artifacts that are named by the noun writing.

In this chapter I argue that the materiality of writing, although often overlooked, is actually at the heart of a number of current controversies within literacy studies, and that this materiality must be acknowledged to fully appreciate the nature of literate acts. Further, understanding writing as inextricably based in the material world can provide a theoretical basis from which to argue about the most recent iteration of the Technology Question: What is the nature of computer technologies, and what is their impact on writing?

I am using the term *material* to mean having mass or matter and occupying physical space. The implements of writing—pens, pencils, keyboards—have mass, as do written products. Even pixeled screen images, although they may not seem material in the same way as do marks chiseled on a clay tablet, depend upon several kinds of material apparatus both for creation and for perception and use (e.g., input devices, monitors, electrical systems, and semiconductor chips). Because this analysis extends beyond what is conventionally seen as the domain of Marxist or neo-Marxist examinations of technology, I have tried to avoid Marxist terminology. However, I do take from Marx and Engels' historical materialism (1846) the notion that the material world matters; that is, that the materially-based conduct of human activities has profound implications for the development of human culture and the shape of human consciousness. Further, my use of the word material is not meant to invoke conventional binary distinctions like material/immaterial, physical/mental, body/mind. Rather, texts written or read are at once material and immaterial, and writers and readers engage one another in realms that are both physical and mental. Indeed, as I explore in the final chapter of this volume, overcoming the culture–cognition impasse in writing scholarship will require refiguring writing, in all its complexity, as of the body *and* of the mind.

Writing is situated in the material world in a number of ways. It always occurs in a material setting, employs material tools, and results in material artifacts. Writers sit in well-appointed desks in offices, or they slouch in less well-appointed ones in classrooms. Sometimes writers forego a desk altogether, preferring a kitchen table, or a lap, or the dashboard of a car. Writers use stubby pencils or felt-tip pens, cheap ball-points or lap-top computers; often writers use a number of these material implements in tandem. Writers compose speeches on backs of envelopes, makes lists on scraps of paper, write essays in spiral notebooks, and compose lab reports or love letters on word processors. Indeed, an observer from another culture might be surprised by how much time people in Western society spend typing on keyboards, or—more surprisingly, perhaps—how much personal, intellectual, economic, and even physical work gets done with pen or pencil in hand. In short, such a visitor would be astonished to see how engaged individuals within Western culture are with the material tools of literacy.

But the materiality of writing, or the materiality of language that is writing, also remains a central puzzle within literacy studies. The Technology Question is present in debates about the nature of oral and written language, in controversies over the relationship between speech and writing, and in discourse about the political and educational implications of that relationship. The Technology Question, unresolved, lurks in discussions about the nature of writing, from Plato to Derrida to the pages of contemporary journals, where scholars argue about writing's relationship to knowledge, to truth, and to power. The Technology Question is evident—indeed, is often begged—in arguments that computer technologies will revolutionize communication, education, and business, or that computers will bring about a wholesale transformation of human thinking and human culture.

In the next sections I review three instances of the Technology Question within literacy studies—one philosophical, one historical, and one sociopsychological. First, the philosophical debate between Plato and Derrida on the nature of writing illustrates the stakes of the Technology Question. That is, both of these philosophers recognized that determining the nature of writing is not an idle or superficial exercise, that at a very real level, questions of writing are questions of truth, knowledge, and power. A second set of scholars who have examined the Technology Question, historians Eric Havelock, Walter Ong, and Jack Goody and Ian Watt, provide empirically-based investigations of the Technology Question, particularly as it concerns the rise of literacy in ancient Greece. Third, the work of Lev Vygotsky and, later, Sylvia Scribner and Michael Cole provide a corrective to some of the dichotomization of speech and writing, and the confusion of cultural and cognitive effects, that are present in the work of Ong, Havelock, and Goody and Watt.

These three examples of scholarship on the Technology Question also illustrate that it is present in a wide range of issues within literacy studies, although its presence is often latent. While all three of the bodies of work examined here are concerned in an essential way with the Technology Question, each is less than explicit about that concern. Indeed, despite the fact that the material tools and artifacts are inherently bound up in acts of writing, there has been scant explicit and detailed attention focused on this materiality in contemporary discussions of writing. Opening the Technology Question up to detailed and systematic examination would lead to a richer and more complete picture of the complex act of writing. It would also help to adjudicate conflicting claims about computer technologies for writing (i.e., whether computers' effects will be humanizing or dehumanizing, democratizing or totalizing, etc.). Further, addressing the Technology Question is vital to understanding the nature of computer technologies for literacy, their power in shaping literate acts, and people's relationship to them.

Finally, the three bodies of work reviewed here illustrate a further dilemma implicit in the Technology Question: Are the changes that writing evokes changes at the level of culture or at the level of individual cognition? If the changes occur at both levels, what is the relationship between them? How can and do technologies, including writing, impact both cognitively and culturally? This returns, of course, to the cognitive/cultural impasse in writing studies more generally: What is the relationship between writing as a cognitive act and writing as a cultural practice? Exploring the Technology Question can provide a way into—and possibly a way out of—this dilemma. This issue is discussed more extensively in chapter 9 (this volume).

THE TECHNOLOGY QUESTION IN PHILOSOPHY

As scholars from Eric Havelock to Jay Bolter have argued, writing is a technology; that is, it is a set of materially embodied symbolic tools that humans use for the goal-directed accomplishment of work—work that is communicative, economic, or intellectual, or, more likely, work that is all of these at once. As a technology, writing extends human beings' ability to communicate with others across space and through time; writing as a technology makes possible literature and history, law and government as we understand them, and certain kinds of philosophy—although writing also makes possible bureaucracies, tax audits, acts of libel, junk mail, and so on.

Philosophers have understood that the union of the physical world of the body with language—the symbolic system that is the highest act of mind—is profound, but they have not agreed on its implications. Plato (1973) and Derrida (1981), sitting at two ends of a 2500 year span of Western philosophy, provide the most pointed example of the philosophical arguments about the Technology Question. Both Plato and Derrida recognize the stakes of the Technology Question: They reorganize that writing is inherently bound up with issues of truth, knowledge, and ultimately power.

In Plato's *Phaedrus* (1973), Socrates denounces writing at length. He argues that writing is a shadow, a derivative of "living and animate speech" and therefore at a further remove from true knowledge than is speech. Note that Plato is primarily concerned with the psychological aspects of writing's impact: Writing gives the illusion of wisdom while in fact fostering forgetfulness. Further, writing, unlike speech, can neither answer queries put to it nor distinguish between "suitable and unsuitable readers." Writing is compared to a child who needs its parent (speech) to defend it, and the very best that might be said about writing is that it can provide a pastime for wise men who are past their prime (sect. 275-76).

Clearly, Plato is highly ambivalent about writing. Earlier in this dialog, Socrates calls the manuscript Phaedrus hides under his cloak the "actual speech" of Lysias and entreats Phaedrus to show it to him (sect. 228). And, of course, Plato himself was a writer of many texts. For present purposes, it is not important to establish precisely where Plato stands *vis a vis* writing; rather, he is provided as an early theorist who recognizes the significance of the Technology Question and devotes considerable attention to it, despite the fact that his approach may not be, in the final analysis, completely consistent.

Through the cumulative power of these multiple indictments of writing, Plato tried to close the book, as it were, on the Technology Question. He failed, of course, because Derrida, twenty-five centuries later, is still arguing with Plato over the nature of writing.   Derrida's larger goal is the critique of Western metaphysics (Johnson, 1981), and in "Plato's Pharmacy" (1981) he takes on a central part of this project, deconstructing Plato, "the father of *logos*."   For Derrida, *Phadrus* is the "inaugural gesture" (p. 128) of Western philosophy, and in his reading of it Derrida turns Plato on his ear. For Derrida, writing is not ancillary or secondary or derived, but is always already there. The dichotomy that Plato sets up[1] between speech and writing already presupposes the technological system that makes it possible—writing. According to Derrida, Plato has to have writing in order to attack writing: He (like Rosseau and Saussure) wants to put writing "out of the question" (p. 158), yet to do so, he must borrow both the medium of writing and its analytical/theoretical system. Further, although Plato sees writing as absence, the "supplement of a supplement" (p. 109), the writing itself gets away from him, "endlessly vanish[ing] through concealed doorways" (p. 128). Because what writing supplements (i.e., speech) turns out to also be a supplement or an absence, Plato can define and defend speech only through writing. Jasper Neel (1988) paraphrases Derrida: "Whatever is supposed to precede and inform writing, whatever is supposed to escape play or be primary or be present in its own right always turns out to operate just like writing. Writing, in other words, created the West, not the other way around" (p. 118).

Is writing an aid to memory, or is it a dangerous, shadowy illusion of wisdom? Is writing a drug that dulls the memory, or merely a pastime? Is writing the *pharmakon* (drug/remedy), or is it the *pharmakos* (scapegoat)? Is writing a supplement to philosophical truth, or does it in fact make philosophy possible? These questions, debated across the centuries by Plato and Derrida, are all variants of the Technology Question: What is the nature of language made material, what is the nature of writing? And what, as a consequence of writing, happens to human thinking and human culture?

For Plato, the effects of writing are most directly psychological: The material implements and artifacts of writing are a psychological crutch, and a tainted one at that, given its remove from true knowledge. Plato's critique of writing is built on firm distinctions between speech and writing, and this distinction is mirrored in the material/immaterial split in Western philosophy that is often traced to Plato. Derrida's response to Plato's psychological concerns, on the other hand, occurs mostly at the level of writing as system. He wants to deconstruct Platonic binaries—particularly here speech and writing, but also body/soul and immaterial/material. To do so he addresses not Plato's psychological concerns but rather how writing works as a cultural system. The stakes in this debate about the Technology Question are huge for both Plato and Derrida: Maintaining a distinction between speech and writing is absolutely imperative for Plato, both politically and philosophically. If, on the other hand, Derrida can deconstruct Plato's duality of speech/writing, one of the most powerful of the Platonic binaries, he is well on his way to cracking the Platonic system as a whole.

I use the argument between Plato and Derrida about writing to illustrate that the Technology Question is a long-standing one with profound implications, politically and philosophically, as Plato and Derrida both understood. Further, the dichotomization of speech and writing that Plato insisted upon (and that Derrida attempted to deconstruct) remains a common theme in other discussions of the Technology Question. This is illustrated—again returning to Plato's Athens—as the historical scholarship on the advent of western literacy is examined.

THE TECHNOLOGY QUESTION IN HISTORIES OF ANCIENT GREECE

A second, quite different body of work concerns the historical analysis of changes wrought by writing on preliterate civilizations. Literary theorist Walter Ong, classicist Eric Havelock, and anthropologist Jack Goody each engage the Technology Question in their comparative historical analyses of ancient Greece pre– and part–literacy.   Each of these scholars is interested in exploring the implications of materially supported alphabetic systems on Greek culture and Greek thought. These scholars' work is vital to examinations of the Technology Question because they take many of the notions, explicit and implicit, in the treatises by Plato and Derrida and explore them through empirical observations of cultural systems and textual artifacts. While these scholars' methodologies are significantly different from one another, there are important parallels in their claims and conclusions.

Ong's (1982) book, *Orality and Literacy: The Technologizing of the Word,* is wide ranging and demonstrates an impressive familiarity with work in diverse fields, from ethnographic anthropology to semiotic theory. Using ancient Greece as an exemplar, Ong examines the nature of thinking and being in primary oral cultures, cultures that are so radically different from Western culture, that Ong admitted his success in this venture can only be partial. Ong acknowledged that his comparisons are of extreme cases: contemporary Western cultures that are "hyperliterate" and primary oral cultures that do not exist except in isolated ways today.

For Ong, writing transforms human consciousness by moving language from an aural realm, where it unfolds across time, to a visual realm, where it takes on a primarily spatial quality. According to Ong (1982), the sense of sight isolates individuals outside and at a distance from what is seen; similarly, sight-based language (written or printed texts) fosters contemplation, analysis, and critique. The sound-based temporal world of speech is totalizing; it "pours into" and "envelopes" (p. 72) the listener, and its centralizing and unifying character shape thought culture. Therefore, writing, what Ong calls "the most monumentous of all human technological inventions," translates sound into space and so "transforms the human life world" (p. 85).

Ong elevates the Greek alphabet above other scripts and syllabaries, claiming that it alone has the simplicity for truly widespread use and widespread effects. For instance, the Chinese system, in contrast to the modern alphabet, is cumbersome and elitist, and Ong claimed that it will "no doubt" soon be obsolete, replaced by the Roman alphabet.[2] Ong is at his best when he examines the paradoxes of literacy: Writing has been closely associated with death, as in the notion of a lifeless written text, but this lifeless object can also be perpetually "resurrected into limitless living contexts" (p. 81); or the idea that writing, because it is artificial, alienates us from the natural world and therefore heightens our humanity. Writing, which is neither natural nor inevitable, is nonetheless a supreme achievement of humankind because "artificiality is natural to humans" (p. 82).

Ong's apparent purpose—suggested by key terms like "consciousness" and "ways of thinking"—was to examine the cognitive effects of literacy, and indeed he has been most often read that way (Brandt, 1990; Heim, 1987). Despite this ostensible focus, however, Ong readily moves from cognitive claims to cultural ones and back again. In the most widely read part of the book (i.e., chapter 3, "Some Psychodynamics of Orality"), many of the characteristics Ong outlines describe patterns of thinking—aggregative, additive, copious—but others seem to be used to describe primary oral cultures, such as traditionalist and homeostatic. In any case, Ong is not interested in examining in any detail the actual relationship between individual and cultural changes wrought by writing, or the mechanisms by which one kind of change mediates another.

Classicist Eric Havelock, with his focus on cultural effects, provides a complementary perspective to Ong's. In a career spanning more than thirty years, Havelock (1986) has attempted to treat what he calls the "oral-literate problem" (p. ix) in the context of Greek philosophy, literature, and politics. Whereas Ong's book is far-reaching and eclectic, synthesizing a great deal of diverse prior research, Havelock uses more primary source material to make a narrower argument, but one that is similar in kind to Ong's. Specifically, Ong discusses literacy and writing generally, whereas Havelock's (1982) thesis is it was the invention of the Greek alphabet per se—specifically the addition of vowels to the Semitic writing system, allowing a more accurate sound to sight correspondence—that constituted the "literate revolution in ancient Greece." Indeed, Ong's argument in *Orality and Literacy* is based in important ways on Havelock's primary research; Havelock, in turn, specifically acknowledges the intellectual debts he owes to Ong's *Orality and Literacy*.

Havelock (1986) insists that primary orality is well nigh impossible for our literate minds to conceptualize because "all our terminologies and the metaphors involved are drawn from an experience that is literate and which we take for granted" (p. 63). In "The Preliteracy of the Greeks," Havelock (1976/1977) synthesizes a great deal of his previous research and lays out a series of nine conclusions about literacy (and preliteracy) in ancient Greece. Most of Havelock's conclusions deal with cultural causes and implications of literacy: that the development of the Greek alphabet (approximately 700 BCE) constituted a monumentous and unique event in the history of human culture; that classical Greek culture, however, preceded literacy; and that nonliterate cultures are not necessarily primitive. Havelock does venture into the realm of the psychological in his discussion of how oral cultures remember, and here he postulates that poetry functions as the mediating mechanism between psychological imprinting and shared cultural memory. However, Havelock stops short of explicating how the literacy skills of *individuals*—primarily traders and craftspersons in ancient Greece—actually translate in a revolution at the *cultural* level.

For anthropologist Jack Goody and his collaborator, literary critic Ian Watt (1968), "the notion of representing a sound by a graphic symbol is itself so stupefying a leap of the imagination that what is remarkable is not so much that it happened relatively late in human history, but rather that it ever happened at all" (p. 9). While Goody and Watt are careful to complicate the literate–preliterate distinction—problematizing, for instance, how literate societies are classified (p. 3)—their ultimate goal is to explicate differences between literate and nonliterate cultures. Hence, they argue against an existing paradigm within anthropology that would deny that a crucial distinction between literate and nonliterate cultures exists. They label such an approach "diffuse relativism and sentimental egalitarianism" (p. 26). Goody and Watt use the case of the rise of literacy in ancient Greece to illustrate how researchers might approach studying specific instances of differences in literacy in other, more contemporary cultures.

Like Ong and Havelock, Goody and Watt identify the development of writing with changes in the space and time dimensions of language use. In the seamless temporality of oral societies, the past and the present remain continuous: Parts of the cultural tradition that are not relevant are forgotten or transformed to maintain homeostasis. In a culture with writing, according to Goody and Watt, there is a disjunction between past and present. Literate cultures understand that the past is past and that it is distinct from the present. And in the tensions that develop between present and past, Goody and Watt claim, literate cultures develop a sense of history, a notion of historical and cultural difference, and the ability to distinguish between error and truth—a distinction that leads to skepticism.

Although history and skepticism are results of changing relationships with time, logical analysis, for Goody and Watt, grows out of the spatialization of language. When powerful concepts like *good*, *truth*, and *justice* are "given physical reality" (17) through writing, they can become objects of analysis. The actual physical reality of these words, in turn, leads to the development of systematic methods for thinking, or logic.[3] Goody and Watt contrast the development of logic in literate cultures to the maintenance of "consistency" (p. 16) in traditional ones. In the face-to-face interactions of the preliterate culture, logical inconsistencies, and the criticism thereof, are overlooked, adjusted, or forgotten.

Like Ong and Havelock, Goody and Watt discuss the implications of the development of writing on both a cultural and a psychological level. The alphabet made writing and reading easy to acquire on an individual level; this, in turn, had important political ramifications for the culture at large. Similarly, the sheer amount of written materials in written cultures means that no one individual can ever participate fully in the total cultural tradition. This leads both to alienation on the part of the individual and to social stratification for the culture at large.

Despite their differences in background and methodology, there are striking similarities in the works of these historical scholars. The example of ancient Greece functions as an exemplar of the cultural and cognitive power of literacy; at times, this example takes on the power of metaphor—or even myth. Ong, Havelock, and Goody all explain writing as time made spatial. In other words, writing turns time into space. In addition, each of them contrasts the decontextualization of the spatial form (writing) with the contextual richness of the temporal form (speech). In a sense, then, Ong, Goody, and Havelock align themselves with Plato's Socrates in seeing writing as once-removed, a derivative of speech or "supplement," in Derrida's terms. However, while Plato can be read as lamenting that writing strips language of its dynamic qualities, Ong, Goody and Watt, and Havelock tend, in varying degrees, to celebrate the abstractness and precision that they believe writing—unencumbered with temporal detail—allows.

For present purposes, the engagement of these historians of Greek literacy with the Technology Question illustrates two important points. First, in emphasizing the time and space dimensions of written language, Ong, Havelock, and Goody and Watt are emphasizing the materiality of written language because, in many ways, what defines material is that it exists in space and time (i.e., having mass and therefore retaining a degree of physical permanence over time). Of course, these scholars are not explicit about their focus on materiality—certainly they do not use that term—but in stressing the spatialization and temporalization of language that writing allows, or rather demands, Ong,

Havelock, and Goody and Watt are in fact defining written language by its links to the material world.

Second, although these scholars each examine both cultural and individual implications of literacy, none of them explicates how, or by what means, the individual translates into the cultural, or vice versa. For a way into understanding the relationship between cultural changes and cognitive changes brought about by technology, I turn now to another group of scholars who have addressed the Technology Question in somewhat different terms.

THE TECHNOLOGY QUESTION IN SOCIO-PSYCHOLOGICAL THEORY

A third group of scholars who have explored the Technology Question can be loosely categorized as sociopsychological theorists. This line of work— beginning with Lev Vygotsky in the 1920s and extending through Sylvia Scribner and Michael Cole in the early 1980s to contemporary neo-Vygotskians such as Jean Lave—has examined the relationship between cultural systems, including but not limited to writing, and individual thinking or consciousness. Vygotsky and Scribner and Cole address literacy directly, whereas Lave deals with mathematics as a cultural system. As I describe below, Vygotskian theory and neo-Vygotskian approaches like that of Scribner and Cole and Lave provide the potentially most useful basis for exploring the Technology Question.

In general, the work of Vygotsky and his followers adds to an examination of the Technology Question in two ways: First, each of these scholars is trying to directly address how culture and cognition mutually construct one another. This move is important because technologies are cultural artifacts that are used by individuals; any theory of technology must be able to account for the relationship between cultural and individual manifestations of technology's effects. Further, the attempt to understand the relationship between culture and cognition is useful in discussing the Technology Question because, as we have seen, philosophical and historical approaches have tended either to sharply separate cultural and cognitive effects (Derrida and Plato) or confuse them (Ong, Havelock). Second, the research of this group of scholars helps to call into question the notion that writing and speech, or literacy and illiteracy (or, analogously, print and computers), are mutually distinctive phenomena. Vygotsky's genetic–historical method, and the empirical research of Scribner and Cole that is built on it, complicate our understanding of technologies and suggest that a sharp dichotomization may be tempting, but is historically inaccurate and pragmatically suspect.

Russian theorist Lev Vygotsky was interested—as were Ong, Goody, and Havelock, among others—in how graphic symbol systems structure human thinking, but he was more explicit than these later scholars in hypothesizing about how this restructuring might take place. For Vygotsky, symbol systems or signs were cultural systems—human-made artifacts and symbols that carried cultural value even as they were put to use by individuals within a culture. Two concepts from Vygotsky—the notion of mediational means and the genetic–historical method—are useful in approaching the Technology Question.

Technological Mediation

Vygotsky was part of a vital intellectual atmosphere in Russia after the Revolution, and he apparently took seriously the notion of developing a psychology based on Marxist principles (see Wertsch, 1985; Kozulin, 1990, downplays the Marxist influence). In addition, Vygotsky was profoundly influenced by Engels' historical materialism as it is laid out in *Dialectics of Nature* (1948). Engels postulated that, in labor, humans interact with nature via material tools. These material tools mediate human encounters with the environment, and, in so doing, transform not only the environment but the humans who use them as well. Vygotsky (1981a) brilliantly extended the concept of tool use to include sign systems, including writing, and he referred to such sign systems metaphorically as "psychological tools." For Engels, labor and the instruments of labor create humans, to the extent that the human hand is as much a product of labor as it is an implement of it. Similarly, for Vygotsky, semiotic signs or psychological tools are the mediational means by which higher psychological functions develop—and therefore the means by which the unique human quality of consciousness is brought into being. Further, psychological tools carry cultural power and cultural history, but they are always instantiated in specific ways in actual use. Human development, then—with development understood as both psychological growth and historical/cultural change—occurs through the creation and use of psychological tools. Although Vygotsky (1986) devotes a great deal of theoretical and empirical attention to speech as a psychological tool, he also includes materially based or materially supported systems like writing, numeric analysis, maps and diagrams, and even works of art as psychological tools (1981b).

The example of speech illustrates several of these tenets of the Vygotskian theory of psychological tools: A child learning spoken language from a parent is engaged in a very individually focused act. However, the language that he or she is learning is not arbitrary or "made up" but is rather the product of her culture. Similarly, the effect of language learning is psychologically profound for the child; Vygotsky (1981a) claimed that such socially supported and culturally sanctioned learning had the capacity to radically transform individual thinking. Once the child has language, then, he or she is able not just to reason about objects and actions in the world, but to communicate about them. He or she is able to use language to modify others', and eventually his or her own, behavior. In this way, individual use of psychological tools feeds back into social activity and the larger cultural system of which it is a part (1986).

Although the example of speech suggests something about psychological tools in individual development (ontogeny), Vygotsky (1966) also saw psychological tools working culturally and historically over time. Casting lots, finger counting, and tying knots as an aid to memory are all ways in which humans historically used materially based objects in the world to support mental activities that have since become internalized: decision-making, arithmetic, and recollection, respectively. As these examples suggest—and as Witte (1992) convincingly argues—Vygotsky's conception of thought extends beyond the purely linguistic. While language learning and use was central for Vygotsky, his interest in both art (1971) and mathematics (1981b) suggests that he was attempting to construct a broad and inclusive theory of psychology.

Despite the fact that Vygotsky was interested in both individual and cultural development, he was not advocating a simple recapitulationist or parallelist model of the relationship between individual and cultural growth; that is, individuals do not recapitulate their culture's development, nor do cultures develop in parallel to the individuals within them. Such a position can be read as implicitly racist, but a close reading of Vygotsky reveals that he was aware of such an interpretation of his work and explicitly argued against it (e.g., Vygotsky, 1966). Further, the complexity of cultural change via tools is underscored by the fact that the "same" cultural tools can be used by different societies in different times to greatly different effects (Scribner, 1985; Scribner & Cole, 1981).

What Vygotsky's notion of mediational means brings to our examination of the Technology Question, then, is this: Tools and signs can have a profound impact on both individual mental functioning and cultural change. Although effects in these two areas are related in complex ways, they are not simply reducible to one another. Further, Vygotsky's concept of psychological tools mediating development (both cultural and individual) suggests that the effects of technological change (e.g., computerization) on writing are profound, but certainly not unitary, easily predicted, immediate, or consistent across contexts.

The extension of Vygotsky that I would like to make is one that is in keeping with the general spirit of his work and underscores the profundity of the Technology Question in writing and the import of technological change in writing tools. Specifically, Vygotsky does not stress the materiality of writing. That is, he tends to describe writing (and other sign systems) *metaphorically* as psychological tools. But writing is the powerful system that it is precisely because it combines the psychological power of the semiotic system of language with the material means to reproduce and disseminate that semiotic system.

For Vygotsky, writing as a sign system, a psychological tool, is analogous to a hoe, a material tool. The hoe mediates my interaction with the physical world in the conduct of my labor of gardening, and the physical world of the garden is transformed, or at least that is my goal. Analogously, writing mediates my interaction with the social world—and is the means of transformation not only of others (when I persuade through my writing) but also of myself (when I learn from it). But what this simple analogy overlooks—and what makes writing even more powerful—is that writing is, or relies on, technological systems as well as sign systems. That is, the hoe is a material tool that except in special circumstances we would not use as a sign or a symbol. But writing is unlike the hoe in that it is material as well as psychological.

Writing has the potential for even more profound transformations of humans because it operates on both of these levels—both its psychological (semiotic) aspect and its material–technological aspect have the potential to transform. Extending Vygotsky's work with psychological tools in this way is useful in understanding why current changes in the material circumstances (i.e., technological tools and contexts) of writing have such a powerful potential and why the Technology Question is of such vital import. In general, Vygotsky's notion of mediation is important in addressing contemporary issues of computer technology and writing because it provides a theoretical basis from which to predict that technology can have real and important, if complex, effects on writing.

The Historical–Genetic Method

The applicability of technological mediation to the Technology Question seems clear: Technology matters, for it can bring about important changes individually and culturally. However, the notion of mediation in and of itself can invite a kind of technological determinism: It can imply that technological change inevitably and straightforwardly leads to cultural or individual change. In countering such determinism, a second Vygotskian concept is useful—that of the historical–genetic method. While certain concepts from Vygotsky have been popular in the educational literature for decades, recently Vygotsky's methodology has attracted the attention of scholars (e.g., Cole, forthcoming).

Because of the influence of Marx, Vygotsky consistently attempted to place psychological phenomena into their historical context. Vygotsky used the term "genetic" in the general sense of "origin" or "antecedents" rather than in the more specific sense as the study of genes or genetics. For him, to study a phenomenon meant to study the history of that phenomenon (Vygotsky, 1981b) and that historical study, in turn, meant studying the phenomenon undergoing change or in process (Vygotsky, 1978). The word *historical* can be broadly interpreted in Vygotskian theory to include: general evolutionary history of the species, the history of individual societies, the history of individuals within a given society, and the history or development of particular psychological systems. As Scribner (1985) points out, this historical analysis can happen at any of several levels, and the integrated psychology Vygotsky was working toward would have attempted to integrate all of these into a single theory of development, broadly defined.

The last of these understandings of history—that of the history of psychological systems—is the one that is the most uniquely Vygotskian, and the one which can be extended and made most useful for examining technology. Understanding 20th-century literacy means understanding the technologies that support it—since without the technologies, literate acts would be profoundly different. Vygotsky's theory of mediation helps us to see tools, signs, and technologies as spatially and culturally distributed systems that function to augment human psychological processing. Viewed in this way, then, technologies—in particular, literacy technologies—are themselves complex systems that might fruitfully be studied genetically, in the Vygotskian sense. What would this kind of historical–genetic study of technology mean, and what gains would it offer? These questions are addressed in more detail in the following chapters (see chapters 6 and 8, this volume). Briefly, a historical–genetic study of literacy technologies would entail looking at technology in process, both in process of use and process of development, and in transition. It would entail examining not only the transformative power of tools on consciousness, but also how the tools themselves get made, and how they get transformed. It would entail reconfiguring what at first may seem brand new technologies as extensions and modifications—albeit sometimes radical ones—of previous technologies, and it would entail studying the phenomenon of technology as a history of that phenomenon.

Taking such a complex historical view of current technologies relieves us of the bind of technological determinism: When the history of a given technology—writing, print, computers—is reconstructed in all its complexity, we can see that a straightforward narrative of technological advance or historical "ruptures" due to technology is not viable (see chapter 8, this volume). When we observe technology in use, we see that, although technological effects are very real, they can be small, subtle, even paradoxical (see chapter 4, this volume). And when we watch technology being developed, we can see that the shape of current technologies is not a given, but rather is the result of complex decision making, economic concerns, politics, and not a little serendipity (see chapter 6, this volume). In short, a historical–genetic approach to technology makes it difficult to continue to posit computers, or any technology, as amorphous, omnipotent agents of change, suggesting instead that a given technology's effects may be varied, elaborate, complicated, and far from immediate. Equally important, a historical–genetic approach to technology opens up a space both for the study of technology and for the active "writing" of it that technological determinism and instrumentalism obscures. I shall return at the close of this chapter to a more thorough discussion of the opening of spaces to discuss, to study, and to write technology.

Neo-Vygotskian Approaches to the Technology Question

Neo-Vygotskians Scribner and Cole (1981) and Lave (1988; 1993) enrich theoretical approaches to the Technology Question through their respective developments of the notion of "practice." Drawing on Vygotsky, other Soviet activity theorists (Davydov & Markova, 1983; Leont'ev, 1978; Wertsch, 1981), as well as Bourdieu (1977) and de Certeau (1985), these scholars place practice in a central position in their theories. In the theories of both Scribner and Cole, and Lave, practice ties together thinking and acting human beings with their cultural, material, political contexts and is therefore a way to integrate agent, action, and world. In exploring the Technology Question, the notion of practice is useful because when literacy is examined in practice, it is seen as intrinsically tied to technology—to tools, implements, and artifacts. A practice account of literacy acknowledges these material tools and technologies; in fact, it would see them as central. But—again as a counter to technological determinism— a practice account would also posit technology as only one of a complex of factors that impinge on thinking and doing in context.

Psychologists Scribner and Cole (1981) developed their practice account of literacy after intense study of the literacy of the Vai in West Africa. Their seven-year project in Liberia was an attempt to systematically examine the cognitive effects of different writing systems. If Scribner and Cole's goal had been to find general, large scale effects of literacy, the study would have been a failure. However, their study is remarkable not only for its thoroughness, but also because it is the first to find real, substantial effects for literacy, at least in some contexts and under some conditions.

Scribner and Cole's practice theory adds a level of complexity to the dichotomization of writing and speech by earlier scholars of the Technology Question, like Havelock and Ong. Arguing against the idea that writing is decontextualized speech and against the "great divide" theories of earlier scholars, Scribner and Cole claim that the practice of literacy is itself deeply contextualized. (A similar argument is made in another vein by Brandt, 1990.) That is, the spatial and temporal contexts of writing may be different than those of speech, but they are no less important. Indeed, individual members of a literate culture, even those who are not actually literate, understand the altered conceptions of space and time that written language requires. In studies where literates and nonliterates were asked to dictate letters of instruction, the nonliterates understood the differing information requirements for readers who were distant to the writer, or who were unfamiliar with the physical context of the task. Scribner and Cole found that nonliterates understood, at least in a limited way, how the practice of literacy transforms space and time dimensions for language users. (Heath,1983, also documented the complex relationships between literacy and nonliteracy in her studies of communities in the United States.)

In general, Scribner and Cole's (1981) work argues against writing as "merely" decontextualized speech, argues against the sharp dichotomization of technological systems, and argues against great divide theories of technological change. Their work also remains the most complete, long-term study of the effects of literacy. Their results, which show real if subtle effects for writing, suggest—as Vygotsky hypothesized—that technology (in this case, writing) matters.

Unlike Scribner and Cole, Jean Lave (1988, 1993) does not address issues of literacy per se. Rather, her work has examined the learning and use of mathematical concepts in everyday life, but her notion of *everyday activity* is one of the most developed accounts of practice in the psychological literature, and her treatment of technology is both complex and subtle and quite applicable to the general understanding of the Technology Question in literacy studies. Indeed, math and literacy share a number of similarities, among them a sort of dual status in the culture at large. At one level, both math and writing exist as subjects for learning in school and objects for academic study; at another level, both exist popularly and actually in the real world as everyday math and reading and writing. The latter form of both math and writing tends to be denigrated in relationship to its academic counterpart (see Lave & Wenger, 1991, especially chapter 5.)

Various technologies are implicated in the everyday practice of mathematics in all of the settings Lave (1988) examined: cooking, supermarket shopping, Weight Watchers meetings. The well-practiced use of these technologies— scales, calculators, even human fingers—is what constitute everyday mathematical competence; this kind of competence is no different in kind that the competence of experts in various domains who must master the use of tools (i.e., engineers, navigators). Lave and Wenger (1991) also acknowledge that technologies carry with them a complex history of use and adaptation that always impinges as well on the practice of those who use the technology. In general, Lave places technologies and artifacts at a central, pivotal position between the individual and the cultural practice within which that individual operates. I return to Lave and her notion of everyday practice in the following chapter.

CULTURAL MYTHS AND A SPACE FOR TECHNOLOGY STUDIES

This review of scholarship in three quite distinct realms of literacy study suggests that the issues surrounding writing technology are pervasive, profound—and far from settled. However, in each of these bodies of scholarship—philosophy, history, and sociopsychological theory—the Technology Question remains for the most part latent. That is, this scholarship does not directly address technology as technology; rather, technology is posited as important (to varying degrees) but is not itself examined in any systematic way. Although not all scholarship within literacy studies needs to focus on technology, leaving the Technology Question latent is a problem in so far as what is latent is often overlooked. Technology is implicated in every literate act, and to ignore this implication is to remain confused about the essential relationship of writing to technology, and about our relationship—as writers, as teachers, as scholars—to both of them.

One danger in keeping this vital aspect of literacy (i.e., technology) latent in our discussions and in our research is that this latency allows or even invites an instrumental view of technology. Such an instrumentalist view sees technology as merely a tool—a neutral and transparent means to produce written language, which is somehow imagined to exist independent of that means. The last decade of work in cultural studies of scientific and other discourses suggests that writing—also a technology—is not transparent, that it carries beliefs and value systems within it, and that to treat written language as if it were neutral or transparent has severe political, theoretical, and practical consequences. (Examination of the "myth" of autonomous text is beyond the scope of this discussion, but see Cazden, 1989; Farr, 1993; Geisler, 1994; Haas, 1994; Haas & Flower, 1988; Nystrand, 1987.) An instrumental view of technology carries with it all the dangers of an autonomous theory of language. When text is seen as autonomous, it is viewed either as nonproblematic and neutral, a view that tends to exclude it from scrutiny and so leave the ideologies and value systems inherent in it unexamined. Or, it is viewed as powerful, above reproach, and beyond questioning, a view that ignores that written language is the product of human motive and serves human purposes; this view creates a situation in which the language "consumer" can be duped, manipulated, or misled.

Similar dangers lie in the instrumental view of technology. In a previous essay (Haas & Neuwirth, 1993), three interconnected cultural "myths" about technology within literacy studies were detailed. These myths obstruct both a true understanding of writing technologies and an active involvement with them: the transparent technology assumption, the all-powerful technology assumption, and the assumption that technology is not our job.[4] These myths about technology place literacy teachers and scholars in a subordinate position to technology, removing them from the realm of technology development and critique and setting them in positions to be merely receivers of technology. Chapter 2 examines two of these myths (transparent technology and all-powerful technology) in some detail, and Chapter 7 shows how these myths are operating not just in literacy studies generally, but even within the specialized literature about technology. Here, I outline the scope of the two myths and suggest that they are an inherent danger in keeping the Technology Question latent in scholarship on literacy.

Like the autonomous text myth, the assumption that technology is transparent posits a kind of distortionless window, through which essential acts of reading, writing, and thinking are conducted. The "technology is transparent" myth sees writing as writing as writing, its essential nature unaffected by the mode of production and presentation. The most serious drawback to the transparent technology assumption is that it encourages an overly positive, whole-hearted acceptance of computer technology without any consideration of possible negative effects of that technology. Viewing technology as transparent encourages a belief that writers can use computer technology without being shaped by it, and therefore discourages any examination of how technology shapes discourse and how it, in turn, is shaped by discourse.

A second cultural myth operating within literacy studies is the assumption that technology is all-powerful and self-determining. In this view, computer technologies will have far-reaching and profound effects, effects that will be almost wholly positive and always inevitable. In this view, we must simply stand back and watch as the computer revolution remakes literacy, language, and culture. When the "technology is all-powerful" myth is operational, individual practices and motives, as well as cultural habits and beliefs, take a subordinate position to technology, which is seen as determining itself. Together, these myths, which are really two sides of the instrumentalist view of technology, contribute to a division of labor in which scholars in the humanities and many of the social sciences believe that "technology is not our job," whereas scholars in other, more technical domains believe that "technology is our *only* job." As I suggest in Chapter 2, Technology Studies will require that each of these groups rethink this faulty view of division of labor.

The goal of this book's first section (chapters 1 and 2) of this book is to open up a space within literacy studies for the examination of the Technology Question. Such an examination will entail looking *at,* rather than *through,* the literacy technologies we use every day. This will be difficult, and indeed not always practical. In the conduct of most work it is important to be able to treat technology transparently; after all, we have classes to teach, books to write, bills to pay, and children to raise. Looking self-consciously at every technology would be paralyzing. However, I believe that opening a space for the discussion of technological issues within the mainstream of literacy studies is crucial. Such a space would make possible the active engagement of scholars of literacy in questions of technological use and development—an engagement that is now precluded by cultural myths of transparent and all-powerful technology. As Chapter 6 illustrates, technologies are not created in a vacuum; they do not emerge, full blown, from the head of IBM. Just as language carries ideology within it, so too does technology.

The Technology Question, as it is argued in philosophy, historical studies, and educational theory and practice, is still open to debate, and I believe this is all to the good for those of us interested in the theory and practice of writing. The stakes in this debate are huge (as Plato long ago recognized). Literacy scholars need to do more than merely observe as the discourses of our culture "make" technology and as that technology, in turn, remakes discourse.

FOOTNOTES

[1]Jasper Neel (1988) notes that Derrida reads the *Phaedrus* "straight;" i.e., for Derrida's deconstructive reading to "work," Socrates must always and simply "speak" for Plato. Derrida therefore cannot acknowledge all the irony or "play" that is present in the dialogue.

[2]Ong's worry about the 40,000-character Chinese typewriter overlooks the possibility of a word processor that—like the human hand—can construct the characters. Like many scholars of western literacy, Ong evidences a latent bias against Asian writing systems. The tenor of *Orality and Literacy*, like that of Havelock (discussed later), is that the Greek alphabet alone leads to logic, philosophy, and higher culture. Although the case to be made for alphabetic systems is strong, it is not clear cut, and Ong's tendency to credit Western (alphabetic) societies alone with advanced culture and thinking is clearly suspect.

[3]It is important to note that, to support their claims in this section, Goody and Watt rely not on empirical or primary evidence, but on the writings of Plato—a move that is somewhat problematic, given Plato's strong beliefs about writing.

[4]The following section is drawn from my published collaboration with Neuwirth, as well as from many conversations we have had about these issues; I am indebted to her for both.

2

TECHNOLOGY STUDIES

The previous chapter argued for the materiality of literacy and set up the Technology Question as essentially a question about the materiality of literacy: What is the nature of material language (writing)? What are its implications? And what happens when the material forms of literacy change? This chapter examines what kinds of systematic inquiry will be necessary in order to address the contemporary version of the Technology Question: What are the implications of computer-based writing tools for the processes and practices of literacy?

The materiality of writing becomes profoundly obvious when technologies change—when writers move from the heft of the manuscript and the feel of a new Blackfeet pencil, to the bright, wired-up, whirring box and clicking keyboard on the desk. During the 1980s many people made this move, from producing texts with pencils, pens, and/or typewriters, to producing them with computers. Much of the research reported in Part 2 of this volume had its beginnings then, when people were interested in telling their own stories of the move from older technologies to newer ones, and were willing to share those stories with me. In interviews I conducted for almost ten years, beginning in the early 1980s, writers told of their experiences of making the move from one set of material tools to another, profoundly different one. When writers exchange one set of material tools for another—or, more accurately, when they add another set of literacy tools to their repertoires—aspects of writing are foregrounded that may not have been noticed before, including the writer's physical relationship to texts and the tools of text production. For example, many writers I interviewed mentioned tactile and visual changes in their understandings of and interactions with texts on computer screens. These writers often sensed that these changes had implications both for the form, structure, and quality of written texts and for the shape of their own writing processes (see chapter 4, this volume; see also Haas, 1989c, and Haas & Hayes,1986).

Both popular and scholarly treatments of writing with computers throughout the 1980s and into the 1990s have stressed the profound differences in writing and written texts that computer technologies have engendered. But a general sense that writing is different with computers is not the same as a clear articulation and careful examination of those differences and their implications. Teasing out when and how technology changes writing, when it does not, and the implications of both is one of the challenges of an enterprise I call Technology Studies: a concerted, focused attempt to examine technologies of writing—historically, theoretically, empirically, and practically. This chapter sketches out what this enterprise might look like, what its tenets and scope might be, and the tasks it might undertake. I hope it can serve as a catalyst, a way into discussions of the complex relationship between writing, in all its cultural and cognitive complexity, and the material technologies that make writing possible.

We are currently at an historical moment that is ideal for this kind of critical inquiry about technology. Computer-based literacy technologies are still new enough that writers notice them. That is, many writers can articulate the advantages and disadvantages of computer technologies and can make conscious decisions to work around these technologies by employing the more traditional technologies of pen or paper at certain junctures in the writing process. Contrast this kind of conscious "noticing" and self-management of technology with the transparency of older technologies, such as the alphabet, the directionality of printed text, or paper. Although these older technologies certainly have shortcomings, most writers can neither articulate these shortcomings nor make choices to work around them. As users and consumers, people prefer their technologies transparent: They do not like to have to think about the features of their word processors any more than they like to think about shifting gears in an automobile, and they prefer to look through a given technology to the task at hand. In the conduct of inquiry about technology, however, scholars are wise to strive to look at the technology itself, rather than through it. Technology Studies should be an enterprise in which scholars consciously and studiously attend to the technology itself—its shape, scope, and history—as well as to its various consequences. Indeed, it is only by examining a technology's scope, shape, and history—by looking at rather than through it—that its consequences can be truly judged.

In the remainder of this chapter, I define the scope and general tenets of Technology Studies.   I also examine what I see as two critical barriers to Technology Studies: cultural myths about the nature of technology and a lack of theoretical grounding for examinations of the contemporary iterations of the Technology Question.

THE ENTERPRISE OF TECHNOLOGY STUDIES

What happens when the material forms of literacy change? For example, what happens when students chart General Lee's offensive into Pennsylvania in 1863 through hypermedia, rather than tracing it on a map in a book? What happens when workers share information through e-mail, rather than around the water-cooler, or when scholars conduct research via the InterNet, rather than by traipsing through dark and dusty library stacks? And what happens when those scholars produce on-line rather than paper documents? An initial response to these questions might be that these familiar literacy activities are radically remade in new, computer-supported environments, and indeed this has been the response from both scholars and the popular press. Certainly, anyone (including most readers of this book) who has made the move from writing with print-based materials to computer-based ones can attest to the sense of newness and difference that attends this move. However, serious inquiry about technology requires an unpacking of just what this sense of newness and difference entails. One of the central projects lying ahead for Technology Studies is to move from a general belief that writing is different when writers use computers to a clear articulation and careful examination of those differences.

One way to begin such an examination is to address specific questions about technology. Doing so underscores that writing is at once *individual*, an act of mind; *cultural*, an historically based practice; and *material*, inherently dependent on physical, space-and-time artifacts. For instance, take the example of a scholar producing an article or monograph. Certainly such an activity is an individual one, particularly in the humanities, where scholars usually work alone to produce "original" contributions to knowledge. Whether searching for obscure texts via the InterNet or laboring over the prose of an introductory chapter, the scholar's activity is, in many ways, a solitary work of the mind. However, simultaneously, the scholar's writing activities are inherently cultural, beginning with the institutions and disciplines within which he or she functions. These institutions both shape the scholar's contributions and have the power to give them sanction (or not). Even the scholar's "original" ideas are in some ways the product of a certain cultural and historical milieu. At the same time, each step along the way—from cruising the InterNet for information to polishing final prose—is dependent in complex and vital ways on material technologies. Perhaps the most obvious examples to contemporary observers are the monitor, keyboard, chips and circuits of the machine that support both the search for other texts and the production of the scholar's own. But more than likely, this writer's processes are also supported by pens, pencils, paper, print volumes, and maybe even his or her secretary's typewriter. In short, this act of writing—like all others—is a complex of individual thoughts, cultural practices and beliefs, and physical, material technologies. And understanding this act of writing—or any other—requires that we address it in all its cognitive, cultural, and material complexity. And this in turn will require scholars trained in diverse disciplines to work together.

Technology Studies Crosses Disciplines

In order to examine the Technology Question as it is manifest in particular, contemporary acts of writing, the complex and symbiotic relationship between culture, cognition, and technology needs to be examined. This is the ultimate goal of Technology Studies—to understand how material technologies both constrain and enable acts of mind, on the one hand, and how cultures produce, adapt and are affected by material technologies, on the other hand. Obviously, such a project will require as well that we address the relationship between a material culture and materially supported cognitive acts. The complexity of such a project may seem overwhelming, given the ubiquitousness and power of reading and writing in our culture; the coordination of mental, physical, and affective efforts that writing requires of individuals; and the diversity of literacy technologies themselves.

This task is both more and less daunting because it is clearly, of necessity, an interdisciplinary one. It is less daunting because no one researcher would be responsible for exploring all aspects of technology and literacy. Clearly, examining how culture, thinking, and technology constitute one another in and through writing will cross a number of disciplinary boundaries and require specialists with an ecumenical spirit able to use a range of methodological approaches to study technology. Historians can pursue questions about the evolution of writing technologies and trace their impact over time; cognitive psychologists can examine people's in-time use of literacy technologies, and the relationship between the material objects and cognitive processes of writing, while social psychologists and organizational behaviorists can examine technology-in-use in a variety of group, organizational, and institutional settings; critical theorists might explore the relationship between power and technology development, both contemporarily and historically; educational researchers could study how technologies change, and are changed by, the classrooms and other real-world learning settings into which they are imported; rhetoricians could examine the arguments made about technology, or the assumptions about technology that operate in given cultural contexts; computer scientists can work to refine and develop tools to meet communication needs in a variety of organizational contexts; and linguists could explore changes in language use that accompany technology development and technology use. Of course, none of these research projects in and of themselves sound particularly new; such efforts are already underway in a number of places, and have been for some time.

What would make the enterprise of Technology Studies new is also one of the things that would make it daunting: active collaboration, frequent communication, and professional interaction across disciplinary and institutional lines. Opening up channels for collaboration and communication between researchers in divergent areas is notoriously difficult, even (or perhaps especially) in academic institutions. But understanding the symbiotic relationship between writing—in all its forms as cultural practice, social interaction, and cognitive process—and the material technologies by which writing is accomplished (from clay tablet to laptop) will require not just scholars from a range of disciplines pursuing related questions, but, at the very least, a conscious attempt to learn about and take into account what other scholars do. That is, the historian looking at large-scale technological change over time would benefit from understanding the sociolinguist's fine-grained look at language use; the critical theorist examining cultural constructs of technology has much to learn from the rhetorician's analysis of technological argument; and the psychologist looking at individuals' interactions with material technologies is reminded—through work in history, rhetoric, and critical theory—of the larger place of both technology and literacy in our culture. And just as the computer scientist who works to develop new literacy technologies needs to understand what the educational researcher does about technology in use, or what the critical theorist does about the cultural uses of technology, humanistic scholars from all disciplines need to understand a bit of what the computer scientist knows: how computers work and how they are made to work.

Ideally, however, those involved in pursuing questions within Technology Studies would collaborate across traditional boundaries in actual hands-on intellectual projects that would need and use the diverse skills and knowledge of computer scientists, linguists, historians, designers, rhetoricians, engineers, psychologists, and critical theorists. It is probably in these circumstances—where scholars from diverse disciplines work together on common projects—that Technology Studies has the greatest chance of taking hold. In fact, some of the best contemporary work in Technology Studies is coming from research sites—including U.S. and European universities and corporate research centers—with just such interdisciplinary teams in place: Stockholm's Royal Institute of Technology (KTH), where, housed in the Division of Computer Science, psychologists, communications theorists, and computer scientists are working to develop computer writing tools that mimic the three dimensionality of traditional writing technologies (Eklundh, Fatton, & Tomberger, in press); Rensselaer Polytechnic Institute, where rhetorician Cheryl Geisler and computer scientist Edwin Rogers are collaborating with engineering students and corporate sponsors to develop and build a computerized collaborating writing and design workspace for engineering students (Rogers, et al, 1994); Bellcore, where psychologists Dennis Egan and Tom Landauer and computer scientist Joel Remde have developed a hypertext system that is theoretically and practically based, using what they call "formative design-evaluation," in which empirical studies and design constitute an iterative series (Landauer, Egan, Remde, Lesk, Lochbaum & Ketchum, 1994); Carnegie Mellon University, where rhetoricians David Kaufer and Christine Neuwirth are working with colleagues in computer science, social science, and graphic design on projects aimed at understanding collaborative on-line writing and developing systems to support that writing (Neuwirth, Kaufer, Chandhok, & Morris, in press); the Laboratory of Comparative Human Cognition at the University of California at San Diego, where psychologist Michael Cole and his colleagues—applied linguists and educational psychologists, as well as community workers and public school teachers and administrators—are studying how technology systems and children change one another (Cole, in press). This list is, of necessity, partial; but these research teams—working across disciplinary, institutional, and even national boundaries—are exemplary because they bring together scholars from a range of disciplines, pursuing vital questions about technology and literacy, and disseminating their results widely to academic, industrial, government, and educational forums.

This kind of collaboration, communication, and interaction across disciplinary lines will be difficult to bring to fruition. Technology Studies will require cross-disciplinary presses and journals (e.g., Lawrence Erlbaum Associates' technology series and the Society for Literature and Science's new journal *Configurations*) and on-line groups for discussion and argument, as well as forums—conferences, meetings, symposia—in which scholars can meet face to face. It will also require some loosening of the institutional structures that impede active collaboration between individuals in different departments and colleges, and between industry and academia. But initially and primarily, researchers working in the diverse areas of Technology Studies must make their own audience as they attempt to reach—or, more accurately, construct—readers who share the larger goals of understanding technology and literacy in all its forms. This volume is one attempt to create such an audience: I hope that the book can speak to my colleagues in computer science as well as in English; to scholars in the human sciences of rhetoric, linguistics, cultural studies, and history, as well as those in the more empirical disciplines of organizational theory, cognitive and social psychology, and education.

One of the tenets, then, of Technology Studies is that it should be consciously and studiously interdisciplinary. Consequently, Technology Studies cannot and should not shy away from, on the one hand, normative studies of value and policy, or on the other, practical studies of development and use. Scholars from critical theory, rhetoric, and education—disciplines that traditionally deal in the murky areas of human values and policy—bring an interest and expertise in addressing questions like the following: What should technology look like? How should technology be used? Who should technology serve? Ideally, these questions could also be taken up by computer scientists and psychologists, who have traditionally been more interested in questions of implementation and use: Does this machine work? What happens when people use it? How does it augment human processing capacities? How can we make it better? An awareness of these kinds of nuts and bolts issues about real, working systems must also undergird the scholarship of researchers considering policy and value questions. Discussions of value and policy are hollow if those conducting them do not have some experience with development and implementation of actual technologies, and technology development is bankrupt if it is not grounded in theory, history, and the thoughtful consideration of consequences. Attempts to understand the relationship between technology and literacy, thinking and culture, are doomed if those conducting them focus too narrowly on one kind of question, or exclude out of hand particular methods.

Technology Studies Focuses on Technology Itself

Another tenet of the interdisciplinary enterprise of Technology Studies would be a continual focusing and refocusing on the technology, a looking at, rather than through, technology. Technology *itself*—rather than merely technology's consequences—must become an object of inquiry. Of course there is interest in technology's consequences, because computers, like other technologies before them, are powerful tools for accomplishing purposeful acts and shaping cultural practice. People are only interested in tools, after all, because those tools can do something for them.

However, theoretical or empirical attempts to understand technological consequences, without attending as well to the shape of the technology itself, stand little chance of success. For instance, empirical studies aimed at understanding the effect of "the computer" on writing in classrooms, or in corporations, must begin with an awareness that "the" computer does not exist; rather, it is instantiated in vastly different ways through use by people in classrooms, homes, offices, and corporations. At the very least, these people use all kinds of computers, and it would be reasonable to expect quite different effects if writers were sharing a few obsolete personal computers running simple word processing programs than if they were using high-powered networked workstations with integrated video, audio, and graphics. In either case, generalizing from one situation to the other would be risky. Empirical studies of technology should look at technology, attending to the range of hardware and software that writers use, as well as the physical setting in which they use it: Is the equipment new, old, or obsolete? Is the machine networked or stand alone? How fast does the machine respond to user input? How is text displayed? Is the system easy to learn? What editing and formatting features are available? How much access do writers have to computers? Is printing available? What are the ergonomics of the workplace (i.e., is it comfortable, well lit, and free of glare, smoke, and excess noise)?

Further, the place of computers in a particular sociocultural setting, the history of computers in that setting, and individuals' feelings and beliefs about technology will all affect what "the computer" is taken to be in any given case. Therefore, reflective, speculative, and theoretical essays must also move beyond using the general term *computers*, or even more broadly, *technology*, as a placeholder that assumes the role of causal agent, without being specified in any clear way. The work of Richard Lanham, one of the most articulate technology scholars within the humanities, illustrates how vague the terms remain in discussions of technology's cultural impact. Lanham (1989), a technological optimist, heralds technology's remaking of reading and writing, and of literature and literary study, but the causal agent in this remaking is sometimes the personal computer, sometimes digitization, sometimes desktop publishing. Certainly all these forms of computer technology are related, but Technology Studies would seek to delineate that relationship and, more generally, to systematically explore (through historical studies, feature analysis, or theoretical inquiries) how particular aspects of computers, particular kinds of computers, and particular uses of computers engender particular cultural effects.

Both instantiations of the *looking through technology* phenomenon (empirical and theoretical) are tied to the myth of technological transparency—the notion that a computer is a computer is a computer. They are also linked to a related myth about technology in our culture—that it is all-powerful, and in the next section, I examine these two myths.   As long as "the computer" remains unspecified, under specified, or too variously specified, attempts to understand the complex, symbiotic relationship between writing and technology will remain disjoint, or even contradictory. Rather, Technology Studies must focus in an exacting way on technology itself. This is not meant to suggest that inquiries should be limited to studies of the black (or gray, or white) box that sits on the desk. Rather, if technology is to be understood, it must be examined broadly, in all its cultural, historical, and material manifestation. Indeed, if technology is understood, as Heidegger (1977) would have it, as a complex of processes, objects, needs, and uses, then the scope of Technology Studies can be broad indeed: studies of the processes of development of literacy technologies, the social and cultural events that utilize those technologies, the institutional and individual uses to which technology is put, as well as careful examination of the actual objects called computers.

TECHNOLOGICAL MYTHS THAT IMPEDE
TECHNOLOGY STUDIES

As I suggest earlier, there are a number of institutional impediments to the conduct of Technology Studies, particularly boundaries between and within cultural institutions, including academic disciplines. Much of contemporary society is structured through division of labor and the making of and deference to experts. Certainly these institutional structures have benefits, including a certain economy of effort and training and a sharing of large amounts of information and knowledge that is beyond the ken of any individual. The conduct of Technology Studies, however, will require working through and across existing borders between disciplines, or at least make those borders a bit more fluid. As difficult as institutional structures may be to overcome, however, there are several implicit beliefs about technology that also provide impediment to the conduct of Technology Studies. These cultural myths, or assumptions, about technology are particularly insidious because they lurk, unexamined, in thinking about and definitions of technology and they color both how problems of technology are delineated and what strategies are brought to bear in their solution. More specifically, these assumptions place us—as scholars, as teachers, and as users—in a subordinate position to technology. That is, these myths or habits of thinking take people out of the realm of technology development, technological critique, and technological inquiry and set them in positions to be merely receivers or consumers of technology (for a more elaborate discussion of these myths, see Haas & Neuwirth, 1994).

The two myths treated here are closely related: One asserts that technology is transparent, whereas the other asserts that technology is all-powerful. While seemingly disparate, these two assumptions actually share an instrumental view of technology. That is, accepting these assumptions means believing that writing and technology are somehow separate and distinct entities, and that they exist independently of one another. This instrumental view of technology is of course connected to beliefs about the nature of institutional and disciplinary boundaries: When technology is seen instrumentally, it is possible to believe that technology is the province only of technologists, experts from another domain, whose job it is to "do" technology, whatever that might mean. And the work of humanists, educators, or cultural critics is seen to be the study of discourse, or learning, or culture as it exists independently from technology. I would argue instead that understanding writing, culture, or technology are—in the late 20th century, as always—part and parcel of the same scholarly the late 20th century, as always—part and parcel of the same scholarly enterprise. Or that they should be.

The Transparent Technology Myth

The myth that technology is transparent posits that technology is a kind of distortionless window: Writing is not changed in any substantive way by the transparent medium through which it passes. In this view, writing is writing is writing, unchanged and unaffected by the mode of production and presentation. The essential processes of literacy are universal and unchanging: Writers and readers simply exchange their pens for word processors, transfer their books to hypertext, replace their face-to-face conversations with computer conferences, and continue to produce texts and construct meanings in the ways they always have. One variant of the transparent technology assumption acknowledges that writing is different with computers, but limits that difference to an increase in efficiency. That is, this version of the transparent technology myth holds that writers can compose, revise, edit, and produce texts more quickly and with less effort with computers; therefore, using computers increases writers' efficiency, but makes no profound difference in how writing gets done. The belief that technology is a "win" because it increases efficiency is obviously problematic: The very metaphor of *efficiency* equates literacy acts with production acts, a somewhat suspect equation (Olson, 1987).

The transparent technology myth views technology merely as a means of textual production. Writing, in its essential nature, is somehow imagined to exist independently of and uninfluenced by that means. As I argue in chapter 1, however, writing is in its very essence technological, because writing has never and cannot exist separate from material technologies. The danger of the transparent technology assumption, of course, is that when it is operative there is no need for inquiry about technology: If technology is "immaterial," so to speak, there is little need to study it at all. But believing that technology is transparent does not in fact make it so, and does not preclude technology having powerful effects on literacy, effects that we are not prepared to examine or understand if we are operating with a belief that technology does not matter.

The Technology Is All-Powerful Myth

The counterpart to the transparent technology myth is the assumption that technology is all-powerful. In this view, computer technologies are self-determining: They will have far-reaching and profound—but essentially one-way—effects. New technologies for literacy are such a powerful force that simply introducing them to writers will change literacy acts in the most profound of ways, supplanting completely the existing pen and book technologies, according to the all-powerful technology myth. This myth imbues computer technology with a number of qualities, among them that computers are unique and that they are active, independent agents of change. One can see this myth operating in largely celebratory popular accounts of technological change, but it is also operative in some scholarly work as well. Chapter 7 (this volume) presents a detailed rhetorical analysis of some of the claims made about technology within English studies; these claims often implicitly invoke the myths of "transparent" or "all-powerful" technology.

There are several dangers to the technology is all-powerful myth. First, the technology is all-powerful myth errs by placing individual uses and motives, and cultural habits and beliefs, in a subordinate position to technology which determines its own uses and effects. Like the technology is transparent stance, this myth essentially compels us to remain noncritical and nonparticipatory. The belief that technology determines itself and its own uses and effects removes the space where both the development and critique of technology occur. If technology determines its own shape and use, there is little need for an enterprise like Technology Studies.

Further, the myth suggests that the theory and practice of literacy will have to be rebuilt from the ground up: Existing theories, practices, and rhetorics will be useless in the new age of this unique literacy tool, the computer. Consequently, scholarship influenced by this myth is given a kind of *carte blanche*, a freedom from accounting for technology by any existing theory or knowledge, as it looks for strong, unitary, one-way, and often only positive effects for technology, or seeks to celebrate the newness and uniqueness of computer technologies. Scholarship, then, becomes a justification for technology, rather than serious inquiry about technology.

For Technology Studies to be a viable and useful scholarly enterprise, the myths of transparent and all-powerful technology must be overcome. There are several correctives to these myths. The first is a thorough grounding in the histories of other technologies, which, as I argue in chapter 8 (this volume), provides a strong counter to the tendency to read history as a series of technological revolutions. The long and complex history of print, for instance, illustrates that technology is neither transparent (i.e., print had and continues to have real consequences) nor all-powerful because those consequences are the result not of the printing press as a unitary object but are rather the result of a complex of technological, cultural, and historical factors.

Another corrective to these myths is to acknowledge that technologies' effects depend on how they are culturally represented and how people reason about them. That is, technologies are made through our thinking and talking about them, and through our use of them (see chapters 6 and 7, this volume). Therefore, technologies are not static–certainly not static enough to be un-equivocally transparent or all-powerful. Rather, they are modified subtly and constantly by the uses to which they are put, and by the discourse that accompanies those uses. Technologies continue to evolve, not just because of technological breakthroughs but because their contexts of use, and their users, continue to shape them. For example, any effect of computer networks on writing processes is a result of a complex interaction between the technology itself and the teachers and students actively using the networks to achieve their goals (Neuwirth, Palmquist, Cochran, Gillespie, Hartman, & Hajduk, 1994). In short, recognizing the dynamic nature of technologies, the ways in which technologies are constructed and used, and the complicated history of techno-logical advance can help counter overly simplistic myths about technology.

A THEORETICAL GROUNDING FOR TECHNOLOGY STUDIES

To what theories of writing or literacy might scholars interested in technology look for the underpinnings of technology study? What theories of writing will help us look carefully at, rather than through, the material technologies of literacy? What theories of writing might help us examine the relationship between cultural tools and cognitive activity? Despite the ubiquitousness of the tools and artifacts of literacy in contemporary culture and the rapid change in writing tools that the last decade has witnessed, surprisingly few theorists of writing have specifically addressed technological questions, and even fewer have attempted to deal with the broader issue of the material nature of writing.

Hence, another impediment to the enterprise of Technology Studies is a dearth of theory that can undergird attempts to examine the relationship between technology and literacy. The lack of coherent theory is due to two related problems: the tendency of writing and discourse theorists to fall victim to the dual myths of transparent and all-powerful technology, and the inability of literacy studies broadly conceived to deal with materiality, particularly the embodied materiality of writing.

Even the best examples of Technology Studies cannot bridge the gap between technology's role in shaping individuals' writing processes or practices and the larger cultural impact of technology that constitutes historical-cultural change. That is, studies of technology tend to focus either on the fine-detailed, real-time processes of technology development, learning, or use; or they examine the broad sweep of change at the cultural and historical level. Seldom, if ever, is this question addressed: How do we get from one to the other? How do we move from discussions of technology's role in thinking to discussions of its role in culture, and back again? This situation, of course, mirrors a larger gap in current understanding: the murky, always-assumed, but never specified relationship between writing as cognitive process and writing as cultural practice, and the relation of both to the material world. Indeed, as chapter 9 (this volume) suggests, Technology Studies may provide a highly specified and materially present instantiation of the cultural–cognitive impasse. At the end of this section I examine the work of scholars studying what I call "embodied practice"; this scholarship may provide a promising beginning for a theoretical accounting of the materiality of literacy and a theoretical grounding for technology studies.

First, however, I briefly examine three bodies of theory that have influenced recent writing research and pedagogy in important ways: cognitive theories of writing, classical rhetorical theory, and postmodern theory. Although an extended critique of these theories is not attempted here, I do want to suggest how each of them has avoided or oversimplified the Technology Question, and why I therefore find them less than useful in addressing questions of technology and literacy. Classical rhetorical theory and cognitive theory have either ignored or only indirectly treated questions of technology; in effect, for much of these two bodies of theory, technology is transparent. A number of scholars have drawn on postmodern critical theory to discuss technology, but these treatments tend to treat technology as all-powerful; they fall prey to the inherent technological determinism of postmodernism.

Cognitive Theories of Writing

The cognitive process theory developed by Linda Flower and John R. Hayes (1981a) is probably the most widely known of cognitive accounts of writing, both within English Studies and outside of it. In their influential article in *College Composition and Communication*, Flower and Hayes define the component parts of their model: a *task environment*, consisting of the rhetorical problem and the "text produced so far"; the writer's *long-term memory*, containing knowledge of topic, audience, and writing plans; and the *writing processes*, with which Flower and Hayes are most concerned: planning, translating, and reviewing, as well as a monitor function to manage the process. The model, virtually unchanged, also appeared in a lengthy piece (Flower & Hayes, 1984) that was the last that Flower and Hayes published on the cognitive model *per se* (Flower & Hayes, 1984). In general, the model treats technology as transparent: Material tools and artifacts only enter into the model in the most tangential of ways.[1]

Because Flower and Hayes are concerned almost exclusively with cognitive operations, there was little mention of the material world of artifacts and tools. Granted, the text produced so far is presumably a material artifact, but it is not treated as such and is in fact only discussed very briefly: two paragraphs in the 1981 piece (1981; p. 371). When Flower and Hayes discuss writers' notes as augmenting memory, they indirectly touch on the technology of paper, which supplies the medium for "abstract representations" (1984; p. 135) that aid writers when they plan written text.

Further, the act of translating, where writers put "ideas into visible language" (1981; p. 373) is the most likely place to treat the tools by which writers actually render their meanings into material artifacts, but for Flower and Hayes translating is exclusively a mental operation. Indeed, the translating box in the cognitive model is the emptiest and least developed. In separate set of studies, Kaufer, Hayes, and Flower (1986) examined the translation process more directly, including some attention to written material artifacts. But here again, the emphasis is on the cognitive processes of planning that the written artifacts support, rather than on those artifacts themselves.

In addition, Flower and Hayes do not attempt to account for computer technology, and there is no acknowledgment that writers might use tools other than pen and paper. Given that much of the actual research was probably done in the late 1970s, this may not be surprising: Even at Flower and Hayes' highly technological university, Carnegie Mellon, computer writing tools were probably not commonplace when this research was conducted. The articles hint that writers were using pens or pencils and paper: One writer reports "doodling on this scratch sheet" (1981; p. 383) and another reports "X[ing] out" a section of text (1984; p. 128). Interestingly, Flower and Hayes draw upon computer examples in their article when the discuss the nature of expert and novice representations (1984; p. 134). But these examples are all about programmers writing code or users trying to read manuals; none of them deals with computers as objects of text production.   As Geisler (1994) notes, Flower's later work moves away from an accounting for the cognitive processes of writing *per se* (see, e.g., Flower, 1988; Flower, Stein, Ackerman, Kantz, McCormick, & Peck;, 1990).

Robert de Beaugrande's 1984 *Text Production: Toward a Science of Composition* attempts to catalogue and describe the components of written composition. In some ways, de Beaugrande's is the most overtly technological of the cognitive process models in that it uses the most detailed and pointed analogies between the human mind and the central processing unit (CPU) of a computer. For de Beaugrande, the mind is a processing and production system, and he uses computer terms (e.g., memory, feedback loop, goodness of fit) to describe the process of writing. In addition, he explicitly mentions technology, including a description of the benefits of spell-checking (p. 231) and a testimonial to the benefits of computer revision in producing his own book (p. 290).

However, there is no explicit, developed account of technology in de Beaugrande's actual model, nor does he discuss materiality in any detailed way. A close reading reveals that there is actually a potential space for technology in de Beaugrande's theory: What he calls the resources of text processing include what is available to be processed in the immediate situation—and these might be construed to include technology, but technology is not explicitly considered. For de Beaugrande, like for Flower and Hayes, there seems to be little cognizance that writers live and work in a material space, creating material artifacts using material technologies. The notion that these material constraints might impinge in any way on the processes of composing, which these theorists seek to examine, is not acknowledged.

A third influential set of theorists in the cognitive tradition—Marlene Scardamalia; and Carl Bereiter; and their collaborators—do offer one detailed treatment of how physical constraints might constrain young writers. In an article written in the early 1980s, Scardamalia, Bereiter, and Goelman (1982), treat what they call the "conditions of text production" (p. 175) and examine how these production factors might inhibit high-level cognitive activity in written composition.   The authors of this piece do not explicitly address technology, nor do they discuss production factors explicitly as material constraints.   But the production difficulties of young children upon which Scardamalia, Bereiter, and Goelman focus are in fact materially based. The first of these difficulties, the loss of ideas from short-term memory due to children's slow rate of production, is presumably less troublesome in adults because they have mastered the technologies of written textual production.   The other difficulties that children have with writing is the interference of higher level processing with "the demands of the written medium" (p. 177) and the lack of external cueing in the form of an interlocutor. Underlying all of Scardamalia and Bereiter's work is a belief that conversation is natural to children, and that their difficulties with written composition lie in the fact that it is unlike the oral conversations with which they are so familiar. Given this assumption—an opposition of conversation with composition—it is not surprising that technology remains transparent for them. The dichotomizing of writing as distinct from speech means that all writing—in whatever medium—is conflated into something that is not speech.   Although materiality is not quite as transparent in Scardamalia and Bereiter as it is in Flower and Hayes or de Beaugrande, it is seen as a constraint, something that skilled writers, facile with the tools of text production, have overcome (see Geisler, 1994, for a further critique). Materiality and technology are not seen by any of these cognitive theorists as inherently a part of writing, and therefore these theories are less than useful in providing a grounding for Technology Studies.

Classical Rhetorical Theory

Chapter 1 (this volume) suggested that Plato can be considered the "originator" of the Technology Question as it has been formulated in Western philosophy; he may have been the first scholar to thematize (albeit rather unsystematically) issues of materiality as they are connected to writing. However, although Plato may acknowledge the Technology Question, his ambivalence about writing and about materiality generally make him an unlikely candidate to furnish a theoretical ground for Technology Studies, as I am conceiving of it.

   In both Plato's philosophy and in his politics, the body, materiality, and technology are all suspect. The body, concerned with material or physical unrealities, is inferior to the mind, which deals with true essences. The body and its material nature are not only inferior to the mind, they may also be considered dangerous or even evil. Derrida (1981) is correct in noting that Plato transfers his ambivalence about (or even hatred of) the body to the material artifacts of writing.

Christian Neoplatonism, of which Augustine is by far the most influential exemplar, retains Plato's suspicion of the body and of the material world generally. Augustine's (1977) *Confessions* contains a forceful renunciation of sexuality and the body in favor of a disciplined Christian life of contemplation and study. Augustine does not denounce written texts as Plato does; indeed, Augustine sees his work as the interpretation of written texts, the Scriptures. His *On Christian Doctrine* (1958) describes rules and precepts for reading that will bring the reader closer to the love of God (see Book 1, sections 39 and 40). However, Augustine maintains a strict distinction between knowledge and truth, on the one hand, and words, on the other—between "things" and "signs" (Kennedy, 1980; pp. 153-55). Indeed, some scholars credit—or blame— Augustine as much as Plato for the bifurcation of body from mind (or soul) that is so prevalent in Western thinking (e.g., Brown, 1988). In any case, the antimaterialism of Plato and the Christian Neoplatonists not only falls short of providing a theoretical grounding for Technology Studies, but it also illustrates some of the entrenched ways of thinking that a serious consideration of the materiality of literacy must overcome.

The art of memory, the fourth of the five ancient rhetorical canons, provides another possible cite from which to discuss materiality in terms of classical rhetorical theory. Although this fourth canon is sometimes dismissed as "mere" memorization of speeches (Reynolds, 1993), Frances Yates' (1966) extensive work on the nature of memory in classical and medieval rhetoric suggests the complexity of memory: This ancient art included memorizing in order, holding in memory, retrieving from memory, imprinting on memory, and improving the memory. For the Greeks and Latins, memory was of vital importance precisely because written artifacts were not yet available to do some of this mental work. Further, and more to my purposes here, Yates argues convincingly that the ancient art of memory was materially based: of paramount importance was the selection of a series of *loci* (literally places), most often parts or locations within an architectural structure. The rhetor then imagined himself moving through the structure, retrieving objects in the order in which he or she had "placed" them there (p. 3). Further, the anonymous author of the *Rhetorica Ad Herennium*

(1937) suggest that the objects to be placed at the *loci* might be extraordinary or peculiar human images, including particularly bodily images.

How is the materiality of memory tied to issues of technology? This is a question that has, for the most part, not been taken up by scholars of classical rhetorical theory, who, like Yates, have primarily dealt with memory in historical terms. Two exceptions are Gronbeck (1993) and Crowley (1993), although Gronbeck's focus is on electronic media such as television, rather than with writing technologies *per se*. Crowley (1993) has takes up the notion of memory as it has operated in contemporary writing theory and argues that a restoration of the importance of memory could aid in the construction of a postmodern rhetoric. She also provocatively examines the relationship between modern conceptions of memory and the development of both literacy and literacy technologies. With the exception of Crowley, most scholars interested in memory, then, have looked at it historically rather than contemporarily, and have not explicitly made the connection to writing technologies. Technology remains implicitly transparent for most classical rhetorical theory, possibly because of its origins as the study of spoken discourse.

Postmodern Theory

A third body of work that has had a great deal of contemporary currency in the study and teaching of writing is postmodern critical theory. Derrida, Foucault, and, to a lesser extent, Barthes have probably been the most influential of the postmodernists within discourse studies. They have provided a way into the study discourse that emphasizes the social and cultural construction of language and its fundamental instability. This section briefly treats Derrida and Foucault, poststructualists who are most often invoked in discussions of technology, and how their work has been used in contemporary postmodern approaches to the technologies of writing.

As I detail in chapter 1 (this volume), Jacques Derrida's (1981) critique of Plato as the originator of western metaphysics is centered squarely on Plato's conceptions of writing. Plato's beliefs about writing—indeed his problem with writing—is that it is material, and therefore suspect. Derrida is useful for those interested in Technology Studies because he rightly points out that writing is very much more than transcribed speech. Indeed, for Derrida, language is never primary or essential, not even in its spoken form. All discourse is "written," in that it is already embued with ideology. Derrida also helps clarify that what is at stake in debates about writing (and, I would argue, all debates about technologies) are vital issues of power and knowledge. However, Derrida's project is one of critique, not one of construction. That is, although his work puts the Technology Question on the table, at least *vis a vis* the technology of writing, and opens up for critique the notion that the relationship technology or writing and truth is a simple one, Derrida does not provide the grounds from which to begin the constructive project of Technology Studies.

When the work of Michel Foucault is invoked in discussions of technology, it is usually in connection with his 1975 work on penal theory and the history of the modern prison, *Discipline and Punish*. Foucault argues that what characterizes the modern prison is its shift from punishing prisoners physically to controlling their minds through surveillance and other indirect means. In addition, Foucault finds that this same kind of disciplinary surveillance underlies much of contemporary society, controlling citizens' behavior in ways that are subtle and hard to detect, yet very powerful. Foucault does not address technology *per se* in *Discipline and Punish*, but the means by which modern prisons (and modern society) control behavior are highly technological. Foucault uses Jeremy Bentham's Panopticon as a metaphor for the insidious surveillance of the modern prison. Bentham's design of the Panopticon was a serious proposal for an artifact that would aid in the liberal reformation of prisoners. Foucault, however, is less interested in the actual technology of the Panopticon than in how it functions to control behavior—both within the prison and outside it.

Foucault's work cannot provide the theoretical grounding for Technology Studies for a number of reasons. First, he posits technology unitarily: The Panopticon is an abstraction. Although positing technology abstractly as an instrument of oppression and control may provide a way into discussions of power, is not as useful in helping us know how to begin to examine actual existing technologies. Further, in his discussion of the move from bodily to mental punishment, Foucault in fact reconstructs and reifies the body/mind distinction (Hayles, 1993); this distinction provides a serious impediment to understanding writing as both an act of body and an act of mind. This more holistic view of writing will be imperative in order to appreciate the relationship between writing and its technologies.

Postmodern approaches to technology have tended to avoid the transparent technology trap. After all, the transparency assumption draws upon notions of efficiency and commonsense (see Haas & Neuwirth, 1993), which postmodernism severely calls into question. However, postmodernism's insistent move away from any kind of agency means technology must be posited as self-determining, if not all-powerful. Further, in works like Mark Poster's (1990) *The Mode of Information* or George Landow's (1992) *Hypertext*, modern information technologies and postmodern or poststructuralist theories are often used to reify one another. Theory and technology exist in a kind of circular relationship, with theory used to somehow legitimate modern technology, which itself is seen as underscoring the aptness of contemporary theory. And what this means is that technology itself—where Technology Studies should focus its efforts—is seldom examined in any critical way. What those interested in Technology Studies can take from postmodern and poststructural theories is the recognition of the cultural construction of knowledge and the basic instability of language—and other cultural systems. However, the "postmodern impasse" that Faigley (1992; p. 20) identifies in his treatment of postmodern theory and writing instruction—that is, postmodernism's inability to sustain a constructive as well as a critical inquiry—is at the heart of the problem of postmodernism for Technology Studies.

Toward a Theory of Technology

As I suggest in the Preface, my goal in this volume is to argue for the materiality of literacy and, more specifically, to explore the relationship between material tools and the practice and process of writing. The studies presented in Parts 2 and 3 provide an empirical grounding for my claim that, through the embodied actions of human beings, cultural tools and cognitive activity construct one another. In the remainder of this chapter, I turn to a brief examination of diverse scholarship that can, by providing further theoretical grounding for Technology Studies, help in understanding the symbiotic relationship of cultural tools and cognitive activity, and the material, embodied link between them.

At first glance, the work of the three scholars treated here might appear to be quite unrelated: Jean Lave (1988) is a cognitive anthropologist studying the nature of competence in mathematics; Mark Johnson (1987) is a philosopher interested in reason and imagination; and Paul Connerton (1989) is working at the intersection of sociology and critical theory on the role of ritual in societies. However, the work of these scholars can be joined loosely under the term *embodied practice*. In so doing, the work draws upon—either explicitly or implicitly—a body of common theory, including the writings of Vygotsky

(1981a, 1981b, 1986), Bourdieu's *Outline of a Theory of Practice* (1977), and de Certeau's *The Practice of Everyday Life* (1985).[2] Lave, Johnson, and Connerton are all concerned with how cognition or thinking—mathematical reasoning for Lave, memory for Connerton, imaginative thinking for Johnson—is both defined by and has its roots in the everyday, embodied experiences of human beings. Lave is careful to note that, in positing "the everyday" as a concept, she is not suggesting an essential division between "domestic life and work, domestic life and public domains, routine maintenance and productive activity, or manual routines and creative mental work" (p. 14-15). Rather, "the everyday world is just that: what people do in the daily, weekly, monthly, ordinary cycles of activity" (p. 15), and the scientists no less than the grocery shopper no less than the schoolteacher are all, for Lave, engaged in everyday activities.

Technologies of every sort saturate the world of everyday activity: the schoolteacher's books, maps, and ruler; the shopper's list, scales, and pocket calculator; the scientist's test tubes, computer, and table of periodic elements. In a later volume cowritten with Etienne Wenger (1991), Lave discusses the role of technologies and artifacts in everyday activity and particularly in the learning of cultural practices. It is vital to understand the technologies and artifacts used in any human practice—from navigation to shopping to engineering—because the heritage of any given practice is carried in its technologies. Technologies and other artifacts "encode" the knowledge of a community and allow for certain kinds of cultural activity and not others; in this way, then, technologies impact on the individuals who use them. Lave and Wenger use the example of the alidade used by quartermasters to illustrate that a tool embodies the thoughts, actions, and biases of unknown numbers of users as it has been developed, used, and adapted over the course of the history of the practice of navigation (p. 101). Certainly, writing systems and writing tools provide an analogous case.

To understand the mechanism by which these cultural tools impinge on cognitive activity, the work of Connerton (1989) and Johnson (1987) is useful. Connerton and Johnson both posit embodiment as a critical feature of human social and cognitive practice. That is, human beings act through a physical, material body,[3] bounded by time and space. According to Johnson, this embodiment includes "the patterns of our bodily movement, the contours of our spatial and temporal orientation, and the forms of our interactions with objects" (p. xix). These scholars' projects have quite different foci: Connerton want to argue that social structures are difficult to change because of the habitual performative embodied acts that comprise cultural activity, whereas Johnson seeks to explore how bodily actions "work their way up" into cognitive meanings and patterns.   But for both, the actions and sensations of the body are inherently and intimately tied to the workings of the mind: in a very real way, people cannot think without their bodies. For Connerton, activities as diverse as appropriate table manners and jazz piano playing are strongly based in bodily movements and feelings; embodied "habit-memory" (p. 84) provides the location through which much cognitive activity takes place. Johnson's inquiry is centered more squarely on cognitive activity as it is usually defined—that is, reasoning and understanding—and his method is to examine the metaphors of everyday discourse. In his undertaking to put "the body back into the mind" (p. xxxvi), Johnson postulates that everyday understanding, abstract reasoning, and even imaginative creativity are all embodied. That is, these acts of mind are made possible by image-schematic structures (also called *embodied structures*; p. 28-9) which are learned through habitual ways of interacting with the spatial/ temporal world. In other words, these cognitive activities are learned, in a very real sense, by our bodies.

Although neither Johnson nor Connerton address issues of technology *per se*, their notion of embodiment and its role in cognition provides a way to examine how technologies—material artifacts and tools manipulated by the body—can have profound effects on thinking. Their work underscores the materiality of literacy: –how utterly bound to the physical world of bodies is writing, one of the most awesome products of the human mind. In general, the work of scholars interested in embodied, everyday practice can be useful in approaching questions about the relationships of technology and literacy, and of culture and thinking. Lave's work is useful in understanding the complex nature of technology and its artifacts, and recognizing that cultural tools and cognitive activity constitute one another; Connerton and Johnson help us see how the embodied actions of human beings mediate cultural tools and cognitive activity.

This chapter has suggested the scope of Technology Studies, the impediments that lie in its way, and the kind of theoretical grounding that will be most useful for those interested in pursuing the Technology Question in literacy studies: How do the cultural tools of writing and the cognitive activity of writing constitute one another? The second part of this volume examines how material technologies impact in subtle but important ways on the thinking processes of adult writers, and in Part 3, I turn to the question of how human beings create their literacy technologies, through embodied actions and through discourse.

FOOTNOTES

[1]John R. Hayes has recently proposed an adaptation of the 1981 Hayes and Flower process model of composing which recognizes technology as part of the task environment (personal communication, 1993). Neuwirth and Kaufer (1989) offer one account of the role external representations can play in composing.

[2]Of these three theorists—Vygotsky, Bourdieu, and de Certeau—I believe that Vygotsky's work is the most directly applicable to the Technology Question in literacy studies. Aspects of his theories are treated in some detail in chapters 1 and 8. I choose to use Lave, Connerton, and Johnson here, rather than Bourdieu and de Certeau, because they more explicitly address questions of technology, literacy, and materiality.

[3]Although "the body" functions as a cultural construct, "embodiment" is always specific and contextualized and tied to the life of an individual human being. See Hayles (1993) for a succinct discussion of the differences between embodiment and the body.

THE ROLE OF TECHNOLOGY IN THE
COGNITION OF LITERACY

3

READING ON-LINE

This chapter begins an exploration of how computer technologies impact on the cognitive processes of individual writers. In particular, this chapter examines how reading and rereading are changed when writers use computers. In keeping with chapter 2's argument that Technology Studies should look at, rather than through, technology, the intent here is to focus on computers themselves, rather than simply on computers' effects. Consequently, several different display and presentation variables are examined, and the chapter concludes with a frame-work of features of computer writing systems that helps to account for the findings presented here. One of the most important findings of these studies is that a computer is not a computer is not a computer; that is, there were strikingly different results for different computer systems. These findings suggest that the computer is not an all-powerful monolith, and that computers' effects are not unitary. Rather, computers can—depending on how they are configured and how they are used—have vastly different effects on writers and writing.

EXAMINING MISMATCHES BETWEEN COMPUTERS AND WRITERS

Discourse about technology, within contemporary culture generally and within literacy studies in particular, tends to be positive, enthusiastic, or even hyperbolic about the potential of computers to assist writers and improve writing. Ellen Barton (1994) identifies what she calls *the dominant discourse* about computers as celebratory discourse that extols the virtues and benefits of technology, and she describes this dominant discourse as it operates in both the culture at large and in literature about computers and writing. Chapter 7 (this volume) presents a rhetorical analysis of recent articles about computers and writing that traces celebratory claims about computers to a set of underlying cultural beliefs about technology. However, there is another source for positive and celebratory discourse about computers for writing—one that may seem more immediately obvious to most computer users. Enthusiasm about computers can also be traced to the advantages that the machine itself offers writers as it streamlines and simplifies much of the work of writing. For many writers, text production is quicker with a keyboard than it is with a pen, and the text itself is usually more legible as well. Computer-based word processors make adding, deleting, and moving text much less onerous than with pen-and-paper technology, and writers can use grammar- and spell-checking programs to eliminate many common errors. Desktop publishing programs allow writers to move their texts from drafting through production themselves, often with integrated sound and graphics, and networking capabilities can link writers across a classroom or across an ocean.

This "visionary view" (p. 3) of technology, as Bruce and Rubin (1993) call it, has fueled important developments in computer writing tools, as well as a great deal of educational innovation. It is certainly not my intention to criticize this enthusiasm for the potential benefits of technology. However, contemporary cultural and disciplinary narratives about computers and writing often paint a rather one-sided picture: that is, a picture of writers freed of the constraints of pen and paper and writing processes transformed by computers; a picture of written texts that are more complex, more sophisticated, and better than they had been before; and a picture of radically new and unique textual genres. However, common sense alone would suggest that no technology is wholly or exclusively beneficial, and indeed, meta-analyses like Hawisher's (1986, 1989) of research on computers and writing suggest a much more complicated picture.

In this chapter, and in the three that follow, I focus not on the benefits of computers for writers—of which there are many—but rather on the problems that computer writers have with various aspects of the machine. The focus is on existing problems, rather than on potential benefits, for several reasons: first, examining problem areas, or "mismatches," between technology and writers allows a more detailed and complicated examination of the technology than does exclusively positive focus on the computer's benefits. Seeing only the benefits of computers for writers assumes that technology is straightforward, nonproblematic, and transparent. Second, examining where existing technology falls short opens a space for the critique of existing technologies and a position from which to argue about the likely benefits of technology in a given situation.   Finally, a focus on what technology *cannot* do can provide the grounds for discussions of technology development within literacy studies— how the next generation of computer tools could and should better serve writers.

This chapter begins with a discussion of a series of interviews of computer writers and their reported reading problems when writing with a computer. Three studies of reading-related writing tasks—spatial recall, retrieving information, and reading to revise—are then presented. The feature analysis that concludes the chapter places these findings into an explanatory context and argues against the notion of technological transparency. I propose four system factors—size, legibility, responsiveness, and tangibility—that make a real and significant difference in how writers read their own texts on-line.

WRITERS' READING PROBLEMS AND THEIR USE OF HARD COPY

Over the course of about ten years, beginning in the early 1980s, I interviewed over 30 computer writers about their experiences using, and learning to use, a computer for writing. The first of these interviews took place in 1983, and the last in 1991. The interviews took place at an historical moment, the 1980s, when many writers—in academia and in the culture at large—were moving from producing texts with pencils, pens, and/or typewriters, to producing them with computers. As I argue in Chapter 1, this move from one set of powerful cultural and material tools to another is a profound one, and the writers interviewed seemed to sense this: They were eager to share their stories of moving to computer writing and seemed sincerely interested in discussing the advantages and disadvantages of computers, as well as in describing how they had adapted their processes to this new writing tool.   A detailed report of these interviews is not provided here. Rather, I focus on one particular set of problems that writers reported: problems in reading their own texts on-line. There were commonalties in how these reading problems were discussed and described that extended across writers, tasks, and computer systems.

The writers that I interviewed varied in age (from 18 to 52 years) and discipline: They were about evenly divided between those with backgrounds in the humanities, in science, and in engineering. All the writers were either employed or attending undergraduate or graduate school at Carnegie Mellon University when they were interviewed, and about two-thirds of the interview subjects were male. Writers were using their computers for a variety of tasks:

short papers and lab reports for students; technical documents of various length and memos for the university employees; and academic articles, theses, and books for the graduate students and faculty. The writers had been using the computer for various lengths of time, ranging from three months to over twenty years. Open-ended questions allowed for unanticipated responses (e.g., "Tell me about your experiences using a computer for writing" and "Can you describe in detail how you go about producing a text using your computer?"). In addition, to these interviews, a subset of ten writers were followed more closely as they used computers for writing over the course of four months. They kept process logs (Nelson, 1990) of their computer writing, noting when and why they printed hard copies of their texts. The logs also contained information about the kinds of writing tasks in which writers engaged and the length and difficulty of those tasks. In general, the process logs tended to corroborate the information that these writers, and others, had given me in interviews (see Haas, 1989c).

The kinds of systems that the interview subjects used and had used varied greatly. At the "low end" of technological sophistication, some of the writers (especially those interviewed in the early 1980s) used a terminal with a CRT display connected to a mainframe. However, some writers used high-powered networked workstations with advanced displays. Still others used IBM PCs or Apple McIntoshes. Almost all the writers had ready access to printing facilities, either in the room where they worked or in an adjacent room.

The ways and extent to which the writers used their computers for writing also varied. A few used it the computer "mainly as a fast typewriter," an efficient way to get a quick well-formatted copy. Others used the machine for low-level revising and editing, taking advantage of the case with which changes can be incorporated into the text-level and sentence-level options tested. (Low-level revision includes word changes and sentence-level editing; "sentence-level options" are choices about word order, syntax, and word choice.) Many writers used the computer throughout the entire writing process, beginning with preliminary planning, brainstorming or freewriting at the terminal, through changes in organization and wording, to proofreading and final editing. Almost all writers said that whether they used the computer exclusively—without any pen and paper or hard copy—depended upon the task they were doing.

Despite differences in level of use, there were many commonalties in the comments that the computer writers made. All the writers felt positive about using the computer for writing. The advantages they mentioned included: text generation that is quicker and "freer"; neatness of the text as it appears on the screen; the variety of formatting options; ready access to other writers via the network; file systems for managing large numbers of texts or large amounts of information; facilitated revision, at both a local and global level; and the sheer fun of using the machine (e.g., one user compared it to doing a crossword puzzle or reading a mystery at the end of a hard day; see also Eklundh & Sjoholm, 1991).

However, these writers also mentioned disadvantages of the computer systems they used for writing, and some of the most frequent complaints about the computer were that it caused reading difficulties. Reading is an important part of the writing process. Writers move back and forth between writing and reading as they produce text; they reread to evaluate and to revise, both globally and locally; they reread to detect coherence problems and to proofread. The writers I interviewed found that the computer put constraints on their ability to read their own texts, and their complaints took several forms. Many writers found it difficult to access large parts of their writing or move quickly to a specific place in the text. Possibly it takes less time to shuffle through several sheets of paper to find a particular paragraph than to move through comparable screens of text. Pen-and-paper writers might also be aided by being able to spread out three, or four, or a dozen sheets of paper in front of them, getting a sense of the text as a physical object. Other writers reported that the "intimacy" that they had developed with pen and paper is difficult to achieve on the computer. Still others found it difficult to reorganize their texts on-line or to detect errors.

Research in human factors adds credence to these writers' reported problems. Several studies have found that reading is slower and less efficient on the computer. Gould and Grischkowsky (1984) found reading to be significantly faster and slightly more accurate on hard copy than on screen, whereas Wright and Lickorish (1983) similarly found hard copy proofreading to be faster and more accurate. In a separate study, Gould and his colleagues (Gould, Alfaro, Finn, Jaupt, Minuto, & Salaum, 1987) tested numerous variables, including resolution, antialiasing, leading and spacing, even angle of text, to determine what factors led to slower on-line reading.

Most of these writers attempted to alleviate their on-line reading problems through extensive use of hard copy. Even writers who called themselves "adamant" computer writers took it for granted that computer writing does not mean that one forgoes a hard copy. One writer enthusiastically discussed her use of the computer to write, claiming she was writing more and better, and that her process had been completely changed by the computer. "I rely on it completely," she said. She then went on to describe how she got a hard copy of her text after every set of changes, either to make notes or just to read through. Although this writer said that she relied completely on the computer, her reports of how she actually wrote revealed that she was reliant on pen and paper as well.

The degree to which and the point at which the writers needed to see a hard copy of their texts also varied: Some writers cycled through twelve or more versions, getting a clean hard copy after each set of even minor changes; some writers brought hard copy notes with them to the terminal, whereas others did not. Some used hard copy to revise and then typed changes into the file; a few did virtually all real writing with pen and paper, whereas many did virtually everything on-line with minimal supplement from paper. Most writers also said that the difficulty and length of the writing task helped determine if and when hard copy became necessary.

Four Types of Reading Problems

Despite differences in writers interviewed, and in their experiences, there were common patterns in writers' reported reading problems, and in the ways they employed hard copy to solve those problems. In this section, I enumerate four areas of impact in which computers seem to create reading problems for writers and describe how writers attempt to solve these problems.

Formatting

Because many of the texts that writers produce on-line are intended for audiences who will read them on paper, it is not surprising that formatting questions concern computer writers. Formatting concerns took a number of forms. One writer said explicitly that he used hard copy printouts because "I like to see it the way they [his audience] will see it." Other writers were concerned with page breaks or the placement of figures and tables. Formatting concerns were reported by writers who were writing long and short texts, difficult texts and straightforward texts. Formatting concerns were particularly problematic for writers who did not use WYSIWYG ("what you see is what you get") editors—that is, editors in which the screen representation had little or no relationship to the eventual printed document. These writers tended to generate and use more hard copy printouts. Even writers whose text-editors included a preview function, in which they could see a picture of the printed text on the screen often used hard copy to check formatting. Overcoming the constraints of checking formatting usually involved making a best-guess, on-line approximation of the desired format and then printing a hard copy to skim, looking for specific problems and often returning to the computer to make further changes. Sometimes writers repeated these steps several times. Virtually all writers reported at least occasionally using hard copy to check the formatting of their written texts.

Proofreading

Many computer writers reported not trusting their ability to detect errors on-line, and these writers often did their proofreading on a hard copy printout of their texts. Some writers mentioned resolution or display problems (e.g., fuzziness, flicker) that interfered with their proofreading, whereas others were more vague: "I just need it in my hands to check for dumb errors." For some writers, computer-based spelling and grammar checkers tended to compound the problem: If writers learned to depend on the computer tools for low-level error detection, they proofread haphazardly—a dangerous practice given that many problems (i.e., missing pluralization or mistyping one word for another) are not caught by spellcheckers. Proofreading problems, although not as prevalent as formatting concerns, were mentioned by most writers, even those who used advanced, high resolution displays, and these problems also occurred across kinds of texts and texts of different lengths. Given findings such as those by Gould and Grischkowsky (1984) that proofreading is significantly poorer on-line, writers' decisions to use hard copy to proofread seem to be good ones.

Reorganizing

Computers also seem to cause problems in reading to reorganize (i.e., in planning and testing changes that involve moving large chunks of text), although actually executing these changes is of course much simpler when the writer is using a computer. Planning the reorganization, deciding what gets moved where, is often difficult if writers have only one view of the document at once, although split-screen options may help to alleviate this problem. Planning reorganizations can also be difficult because writers can "get lost" in computerized texts that contain fewer spatial cues. In planning their reorganizations, many writers reported using arrows, stars, and other graphic markings that are easy to create and see on paper, but may not be so with most computer systems. Similarly, testing a reorganization may be difficult on-line because the writer has to make the move in order to test it (i.e., in order to see how the text will read after the reorganization, the writer actually has to execute the change). However, with paper, the writer can reshuffle pages in order to read the reorganization before it is actually executed. This kind of move tends to be more difficult when writers are reading from a screen. The problems writers had in reading to reorganize was directly tied to text length: Once a computer text got to be over about four or five full screens, writers said that they tended to plan and test reorganizations on hard copy printouts.

There are, of course, software features that can make reorganizations easier. Certainly large screens can help, as can "search" features which quickly move the writer from one section of a text to another. Using an "undo" feature can also be helpful, although these features usually only undo the most recent command. In general, the fact that planning and executing decisions about text seem to be collapsed for computer writers may be problematic (see Chapter 4). One interview subject, a novelist, lamented the loss of "the history of the writing—those lines you discard and then want to pull back later—with the computer they're just gone."

Reading for a Sense of the Text

When using a computer, many writers also felt constrained in their ability to critically read and assess the shape of their own arguments, to match the actual text with their intentions (Witte, 1985). This problem was mentioned with a great deal of regularity by writers of varying abilities creating different kinds of texts. They often used the words "sense of the text" to describe this problem, or they used spatial or tactile metaphors to describe this problem: "My text is hard to pin down on-line"; "There is a problem getting a feel for the piece"; "It's hard to get your center of gravity in the writing." Getting a sense of the text would seem to be a crucial aspect of judging and revising one's own writing; this may be one way that writers read with the eyes of their readers, and thus judge the success of their arguments or narratives. The text sense problem was so pervasive—and so intriguing, given that current theories of writing say nothing about such a phenomenon—that I examined it in more detail. This more detailed examination of the problem appears in chapter 5 (this volume). Here,

I will simply note that while not all writers mentioned text sense problems, all of those who wrote conceptually difficult texts—arguments of various types, including articles and theses, as well as some coursework assignments for undergraduates—indicated that they at least sometimes had difficulty assessing the shape of their own arguments when they read their texts on-line.

THREE STUDIES OF WRITING-RELATED READING TASKS

The three empirical studies described in this section were designed to learn more about writers' problems reading their own texts on-line. These studies compare readers' performance in various reading tasks—the kinds of reading tasks that are crucial for writing and that the interview participants found difficult on the computer: (a) recalling location of information, (b) retrieving information, and (c) reading to revise. The studies used a variety of hardware and software; in fact, hardware and software variables were explicitly considered in each of the three studies in order to learn more about what features of computing systems contribute to the kinds of reading problems that writers reported in the interviews. Table 3.1 summarizes the differences in computer systems; not every study examined all of the variables described in this table, but each of these variables was the focus of at least one study.

Table 3.1
Summary of Display Variables

	Hardcopy	Standard Computer	Advanced Computer
Screen or page size:			
inches:	8 1/4 x 11	9 1/2 x 6 1/2	9 1/2 x 10 1/2
characters:	58 lines x 72 characters*	24 lines x 80 characters	50 lines x 90 characters
Screen and type:	Black-on-white	CRT display: white-on-black or green-on-white	High resolution bit-mapped display: black-on-white
Fonts:	Non-variable	Non-variable	Variable
Represetation of text size and location	——	Percentages at bottom of screen	Scroll-bar
Commands for changing screen	——	Control keys	Mouse and pointer
Speed	——	4800 baud	16kilo-baud

*In Experiment 1, hard copy page size was the same as standard computer screen size.

Study 1: Recalling the Spatial Location of Information

Writers must be able to locate information in their own texts, for tasks such as
evaluating coherence or making organizational changes. Locating information
in texts partly depends on spatial recall: remembering where (in the text and on
the page) a given item of information appeared. For instance, a writer may recall
that a particular point that he or she needs to develop further was located on the
bottom left of a page about halfway through a manuscript. In a study on spatial
recall, Rothkopf (1971) found that subjects reading from printed texts showed
significant incidental spatial memory; that is, even when readers were not
explicitly reading to recall spatial location, they often recalled the location of
information later. Because computer displays tend to provide fewer spatial
cues, and because writers interact with computer texts two dimensionally rather
than three dimensionally, Study 1 was designed to test whether reading on a
computer screen constrains spatial recall.

Participants

Ten students (six women and four men) in the Master's of Professional Writing
and Master's of Arts Programs in the English Department of Carnegie Mellon
University were randomly assigned to either a hard copy or a computer
condition. All participants had some computer experience and were familiar
with the text-editing system used in the study; readers in the computer condition
were given a brief review of editing commands before their reading session.

Procedure

Participants in both conditions read a 1000-word (nine pages or screens) article
on knee injuries from *Science '83* magazine. They were told to read normally,
neither skimming nor memorizing facts. The texts used in the two conditions
were made as similar as possible, with a line length of 78 characters, a page-
length of 22 lines, and double spacing. Readers in the computer condition read
from a standard 21-line by 80-character green-on-black display; the system
speed was 4800 baud (see Table 3.1 for a summary of display differences).
Readers in the hard copy condition read from pages in notebook that were
identical in size to the computer screen.

Readers were asked to recall the location of eight items. For each item, a full sentence from the text was read to the participants and they were asked to recall: (a) page (or screen) number, and (b) within page location of specific words. Control group members used a notebook with blank pages, similar to the one from which they had read the original text, and they used a pen to indicate where they thought the information had occurred in the text. Computer readers used a computer file the same length as the original file, but filled with blank spaces; they moved the cursor and typed in a number to indicate where the information had occurred. Sentences were read to the participants verbatim, and they were asked to indicate where particular words had occurred in the text or computer file. For example, participants were read a sentence from the original text, such as "Probably the most famous knees in football are those of former Jet quarterback Joe Namath." They were then asked to put a small "2" where they remembered seeing the words "Joe Namath."

Analysis and Results

Each reader was given three scores for each of the eight questions:
1. Text-sequence score (difference between the original page or screen number and the one chosen).
2. Vertical score (difference between the original line or row number and the one chosen).
3. Horizontal score (difference between the original character or column number and the one chosen).

Differences between given answers and correct answers were computed and totaled in each category for each reader. In each category, readers in the hard copy condition scored better than readers in the computer condition. Differences in vertical location (line number) scores were significant at the $p < .05$ level ($F[1;8] = 7.44$); neither text-sequence location nor horizontal location scores were significantly different ($F = 1.05$, $F = 1.27$).

Discussion

The results of this study indicate a difference for spatial recall when information was presented on a computer screen and on paper. The difference in recall of vertical location was the one statistically significant difference. This result might have been expected if the experimental group participants had read text from a scrolling screen, or if the amount of information presented on screen and page varied. But the computer screen did not scroll, and the experimental text had the same number of rows per page as the control group text. The result, therefore, is somewhat surprising. The difference may be due to participants' greater experience with printed text; it may also be due to the fact that readers in the hard copy condition were interacting with text directly in a tactile as well as a visual way. In any case, eroded spatial sense may translate into difficulties locating information in texts and may contribute to the reading problems that the interviewed writers reported.

Study 2: Retrieving Information

This study builds on the results of Study 1, which showed readers remembering the location of specific words more accurately in a paper condition than in a computer condition. In this study, readers were asked to retrieve slightly larger amounts of information in order to answer questions. This study also examined several different computer variables. In particular, it seemed sensible that recent computer design advancements might make this task easier for readers using computers. Therefore, a second computer condition—taking advantage of improved resolution and enlarged screen size—was tested along with the more standard personal computer condition. Participants read texts in three conditions:

- Condition 1: Participants read from a printed text (58 lines by 72 characters) three and a half pages long. The text was printed in Times-Roman 12 by a Xerox 9700 printer.
- Condition 2: Participants read from a standard personal computer (CRT) screen, 24 lines long by 80 characters wide. The text was presented on twelve screens of a gray-on-black display. The baud rate for the machine was 4800. All readers assigned to this condition were familiar with the hardware and software used in the study. Because the text-editor contained "search" commands, and because use of these commands might aid readers in the task, readers were instructed in using these "search" commands before doing the reading task, although only one person had not used them previously. This text-editor used percentage indicators at the bottom of each screen to signal text length and location, and keystroke commands to move through the text.

- Condition 3: Participants used an advanced computing system, Andrew, under development at the time at Carnegie Mellon University (Morris, Satyanarayanan, Conner, Howard, Rosenthal, & Smith, 1986). They read from a Sun workstation with a 19-inch diagonal, bit-mapped, high-resolution, black-on-white display. The window in which the text was presented in this experiment was 50 lines by 90 characters, and the text was presented in five and one-half screens. Text-editing windows contain a scroll bar, which is a graphic device for representing the size of the text and the position in the total text of the part currently being displayed. To change the display (e.g., move to the next section of text or back to a previous one), the user uses points and clicks the mouse in the scroll bar. The text editor was being developed at the Information Technology Center at Carnegie Mellon (see Palay, et al, 1988, for a description of this editor).

This advanced system was used in this reading study, as well as in Study 3, which follows. In addition, the Andrew system was used in the studies of writers that are reported in chapters 4 and 5 (this volume); an account of its development is found in chapter 6 (this volume). The reading studies reported in this chapter examined only a small number of features of the Andrew system; detailed explanations of the system (and illustrations of it) are presented in the later chapters, where user interface and visual aspects are more pertinent.

Participants

Fifteen students, male and female undergraduate and graduate students in Humanities and in Engineering, were assigned either to the paper condition or to one of the two computer conditions. All participants had some text-editing experience. All participants in Condition 2 were familiar with the personal computer and text editor used. Participants in Condition 3 learned the new computer system in brief training sessions, and all demonstrated mastery of mouse and scroll bar devices before they did the reading task.

Procedures

Participants read an 1800-word self-help file for a bulletin-board feature on the computer system in use at Carnegie Mellon University. The document contained tabled lists of commands as well as standard written text. Readers were instructed to read the document as they normally would. They were also told that they would be asked questions when they had finished reading, and that they would be able to access the text to answer the questions.

After they had finished reading, participants were asked six questions that could be answered explicitly by reference to the text and six others that could be answered only by inference from information given in the text. They were told to go to the page or screen where the information—either explicit or implicit—was presented, to indicate verbally when they had found the information, and then to answer the question. They were instructed to locate the information even if they could answer the question without returning to the text. Responses were timed, and answers were used to determine that readers were returning to the correct places in the text. Incorrect responses were fewer than one per subject and were distributed over questions and conditions.

Analysis and Results

Because errors were so few, only the time results were analyzed. One reader in each of the computer conditions gave up before finding the answer to one question. For these readers, 11 response times were averaged for the mean score. Readers reading from the hard copy text performed the task the most quickly; the mean response time was 13.0 seconds in the hard copy condition. Readers using the advanced computer condition did almost as well; the mean response time in this condition was 15.9 seconds. Those readers in the standard personal computer condition were the slowest: It took, on average, 32.7 seconds for these readers to respond to retrieve answers to the questions. Analysis of variance (ANOVA) showed a significant difference among conditions ($F[2;12] = 35.57, p < .01$), and Newman-Keuls tests revealed significant differences ($p < .01$) between the paper condition and the personal computer condition, and between the personal computer condition and the advanced computer condition. There were no significant differences between the hard copy and the advanced computer conditions.

Discussion

The readers reading from hard copy texts retrieved information more quickly than did readers in the computer conditions. However, the results for readers using the advanced computer system—with better display and more sophisticated text advancement method—approached that of readers reading from hard copy. The readers in the standard personal computer condition, however, took over twice as long to answer questions as did their counterparts in the hard copy condition. In general, this study suggests that reading to retrieve information from paper and from this advanced computing system are virtually the same, but that retrieving information in the standard personal computer condition is significantly slower.

These striking differences in performance in the two computer conditions could be due to display variables or to text advancement variables. In other words, the differences in time to answer questions could be the result of display differences in the two computer conditions, such as resolution, screen size, or type of fonts. However, they could be the result of differences in the user interface software: whether readers used keystrokes or a scroll bar, mouse, and pointer to move through the text. Study 3 attempts to differentiate between these two classes of variables.

Study 3: Reading to Revise

Studies 1 and 2 demonstrated that both locating and retrieving information are easier from hard copy than from some computer displays. Apparently, it is easier to perceive the spatial structure of the text and to locate information when reading from hard copy than from some computers. However, one might argue that perceiving spatial structure of a text and retrieving information, although useful, are not nearly as important for readers as is perceiving text meaning. Revision, a critical aspect of writing, for example, requires the writer to form a mental representation of the text's meaning and to evaluate that meaning critically. In Study 3, readers performed a reading-to-revise task that required them to construct the meaning of a scrambled text. The task of reordering a disordered text was chosen because it is a comprehension task with a spatial component, similar to detecting organization problems in a writer's own text. In the interviews described at the beginning of this chapter, several writers indicated that they generated a hard copy of their computer texts to read in order to reorganize.

As in Study 2, several computer variables were tested. In particular, this study examined screen size and text advancement method as two variables that might contribute to differences in readers' performance. The earlier study examined two different computer systems, whereas this study took a more fine-grained approach and varied screen size and text advancement method within one computer system. Each of the computer conditions used the advanced computing system described earlier. Variables of screen size (large and small) and text advancement method (scroll bar or keystrokes) were crossed to produce four computer conditions. The large screen was ten and one half inches long and nine and one half inches wide and held 50 lines of text; the small was six and one half inches long and nine and one half inches wide and held 24 lines of text. This small screen approximated the size of a standard terminal or personal computer screen, whereas the large screen used most of the space available on the advanced machine. In two conditions, readers advanced the text by using a mouse to point to a different section of the scroll bar; in the two other computer conditions, readers used function keys (i.e., page forward, page back, beginning of file, and end of file) to move around in the on-line text.

Participants

The participants were 10 entering freshmen with fewer than 10 total hours spent on a computer prior to the experiment. Choosing computer novices reduced any interference from prior experience with other computers. The participants were trained on the computer system—particularly the use of the scroll bar and function keys—for approximately 3 hours in two sessions before beginning the reading task used in this study.

Procedure

Five nonfiction texts, approximately 1200 words long and similar in readability (Grade 11.5 to 12 as measured by the Flesch Readability Formula; Flesch, 1974), were altered so that complete lines of text were out of order. After scrambling, the lines of the text were numbered sequentially.

Participants read the disordered texts in five conditions. Unlike the two earlier studies, in which groups of writers using different technologies were compared with one another, this study used a within-subjects design; that is, each reader performed the task in each of the five conditions, and then each reader's performance was compared with his or her performance in the other conditions. Because the comparisons are sharper in a within-subjects design, it is possible to see greater effects without increasing the number of participants in the study. The five conditions were:

•Condition 1: hard copy
•Condition 2: large screen and scroll bar
•Condition 3: large screen and function keys
•Condition 4: small screen and scroll bar
•Condition 5: small screen and function keys

The order of the five conditions was counterbalanced. Participants indicated verbally how the lines should be reordered. The task was done orally (using the line numbers) to eliminate interference from motor variables. In other words, the study explored reading only. It was designed to examine how readers made sense of the text; it did not test how or how quickly readers could carry out the reorganizations necessary to make the text coherent.

Analysis and Results

A one-way ANOVA was performed for all five conditions and Newman-Keuls tests were run to determine which of the conditions differed significantly from each other. An additional two-way ANOVA was performed for the four computer conditions to assess the relative effects of screen size and text advancement method.

Readers' performance in the hard copy and large screen conditions were similar, while performance in the small screen conditions was significantly slower. The mean time to complete the task was lowest in the hard copy condition (13.5 minutes), followed by large screen/keys (14.4), large screen/ scroll bar (15.7 minutes), small screen/scroll bar (20.6 minutes), and small screen keys (20.7 minutes). The main effect for conditions was significant at the .001 level ($F[4;36] = 13.39$). The Newman-Keuls analysis of the five conditions (presented in Table 3.2) shows hard copy and large screen conditions differing significantly ($p < .05$) from small screen conditions. However, this analysis showed no significant difference between large screen and hard copy conditions, and no significant effect for text advancement method (the scroll bar/key variable). In the two-way ANOVA (presented in Table 3.3) for the four computer conditions there was a significant main effect ($p < .01$) for screen-size, no significant effect for scroll bar *vs.* function keys, and no significant interaction between the variables.

Table 3.2
Newman-Keuls Tests of Significance
for Reading to Revise Experiment

	Hard Copy	Large Screen		Small Screen	
		Keys	Scroll Bar	Scroll Bar	Keys
Hard Copy	——	8.90	22.03	71.08*	72.39
Large Screen		——	13.13	62.18*	63.19*
Keys					
Scroll Bar			——	49.05*	50.36
Small Screen				——	1.31
Scroll Bar					
Key					——

p<.05; df = 36

Table 3.3
ANOVA for 4 Computer Conditions
for Reading to Revise Experiment

Source	df	SS	MS	F	p
Subjects	9	403.08	44.79	4.25	.01
Conditions	3	325.34	108.45	10.30	.01
screen size	1	316.62	316.62	30.07	.01
mouse/keys	1	3.48	3.48	.33	NS
interaction	1	5.14	5.14	.49	NS
Subjects X					
conditions	27	284.30	10.53		
Total	39				

Discussion

The mean response times, which show an advantage for hard copy and for large screen workstations, seem to bear out the interview reports of difficulties in getting a sense of the text on a computer screen. These results are also consistent with results of previous studies involving recall and retrieval of information. Screen size appeared to be an important variable: The large screen conditions approached the hard copy condition in efficiency, and the small screen conditions were significantly less efficient than the large screen and hard copy conditions.

The manner of moving through the text—whether by scroll bar or by function keys—did not appear to make a significant difference for readers, nor was there an interaction between the two variables. Initial training on the scroll bar took longer than did training on the function keys, yet despite this fact—and in spite of the fact that there appears to be no difference in efficiency for scroll bar or function keys—readers in general preferred the scroll bar because they believed that it allowed them greater precision in moving through the text.

A FRAMEWORK OF COMPUTER FEATURES

This section summarizes in some detail the results of these observational and empirical studies of reading on-line and then presents a framework of computer features that helps account for these findings. The four features—size, legibility, responsiveness, and tangibility—are discussed in more detail in a previous article, cowritten with Wilfred J. Hansen (Hansen & Haas, 1988); in that article, we also identify a number of secondary factors that I do not discuss here.

In the interviews of computer writers, most writers indicated that, under certain conditions, they felt constrained in reading the on-line texts they were writing using computers. These reported reading problems extended across types of writers, types of writing tasks, and types of computers. In particular, writers reported problems checking the format of their texts, proofreading, reading to reorganize, and reading to get a sense of the text, and often their problems were exacerbated if the texts they were writing were long and/or conceptually difficult.

In the three empirical studies that followed these interviews, I examined several computer variables: display, speed, screen size, and text advancement method. In these studies, I found that writers' spatial understanding of text was eroded when they read that text on a standard personal computer. Further, retrieving information was slower on a standard personal computer than it was on either paper or a more sophisticated computing system with an advanced display. In the third study, I found that critically reading to reorganize a text was better when writers used hard copy or screens that displayed more text than when they read from small screens.

As I argue in chapter 2 (this volume), one of the goals of Technology Studies should be to look at, rather than through, technology; that is, technology itself—rather than merely technology's effects—should be an object of inquiry as we seek to understand the relationship between literacy and technology. The studies reported here attempted to look in a detailed way at a range of computer variables, and to tease apart the effects of these different variables on writing-related reading tasks. The remainder of this chapter attempts to bring these variables back together in their technological contexts. Specifically, I argue that when any or all of these four factors (i.e., size, legibility, responsiveness, and tangibility) vary, they can lead to important differences in readers' and writers' behavior. Of course, these variables are not only computer variables, but are present in print texts as well, although in print texts they may be a great deal more transparent.

The first variable is *screen/page size*, and it refers to the amount of text that is visually available at any one time. Obviously, larger screens and larger windows allow readers and writers to view more text at once. Print texts vary in their size as well. Books tend to display more text at once than do computer screens, but less than is possible if writers lay out pages of a manuscript next to one another. Of course, there is a point of diminishing returns in increasing the size of text: A wall-size screen may not offer advantages over a 19-inch screen, and laying out a dozen sheets of a manuscript may not be an improvement over laying out two or three. The results from Studies 2 and 3 support the importance of size in writing-related reading tasks. In addition, the amount of text available was often mentioned by writers in the interviews; size may also be an important part of why writers felt that reading long texts was more difficult on-line.

The second variable in the framework is *legibility*. The studies reported here did not address legibility directly, although earlier studies in the field of human factors have established both the importance and the complexity of legibility (e.g., Booth, Bryden, Cowan, Morgan & Plante, 1987; Gould & Grischkowsky, 1984). Variables such as spacing, antialiasing, contrast, and flicker are all important in legibility, and according to Gould et al. (Gould, Alfaro, Finn, Haupt, Minuto, & Salaum, 1987), there is not a clear formula for determining which of these variables is preeminent in any given situation. The legibility of the paper texts in these studies was significantly better than the legibility of the texts presented on a standard personal computer. The legibility of the advanced computing system was also better than that of the standard personal computer, and—based on the Gould et al. analysis—the paper texts were probably slightly more legible than those presented on the advanced workstations.

Legibility probably contributed to readers' speed in these studies and may account at least partially, if subtly, for the results of the three reading studies presented in this chapter. Legibility of text probably also contributes to readers' comfort level with various media and may help to account for writers' desire to print their texts and read from hard copy, which many of the interview subjects reported doing, even when they could not be precise about why they were doing it.

Responsiveness, the third factor in the framework, includes how quickly the writing/reading system responds to actions taken by the writer/reader. Responsiveness is complex in that it is comprised of at least two components: the speed with which the system begins to respond to a writer/reader's action, and the speed with which the response is completed (Hansen & Haas, 1988, p. 1082-3). Responsiveness for print texts is high for reading, because eye and hand movements are well practiced and automatic for most experienced readers. In addition, although print text is static, moving to a new part of the text requires a repainting of the screen with a computer system, and this can be quite time-consuming (taking as much as a second or more with some systems). In the studies reported here, the personal computer had lower responsiveness than the advanced workstation because its speed was much lower. Of the interview subjects' reported problems, reading to reorganize and critical reading are probably particularly affected by low responsiveness, while proofreading may be less so. However, writers interviewed also mentioned that producing texts with computers is satisfying because it can be so rapid. It may be that pen and paper has less responsiveness for writers, while print texts have more responsiveness for readers.

The final factor, *tangibility*, is a complex of both visual and tactile aspects of interacting with texts. A computer system or other technology has high tangibility when users feel that they are in direct contact with the text. Therefore, what Schneiderman (1992) calls "direct manipulation" of the text is an important contributor to tangibility. Print texts are obviously more tangible in a tactile sense because readers and writers hold the actual text in their hands. In general, pen-and-paper writers are more able to directly manipulate their texts—for example, drawing on them, folding them, reshuffling pages—than are writers using computers, although certainly some computer systems are more tangible than others. That is, pointing a mouse directly at a word the writer wants to highlight is more tangible than using arrow and function keys to select the word.

The confluence of tactile and visual cues into tangibility of text probably contributes to writers' reports of greater sense of text with pen-and-paper documents; certainly the notion of intimacy between writer and text suggests a certain level of tangibility.   In the reading studies reported here, tangibility probably had the greatest effect in Study 3, where writers had to both construct a text meaning and determine how to rearrange the text. It seems that direct manipulation of the text (i.e., increased tangibility) would be an important factor in this kind of task. Similarly, conceptually difficult texts may be easier to read and write with the greater degree of tangibility; this is consistent with interview subjects' reports.

Any changes in literate behavior that computers facilitate or mandate are neither inevitable nor invisible. Rather, they are the result of actual features— in this case, visual and tactile—of the technology. The framework proposed here is partial and by necessity incomplete.   Computers and other writing systems have other aspects that could also be delineated in this way, and certainly other frameworks may ultimately prove more useful. What I have attempted to show through this feature analysis is the necessity and the possibility of examining computer systems in some detail in order to explain technology's effects on writers. The effects found in the studies reported here are small ones, based on the experiences and behaviors of limited groups of writers. However, the vast cultural changes that many predict for computer writing systems would seemingly be made up of a series of small, but critical, changes that computers will facilitate in literacy activities. An ultimate goal of this kind of detailed examination of which features of computer systems may result in what kinds of changes in readers' and writers' activities, is a normative one: to be able to argue cogently about how computer systems should be designed in order to better serve the needs of real readers and writers.

ACKNOWLEDGMENTS

Parts of this chapter appeared previously as "'Seeing it on the screen isn't really seeing it: Computer writers' reading problems," in Gail Hawisher and Cynthia Selfe (Eds.), *Critical perspectives on computers and composition instruction*, pp. 16-29, copyright 1989 by Teachers College Press and used by permission; and "'What did I just say?' Reading problems in writing with the machine," Christina Haas and John R. Hayes, *Reseach in the Teaching of English, 20*(1), pp. 22-35, copyright 1986 by the National Council of Teachers of English and used by permission.

4

MATERIALITY AND THINKING: THE EFFECTS OF COMPUTER TECHNOLOGY ON WRITERS' PLANNING

In the next two chapters, I present clear, direct evidence of how the material tools of writing significantly and consistently alter the mental processes of text production. This chapter examines how computers impact on writers' cognitive processes as they plan their texts and on their planning notes. Chapter 5 examines writers' materially based representations of textual meaning and their physical interactions with written artifacts during the course of text production. Together, the studies presented in these two chapters suggest a picture of computer writing that is subtly, but profoundly, different than writing with pen-and-paper.

In particular, the study presented in this chapter shows planning—a critical subprocess of writing—to be shaped in significant ways by the material technologies that writers use. Not only is planning diminished in total when writers use computers, but the patterns of planning over time and the focus of planning are also shown to be different. Further, there are important differences in the amount and kinds of notes that writers use when they are writing their essays on-line and on paper. These results provide a strong, empirically based counter to the transparent technology assumption—the assumption that what is essentially writing remains constant, regardless of the material technologies employed. Indeed, these results show that the shape of written composition is very different with different media.

This study offers detailed information about what kinds of differences computer technologies facilitate, and how these differences play out in real time through the composing processes of actual writers. In so doing, it argues as well against the notion that technology is monolithic and all-powerful because many of the differences noted here are quite subtle. The fine-grained analysis of writers' processes (via think-aloud protocols) illuminates subtle differences in composing with different material tools—differences that may not be obvious with other methodologies. The textual analysis of notes—artifacts that readers do not usually see—provides another window on writers' thinking processes. Because they focus on subtle but potentially powerful differences in composing, these kinds of analyses can help to delineate what particular aspects of particular technologies lead to particular effects. This delineation, in turn, provides the kind of detailed information necessary for constructive critique of technology. I return to these results in chapter 9 (this volume), where I offer a general discussion of how spatial, visual, and tactile aspects of writing profoundly shape writers' experiences with different technologies.

THE IMPORTANCE OF PLANNING IN WRITING

Theories of the cognitive processes of writing have emphasized the importance of planning (Bereiter & Scardamalia, 1987; Flower & Hayes, 1981a; c.f., Hayes-Roth & Hayes-Roth, 1979). During planning, which may occur both before and during writing, writers make a myriad of decisions about the communication situations, the written product, and their own composing process—decisions ranging from author's persona to intended audience effects to stylistic options. Although writing researchers have defined planning in a number of related, but not identical, ways, it is generally seen as a cognitively complex, reflective activity that is critical to successful writing. Further, writing researchers have found that better writers seem to plan more. Bereiter and Scardamalia (1987) found that the planning of the more mature, adult writers was almost four times as long (in number of words spoken in a think-aloud protocol) as the text they produced from those plans. In addition, young writers in Bereiter and Scardamalia's study were often unable to differentiate writing from planning: When instructed to plan to write, they instead produced text that stood as their final product. Flower and Hayes (1980) also found that expert writers differed from novice writers in both the amount and the kind of planning they did during writing. Not only is planning the hallmark of the expert writer, but planning may be where discovery during writing takes place (Murray, 1984). Planning in writing, like planning more generally, can be valuable because it is reversible, accommodates novel and flexible approaches, and allows writers to make and correct mistakes in a plan rather than in a text (Hayes, 1987). In short, planning is a smart, efficient strategy, both in writing and in solving problems more generally.

Of particular interest are questions about when planning happens and what kinds of planning writers do. A number of researchers have explored the "when" of planning. Planning seems to occur throughout the writing process (Flower & Hayes, 1981b), an integral part of the "ongoing moment-to-moment process of composing" (p. 373). Writers may set and refine goals, and generate and organize ideas at any point during composing. However, prewriting periods may be particularly important as periods of invention, discovery, and planning. Bereiter and Scardamalia (1987) found that fifth-graders' start-up times—the quiet periods before writing began—were much briefer than the start-up times of more experienced adult writers.

It is also during these initial planning periods that writers produce planning notes—textual and graphical cues that the writer produces as a throw-away planning space (Burtis, Scardamalia, Bereiter, & Tetroe, 1983). Kaufer, Hayes, and Flower (1986) described two kinds of notes generated by their experienced writers: topic designators and instructions to the writer. Both kinds of notes serve a metacognitive function: The former remind the writer to include specific content information, and the latter serve as content-less prompts to reach a particular rhetorical goal. Some notes were expanded by writers as they composed formal prose, whereas others were adapted and changed as composing proceeded.

Burtis and his colleagues (Burtis et al., 1983) examined the planning notes of a group of students and adults as they planned in preparation for writing. For the older students (14-year-olds), the notes represented ideas that were later expanded into compositions, much like the notes of experienced writers studied by Kaufer et al. (1986). The notes of the younger writers, however, were in fact first drafts of compositions, which were later edited but seldom elaborated or reorganized. Burtis et al. (1983) found that the adults took very complex and condensed notes, complete with arrows, lines, asterisks, and boxes. In contrast to the linear, text-like notes of the young students, these adults' notes were brief, terse, and diagrammatic. The researchers saw a clear developmental trend, in which notemaking gradually becomes differentiated from writing.

Research has also suggested that there are different kinds or levels of planning: what writers are planning for and where their focus of attention is located during planning. Some researchers postulate a difference between rhetorical plans for the writing situation and plans for the text. Bereiter and Scardamalia (1987) see a special value in planning that takes writers back and forth between content and rhetorical problems spaces. Flower and Hayes (1981b, 1981c) found that expert writers often made rhetorical plans—plans that took into account audience, context, and purpose—but that these kinds of plans were seldom made by novice writers. Types of planning have often been set in contrastive terms: Bereiter and Scardamalia's knowledge-telling and knowledge-transforming (1987) are similar to Flower and Hayes' (1981b) product-based and reader-based planning, both in the focus of each type of planning and in how each type is used by different writers. Novices tend to rely only on the former in each contrastive pair, whereas experts use the latter as well.

Recently, Geisler (1994) has added a level of complexity to our understanding of the profound differences in experienced writers' and students' use of rhetorical knowledge while composing. Rather than simply posit distinct processes and frameworks for expert and student writers, Geisler attempts to account for the movement, over time, from naive representations of content and rhetorical situation (held by student writers) to the more complex, interrelated representations of the expert writers she studied. Her analysis calls into question the accuracy of positing distinct and separate categories of rhetorical and content planning, especially for expert writers.

Researchers have found that different levels of plans for text (however rhetorical those plans may be for expert writers) can be distinguished. Matsuhashi's (1981) study of planning during pausing distinguishes between global and sentence-level text planning and her revision study (1987) sought to classify text revisions on the basis of the changed plans—conceptual or sequential—behind the revisions, rather than the changed words themselves. Burtis et al. (1983) claim that textual planning gradually becomes distinguished from text production during the course of writing development, and they distinguish between two types of textual planning: conceptual planning and content generation.

Clearly, amount and kind of planning during writing may be partly a function of the writer's development, expertise, and knowledge. The situation in which writing occurs may have an influence on planning as well. Many school writing situations may be so impoverished that students see no need or reason to plan (Applebee, 1984). Or, the structure of the school situation may in fact allow students to circumvent instructional goals and engage in less difficult writing tasks which do not require high-level planning (Doyle, 1983).

Other, richer situations may allow writers to tap the rhetorical complexities of a situation and engage in more planning (see e.g., Geisler's, 1994, study of expert philosophers; Berkenkotter, Huckin, & Ackerman's, 1988, account of writing by a graduate student in English).

A STUDY OF THE EFFECTS OF WORD PROCESSING ON PLANNING

Of particular relevance for the current study is another situational variable—namely, the available technologies writers use to compose—that may affect how writers plan. Specifically, the use of word processing or computers for writing may affect the amount of planning that occurs before and during writing. The current study examines the effects of word processing on writers' planning. Since virtually every computer-based writing tool—hypertext systems, mail programs—have word processors build into them, it seem particularly appropriate to examine this most generic of computer writing tools in order to ascertain what, if any, effects it has on writers' composing processes.

Daiute (1985) made early predictions that using word processing would increase planning because writers—elementary school students particularly—could turn their attention away from handwriting, recopying, and checking spelling and focus on more higher level concerns. Daiute's predictions have not been borne out, however, by subsequent research. In particular, studies conducted by Lillian Bridwell-Bowles and her colleagues (Bridwell, Sirc, & Brooke, 1985; Bridwell-Bowles, Johnson, & Brehe, 1987) have explored questions of planning by different kinds of writers. They found that college students spent a great deal of time trying out various ways of formatting their texts by testing various word- and sentence-level options, rather than doing high-level planning. Further, when these researchers interviewed and observed a group of experienced writers, they found these writers to be aware of difficulties in planning their computer texts, and consequently they used pen-and-paper to supplement word processing.

In addition, planning may be inhibited on computer systems that make it difficult to create and manipulate planning notes. Burtis et al. (1983) found that planning notes—used to keep writers on track, to develop ideas, to keep track of goals—are often diagrammatic and nonlinear. Most word processing packages, even today, do not make it easy for writers to create boxes, arrows, and other diagrammatic writing notes. Because of their throw-away nature, writers' planning notes are seldom examined as textual artifacts. In this study, however, I look at planning notes as material traces of writers' planning and hypothesized that different technological conditions might lead to different kinds of planning notes.

Not only may amount of planning be affected by word processing, but there are reasons to believe that the use of word processing for writing may also influence the level or type of planning in which writers engage. First, writers might do more word- and sentence-level planning (i.e., planning concerned with word choice, sentence structure, punctuation, and other surface-level options) when using word processing if that medium encourages writers to focus at the word- and sentence-levels. Further, small computer displays that show only a portion of the text at once might encourage writers to focus their attention on parts of text within a screen rather than think about concerns that extend across screens. Similarly, when using word processing writers might do less high-level text planning (i.e., text planning concerned with text structure and organization, development of a thesis or argument, and choices about audience effect or tone of the piece). First, if writers are devoting more attention to low-level planning with word processing, it is reasonable to expect that they would think less about high level text planning. Second, if notemaking on the word processor is inhibited, writers may engage in less high-level text planning because, as Burtis et al. (1983) point out, notemaking is used by writers to explore, develop, and organize ideas—all high-level text planning activities.

In addition, planning notes may be difficult to create and manipulate when using standard computer systems for writing. Burtis et al. (1983) found that expert writers used planning notes to keep themselves on task, to keep track of their goals, and to explore ideas. Although many multi-media systems allow for the inclusion of graphics into text files, the creation of the kind of quick, nonlinear, and diagrammatic notes that writers often use to think with may be difficult with many computer writing systems, where arrows, boxes, and added emphasis (e.g., directional arrows, checkmarks, stars) may be cumbersome to produce.

The current study was designed to explore these four questions:

•Do writers plan differently—in amount or in kind—when they use word processing versus when they use pen-and-paper?

•Does using pen-and-paper to supplement word processing change the amount or kind of planning?

•Are there differences between experienced writers and student writers in how they plan when composing with pen-and-paper versus word processing?

•Are there differences in the amount or kind of planning notes that writers produce with different technologies?

Procedure

This section describes the setting, methods, and participants in the study; the task in which writers engaged; and the computer system that they used.

Setting

The setting for this study is a private research university set in a medium-sized eastern city. About 6500 students, one third of whom are graduate students, attend the university, which is predominantly White. Male students outnumber females by a ratio of about 3 to 1. The university has a strong technological focus. The largest and strongest departments in the university include the engineering departments, and the computer science school is world-renowned. Even students majoring in arts or humanities may find that their classes contain a strong technological component, either in subject matter (e.g., computer-generated art) or pedagogical presentation (e.g., sophisticated software for mapping arguments in an English class). Similarly, faculty across the university tend to be involved in technological projects, and they use quite sophisticated hardware and software for their daily tasks. At the time this study took place, the university had embarked on a joint project with a major computer manufacturer to develop a prototype educational computing system on campus. Prototype versions of this system were used for this study (see the description of the computing system later).

Although this university is somewhat unusual in its technological focus and sophistication, there are important reasons to study computer-based writing in such a setting. First, in a setting like this one, most writers—students, faculty, and professionals—are practiced users of technology. They tend not to need much training on word processing or other writing software, and their facility with technology minimizes interference from learning or other variables. In addition, as computer technology becomes more affordable and more widely used, other universities may well begin to put this kind of sophisticated technology in place for students and faculty. Hence, although this university may have seemed quite advanced technologically when this study took place (late 1980s), many universities may approach this level of sophistication today.

Method and Design

The study employed a 2 x 3 factorial design, with one between-subjects factor (writing experience) and one within-subjects factor (writing medium). Ten experienced writers and 10 student writers composed essays in each of three conditions: pen-and-paper, word processing alone, and a combination of word processing with pen-and-paper (and hard copy printouts). This "both" condition, which allowed the use of paper with word processing, may more accurately represent the way many writers actually use word processing (see chapter 3, this volume). In the two word processing conditions, writers were free to use a separate window for notes if they wished; in the both condition, they could use pen and paper for notes as well. The conditions were counterbalanced for topic and order.

A think-aloud protocol methodology was used in order to obtain a complete picture of writers' planning behavior. Participants were asked to speak aloud as they wrote. Those writers who had not previously encountered this think-aloud procedure were given a brief two-part training session in which they first saw the process modeled by the experimenter and then practiced speaking aloud while composing a short letter. All sessions were also videotaped. The video tapes of writing sessions were not analyzed for the study presented in this chapter. However, some of them provided data for the profiles of writers interacting with technologies and artifacts, which are presented in chapter 5 (this volume).

Audiotapes for each of the 20 writers' three sessions were transcribed, and the resulting 60 protocols were parsed into clauses, following the general approach developed by Hayes and Flower (1980). Writers' planning notes were also analyzed. To insure that the think-aloud methodology was not affecting the conditions differently, the verbalization rate (clauses uttered per minute) and the composing rate (words written per minute) were compared. Mean number of verbalized clauses was 5.4 in the pen-and-paper condition, 4.9 in the word processing condition, and 5.1 in the both condition. These differences were not significant by ANOVA [$F(2,36) = 2.61$]. The differences in composing rate were not significant: Mean words per minute were 10.8 in the pen-and-paper condition, 11.2 in the word processing condition, and 10.1 in the both condition [$F(2,36) = 2.12$]. Interestingly, the length of the final texts were significantly different [$F(2,36) = 7.06, p < .1$]. The mean length (in words) of the finished texts was 595.7 in the pen-and-paper condition, 767.1 in the word processing condition, and 682.0 in the both condition. For this study, proportional analysis was used to minimize effects of differences in length of writing sessions.

The Writing Task

The three writing prompts were generated using a procedure developed and tested by Hoetker and Brossell (1986). Because all subjects were either college students or campus employees, the prompts dealt with familiar school-related or academic experiences and allowed writers to specify the exact topics. Following Hoetker and Brossell, I also cast the prompts into a common syntactic pattern and tried to make the experimental situation reflect a real rhetorical situation. Therefore, writers were asked to participate in a writing contest (i.e., to write essays that were to be judged by actual readers on the basis of clearly stated criteria). As an added incentive, a cash prize was to be awarded to the contest winner in each subject group. One writing prompt read as follows:

Take the next hour to plan, write, and proofread an essay on this topic:
A social group or activity that many students encounter in college that may affect them in important ways.
In your essay, you should introduce your subject and then either
—explain the subject you have chosen, or
—take a position about your subject and support it.
At least two evaluators will read your essay and assign it a score. The evaluators will be college teachers of English and professional writers. They will be paying special attention to whether you
—state your ideas clearly
—develop your ideas logically and in sufficient detail.
Ten other people will also be writing essays for this contest. If yours is selected as the best, you will receive a bonus of $15.

The other two prompts were identical, except they asked writers to write on "a habit or belief that many students acquire in college that affects their lives in important ways" or "a common practice in American schools that either inhibits or aids learning."

Participants

Twenty writers, 10 students and 10 experienced writers, took part in the study. The 10 student writers were all second-semester freshmen. They were randomly selected from a group of students who had completed two courses with Andrew (the computer system, described later, that was used for the study): one an introductory workshop and one a writing course using Edit Text, the text editor for the Andrew system. The professions of the experienced writers included systems design, teaching, and professional writing. They were selected to participate based on two criteria: Andrew experience (daily use of the Andrew system for at least 3 months) and writing experience, established by having published technical or professional writing or by being recommended by their supervisors as better-than-average writers. One of the experienced writers was Asian, one of the student writers was African American, and the remaining participants were White. Twelve of the twenty writers were male, and 8 were female. Subjects were paid for their participation in the study.

All of the participants were experienced with computers in general and the Andrew systems in particular. The experienced writers all used the Andrew system in their daily work; eight had an Andrew workstation in their offices. They had been using computers or word processors on a regular basis for an average of 6.9 years, and they had been using the Andrew system and the text-editor Edit Text for an average of 1.9 years. The student writers had an average of 4.3 years computer experience, and all had been using Andrew and Edit Text for two semesters. Many of the students had had their own computer at home during high school and over half knew one or more programming languages before coming to college. In short, all the participants were experienced and comfortable with computer technology.

To further ensure that writers were facile with the Andrew system, they each completed a pretest of facility with Edit Text, based on a set of benchmark text-editing tasks developed by Card, Moran, and Newell (1983). The three parts of the pretest were crucial for producing an original document with word processing: typing, correcting errors, and moving chunks of text. All participants were able to complete the pretest, and time scores for all participants fell well within three standard deviations for their subject group. Typing speed was 34.4 mean words-per-minute for experienced writers and 22.42 mean words-per-minute for student writers. The mean times to complete the ten corrections were 1 minute, 12 seconds for experienced writers and 1 minute, 56 seconds for students. The mean times for moving chunks of text were 1 minute, 20 seconds for experienced writers, and 1 minute, 55 seconds for students. This pretesting, and the training that was done in the think-aloud protocol methodology, increased my confidence that the results of the study were due to differences in technology, rather than interference from other variables.

The Computer System

The computing system used in this study was the Andrew system (Morris, Satyanarayanan, Conner, Howard, Rosenthal, & Smith, 1986), developed by IBM as a prototype educational computing system. The Andrew system and its text editor, Edit Text, offer a number of advantages for writers: a large, black-on-white display screen, approximately ten inches high and fourteen inches wide; a bit-mapped display for greater resolution; a mouse-and-menu-driven interface, which lessens the necessity to remember commands and contributes to tangibility; a scrollbar for moving through the text and for indicating the relative length of the document; variable fonts (e.g., bold, italic, larger); a preview program that shows writers a picture of how their finished document will look; and a windowing capability allowing writers to view their document in one window and their notes in another, or so they can see two (or more) versions of their text in different windows. Figure 4.1 shows the Andrew screen as it was set up by one of the student writers, with his planning notes in the upper window and his in-progress document in the lower window.

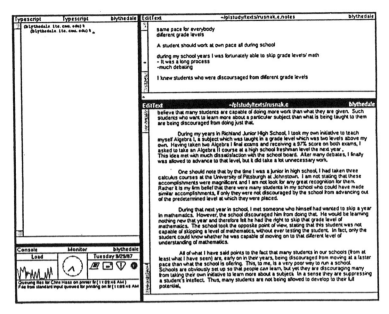

FIG. 4.1. Andrew screen with two windows.

Analysis

The analyses focused on both amounts of planning and kinds of planning. I examined amounts of total planning, initial planning, and planning notes and two kinds of text planning: sequential and conceptual.

Amount of Total Planning

The first analysis sought to examine differences in amount of planning between groups and between conditions. Each clause in the protocols was coded as one of six major writing activities: planning, producing text, rereading text, evaluating text, attending to the medium, and a miscellaneous category that included extraneous questions, inaudible comments, and the verbalizing of computer commands (in the word processing conditions).

Planning. This broad category included setting goals and making plans for what to do or say. Burtis' (Burtis et al., 1983) notion that planning is gradually differentiated from text production makes sense not only developmentally, but also in the context of real-time writing production; that is, planning and translating, or text production, can best be seen as two ends of a continuum, with abstract, high level plans for audience effect or topic at one end, and plans for word choice and syntax at the other. These local word- and syntactic choices are only slightly differentiated from the production of words on the page or screen. Therefore, the category for planning comments was broad enough to incorporate the range of plans for text that writers use.

Comments in the planning category ranged from global, such as deciding on a topic (e.g., "I guess I'll write on fraternities"), to focused, such as trying out various sentence- or word level options. Other kinds of planning comments were procedural or process comments (e.g., "I'll make a note and come back to this later" or "Let's reread it" and rhetorical planning comments (e.g., "I'll try to convince them [audience] of my view" or "I want to sound reasonable"). The following discussion on coding for types of planning offers a more detailed description of the range of planning behaviors.

Producing Text. These comments were verbalizations of the text as it was being produced. Statements were coded regardless of whether they were included in the final text. Sometimes in the written transcript of the writing session it was difficult to determine if word- and sentence-level comments were plans, or if they were actually written down. In these cases of confusion, subjects' notes, drafts, and final texts were examined. In two instances, tapes of sessions were also used to clarify the nature of the comments.

Rereading Text. Statements in this category included subjects' actual rereading of their own texts. The category did not include reading and rereading of the instructions, which were not coded.

Evaluating and Reviewing Text. This category included comments in which the writer reviewed or evaluated previously written text. Evaluative comments ranged from very broad comments, such as "This is horrible" or "I like this," to more specific comments, like "I've spelled *tenure* wrong." Also included in this category are comments in which the writer reviews or sums up previously written material: For example, "So I've covered points one and two [on her outline]," "I've talked about American schools, and I've talked about Japanese schools," and "Now that paragraph sets up the problem."

Attending to the Medium. Comments in this category were direct references to the tools being used (beyond a mere verbalization of a command sequence; see below). These were comments in which the focus of attention moved from the writing task to the medium used to produce text. Some examples of comments coded into this category are "So I'm repositioning the window and moving it here to here," "This [the system] seems slow today," and "I need an eraser."

An extraneous category, accounting for from 3-16% of the protocols, was excluded from the analysis. This category included verbalizations of commands as they were given to the system (e.g., cut, save, center), questions to the experimenter, comments irrelevant to the task at hand (e.g., about the weather or the coffee), statements about the procedure, and unintelligible comments.

A reliability check of this initial coding revealed 89% agreement between two raters and reliability of .85 by Cohen's kappa. The five major categories—planning, producing text, rereading, evaluating and reviewing, and attending to the medium—accounted for over 88 percent of the protocol statements. Excluded from further analysis were the protocols of one student writer, who exhibited no planning behavior at all. This student, who was judged to be an excellent writer by her English teacher, appeared to have a well-articulated writing script (Flower & Hayes, 1980) which allowed her to generate a fairly coherent, if conventional, response to the topic with virtually no overt planning.

Amount of Initial Planning

In addition to total amount of planning, initial planning—or the planning that occurred before writers produced a written sentence—was also examined. The number of planning statements before the generation of text was tallied for each writer in each condition, and proportions were derived relative to the total amount of planning. In other words, I examined the proportion of planning in each condition that occurred before writers began to produce text. In two cases (both in computer conditions), audio- and videotapes were used to establish precisely when writing began.

Amount of Planning Notes

The notes produced during the writing sessions of each writer were collected. Notes produced on-line were saved in a separate notes file. The number of words produced in each condition was tallied and totaled. Final notes only were analyzed because notes produced and then deleted on the word processor were not captured; any crossed out or erased notes in the pen-and-paper condition were similarly omitted from the analysis. Previous research (Burtis et al., 1983) suggests that the making of notes serves an important planning function, allowing writers to explore and organize ideas and keep themselves on task. Writers who planned more were expected to produce more planning notes and, more to the point for this study, that those conditions allowing or encouraging notemaking would evidence more planning.

Kinds of Planning

Writers may plan differently in kind as well as in amount when using word processing versus pen-and-paper. Therefore, I also explored the hypotheses suggested by some previous research: (a) when using word processing, writers would do more word- and sentence-level or sequential planning; and (b) when using word processing alone, writers would do less whole text, or conceptual, planning.

Although I was particularly interested in text plans, I developed a four-part coding scheme to account for each planning statement in the protocols. Each planning statement was coded as either a process plan, a rhetorical plan, a conceptual text plan, or a sequential text plan. In this study, process planning comments were often cues to begin and end, decisions to reread, or decisions to delay a certain activity. Some examples of process planning comments are "I'll reread this," "Come back to this later," and "I guess I'll finish up." Rhetorical plans included comments about purpose or audience, like "How much do they [the audience] know about this?" and "I don't want to sound like a bigot." It seemed likely that there would be differences between subjects and between groups in the use of process plans, but that pen-and-paper or word processing conditions would not affect process planning. Further, determining in any given case whether a plan was rhetorical could be problematic. Therefore, the analysis focused on plans for text.

Matsuhashi's (1987) analysis of different kinds of revision plans provided a useful way to explore these hypotheses about the impact of word processing on different kinds of planning. Drawing on de Beaugrande's (1980) notions of conceptual connectivity, which deals with underlying conceptual relations, and sequential connectivity, which focuses on the lexical arrangement of the surface text, Matsuhashi developed a coding scheme to distinguish two kinds of text planning. Matsuhashi's coding scheme was adapted slightly for this study, but the names of her categories were retained.

Conceptual Plans. Conceptual plans guide the creation of the conceptual meaning and structure of the text and include generating content, exploring the topic, developing ideas, deciding "what to talk about," organizing ideas, and elaborating and coming up with examples. In this study, conceptual planning often occurred in lengthy episodes, especially at the beginning of the writing session, as in this example.

> Let's see what could I write about. . . . what habits did I develop in college? What about smoking . . . drinking . . staying up late. Those are all bad habits. Do kids develop any good ones? I guess kids at [this university] probably do . . .

Other examples include "So now I need to get real specific," "What else could I say about this?" and "Let's see . . . I need to tie all this together in a concluding paragraph."

Sequential Plans. Sequential plans focus on lexical or syntactic arrangement, or the textual expression of meaning. Decisions about word choice or syntactic arrangement as text is produced are the most common examples of this type of text planning. Many of the statements in this category resembled the "proposing and evaluating of sentence parts" identified by Kaufer, Hayes, and Flower (1986) in their analysis of the translating process. Many of the statements coded as sequential planning were interrogatives, including questions like "What do I mean?" or "What do I want to say?" or simply "What?" interjected into verbalizations of the production of text on the page or on the screen (Kaufer, Hayes, & Flower, 1986).

Writers varied in how much they plan (or struggle) to produce text at the point of utterance. For some writers, every written phrase was preceded by elaborate word-level plans; for others, the words seemed to flow off the pen (or the keyboard) without much sequential planning. For some writers, this struggle to produce words may have been where ideas are tried out or even "discovered" (Murray, 1978). The following example shows the nature of these kinds of sequential planning statements. Text that was actually written is in italics.

> Partying can affect the student in . . . let's see. OK. *Partying*, partying provides the student with . . . what? When at college there are many . . . *When a students goes to college* he, he or she? no . .*he finds many more parties than before.*

Also included in this category were concerns with spelling and punctuation, and comments in which the writer referred to "last paragraph" or "next sentence" without any mention of the meaning or function of that paragraph or sentence. Some examples of sequential planning comments are "Should that be a semicolon or a colon?" "Should I say students or kids?" and "I'll make this two paragraphs."

In essence, then, this coding scheme makes a distinction between thought and language. While this distinction is a tenuous and largely theoretical one, I was able to distinguish the two types of planning comments with some regularity: agreement between two readers trained in the coding scheme for types of planning was 91% with a reliability of .76 by Cohen's kappa. The distinctions between Conceptual and Sequential planning—like the distinctions in all of the coding here—were made in context; i.e., raters sorted the planning comments not as isolated statements but as part of a whole writing session.

Results

Amount of Total Planning

The first analysis examined differences in total amount of planning for the two groups of writers—experienced writers and student writers—and three conditions, pen-and-paper, word processing alone, and word processing with pen-and-paper allowed (the both condition). The total number of protocol statements coded as planning were tallied for each writer in each condition; proportions were derived relative to the total number of clauses in each protocol.

I was primarily interested in proportion of planning in each condition—that is, the amount of planning relative to the total length of the writing session and of the protocol—because the length of the writing session was quite varied among individuals and across groups. For example, protocols ranged in length from 4 pages for one student writer to 16 pages for one experienced writer. Proportional analysis reduced the variance and showed the differences between conditions more clearly.

Means for percent of planning, as shown in Table 4.1, were similar for the word processing and both conditions (27.2 and 27.8, respectively), but there was more planning in the pen-and-paper condition (33.9). A two-way analysis of variance (ANOVA) for percent of planning showed a main effect for condition [$F(2,34) = 6.73$, $p <.005$], an effect for group that was just short of significant [$F(1,17) = 2.98$, $p <.10$], and no interaction between group and condition [$F(2,34) = .81$, $p <.05$]. Neuman-Keuls analysis showed that this variance can be accounted for by a significant difference ($p <.001$) between the pen-and-paper condition and the word processing alone condition, and a significant difference ($p <.01$) between the pen-and-paper and the both conditions. The word processing alone condition and the word processing with paper allowed condition both resulted in significantly less planning than the pen-and-paper condition, but there were no significant differences between these two word processing conditions.

Table 4.1
Mean Percent of Planning Statements

	Means (SD)		
	Pen and Paper	Word Processing	Both
Experienced writers	38.5 (12.0)	29.8 (12.4)	32.6 (13.9)
Student writers	28.8 (10.4)	24.3 (12.9)	22.4 (7.2)
Combined	33.9	27.2	27.8

Amount of Initial Planning

The next series of analyses examined the amount of planning that occurred before writers began producing formal text. In the pen-and-paper condition, initial planning was the largest percentage of total planning (42.6), with the word processing condition and the both condition showing similar percentage of initial planning (28.3 and 31.8, respectively). Further, when the groups were broken out, it seemed that the experienced writers were doing more initial planning than are the student writers (as would be expected), although both groups had the most initial planning in the pen-and-paper condition and the least in the word processing alone condition. For experienced writers, the percentages were 48.4 in the pen-and-paper condition, 38.5 in the word processing condition, and 37.5 in the both condition. The percentage for student writers were 36.1 in the pen-and-paper condition, 25.4 in the both condition, and 17.0 in the word processing condition (see Table 4.2).

Table 4.2

Mean Percent of Initial Planning

	Means		
	Pen and Paper	Word Processing	Both
Experienced writers	48.4 (22.0)	38.5 (16.9)	37.5 (20.5)
Student writers	36.1 (23.8)	17.0 (13.4)	25.4 (20.5)
Combined	42.6	28.3	31.8

Results of a two-way ANOVA for initial planning percentages showed a main effect for condition [$F(2,34) = 3.77$, $p < .03$], a main effect for group [$F(1,17) = 5.55$, $p < .03$], and no interaction [$F(2,34) = .48$, $p < .05$]. Neuman-Keuls analysis revealed that this difference in percent of initial planning can be accounted for by a significant difference ($p < .05$) between the pen-and-paper condition and the word processing alone condition.

Planning Notes

More writers took notes in the pen-and-paper condition than in the other conditions. Of the 19 writers, two (one student and one more experienced writer) did not take notes in any of the conditions. In the pen-and-paper condition, all of the remaining 17 writers took notes. Ten writers took notes in the word processing condition only, and 13 writers took notes in the both condition. Table 4.3 shows the patterns of notemaking in the three conditions.

Table 4.3

Numbers of Writers Making Planning Notes in each Condition

	Pen and Paper	Word Processing	Both		
			Pen only	WP only	Both
Experienced Writers ($n = 10$)	9	7	4	1	2
Students ($n = -9$)	8	3	5	3	0
Total	17	10	15		

Not only did more writers make pen-and-paper notes, but the mean number of words of notes was highest in that condition, 69.26 words. The mean number of words of notes taken in the both condition was 51.32, while the mean for the word processing conditions was lowest, 33.89 words. However, there were no significant differences in the amount of notes produced in the three conditions. A two-way ANOVA showed significant differences ($p<.05$) between the groups in number of words of notes taken, but the differences between conditions were not significant ($p<.10$).

I anticipated that writers would choose pen-and-paper for notes when it was available, and that they would produce significantly more notes with the pen-and-paper medium than when using the word processor for notes. However, these expectations about notemaking were not confirmed. Although more writers used pen-and-paper to take notes, and although the number of words of notes was highest in the pen-and-paper condition, the only significant differences were between the two groups of writers.

In the course of this analysis, however, it became clear that the ways in which writers were producing and using notes was very different in the different conditions. Because the protocol methodology employed here was not useful in describing these differences, I undertook a textual analysis of the notes taken in different conditions. Following the presentation of amounts and types of planning (from the analysis of think-aloud protocols), I return at the end of this chapter to a more detailed analysis of the notemaking behaviors of these writers. This analysis provides a suitable conclusion for the study because the profiles of writers' and their planning notes provide a springboard for discussion of why writers may plan less in computer conditions.

Amount of Planning in the Both Condition

One of the intriguing results was the lack of significant results for the both condition. Initially, this both condition was predicted to be very conducive to writers' planning because it would allow them to take advantage of both word processing and pen-and-paper (i.e., the speed of producing text could be retained via the word processor, but planning notes and outlines could still be done on pen-and-paper. However, the mean scores for this condition usually fell between those of the other two conditions (see Tables 4.1 and 4.2). Analysis of percent of total planning and percent of initial planning revealed no differences between the word processing alone and the both conditions. Therefore, although the both condition might be expected to favor planning, the results were inconclusive.

The way that people responded to the both condition may have contributed to the lack of significant results. Although many writers report using pen and paper to supplement word processing for planning notes or for initial writing (Bridwell-Bowles et al., 1987; Haas & Hayes, 1986), the writers in this study varied widely in whether and how they used pen-and-paper to supplement word processing: five of the ten experienced writers and three of the nine student writers treated the both condition as if it were a computer alone condition. They did not make any hard copy notes, nor did they generate a printout in the both condition.

To determine if there were differences in planning between those writers who used pen and paper in the both condition and those who did not, each of the subject groups (experienced and student) was divided into two subgroups. This analysis contrasted writers in a true both condition to writers in what was in fact a word processing alone condition. Mann-Whitney tests showed no significant differences between writers who did and who did not use pen and paper to supplement word processing, either for total planning in the both condition or for initial planning in the both condition [$U = 9$; $U = 10$]. Finally, an analysis was done on the numerical differences in planning percent between the both condition and each of the other two conditions for each group of writers: those who had and those who had not used both media in the both condition. Again, Mann-Whitney tests revealed no differences [$U = 9$].

Kinds of Planning

To examine possible differences between conditions in kinds or levels of planning, two separate analysis were conducted: one for sequential planning and one for conceptual planning. While these two phenomena could occur together (that is, writers could do less of one and more of the other), each could also occur independently. For this analysis, only pen-and-paper and word processing alone conditions were compared, because previous analyses had suggested that the important differences lay here and because there were large individual differences in the way writers used the both condition.

Sequential Planning. This analysis examined the amount of sequential planning as a percent of total planning. As Table 4.4 shows, the amount of sequential planning was almost half again as much in the word processing condition as it was in the pen-and-paper condition (36.2 and 25.3, respectively). A two-way ANOVA revealed no difference between groups in proportion of sequential planning $[F(1,17) = .42]$, but a significant difference between conditions $[F(1,17) = 6.76, p < .01]$, and there was no interaction $[F(1,17) = .22]$. This analysis revealed that there was significantly more sequential planning when writers used word processing alone.

Table 4.4

Mean Percent of Sequential Planning

	Means (SD)	
	Pen and Paper	Word Processing
Experienced Writers	27.9 (15.9)	39.6 (17.9)
Student Writers	22.4 (10.6)	35.4 (13.1)
Combined	25.3	36.2

Conceptual Planning. Conceptual planning as a proportion of total planning was then analyzed. Conceptual planning accounted for 67.7% of the total planning in the pen-and-paper condition and 52.1% in the word processing condition (see Table 4.5). Two-way analysis of variance for percent of conceptual planning shows a main effect $[F(1,17) = 11.76, p < .003]$ for condition, no effect for group $[F(1,17) = .037]$, and no interaction $[F(1,17) = .53]$.

Table 4.5

Mean Percent of Conceptual Planning

	Means (SD)	
	Pen and Paper	Word Processing
Experienced Writers	66.2 (16.5)	53.7 (16.3)
Student Writers	69.4 (7.5)	50.2 (18.1)
Combined	67.6	52.1

A subsequent analysis of the raw number of clauses of conceptual planning underscored the differences for condition and shows a difference between groups. The mean number of conceptual planning statements was half again as much in the pen-and-paper condition as in the word processing condition (75.9

and 52.7, respectively). The patterns held for each group, although the experienced writers had more conceptual planning statements than did the student writers. The mean for experienced writers was 105.3 statements in the pen-and-paper condition and 73.9 in the word processing condition, whereas the student writers' means were 43.2 conceptual planning statements in the pen-and-paper condition and 29.1 in the word processing condition. A two-way ANOVA showed a main effect for condition [$F(1,17) = 8.80, p < .01$], a main effect for group [$F(1,17) = 6.34, p < .05$], and no interaction [$F(1,17) = 1.27$].

Discussion of Planning Results

Result 1: There was less planning with word processing. Writers planned significantly less when they were used word processing than when they used pen-and-paper. There were also significant differences in the percent of planning that occurred before writers began to produce text. These results add credence to anecdotal reports of writers who feel pressed to begin writing sooner when using word processing (Bridwell-Bowles et al., 1987), and they are supported as well by other observational studies, such as Eklundh and Sjoholm's (1991) longitudinal study. Further, these results provide a possible explanation of the text sense problem reported by some writers who use word processing: If a writer plans less when producing a test with word processing, then he and she may experience a difficulty in knowing or recalling that text. This text sense problem is examined in more detail in chapter 5 (this volume).

There are several possible reasons for less planning—and less initial planning—with word processing. Although the amount and proportion of planning was less in the word processing condition, the writing sessions and texts from this condition generally were not shorter. Possibly writers made up for repressed planning with word processing in other ways. In a separate study (Haas, 1989a), I found that although writers planned less in word processing conditions, they reread their texts more extensively than they did in the pen-and-paper condition.

A more likely explanation for these results is that writers began writing sooner and spent less time planning because making changes is easier with word processing. Computers are more responsive (see chapter 3, this volume) both for producing text—because most writers can type faster than they can write—and for making changes to text. That is, word processing is a less expensive medium in which to produce text than is pen and paper, because with the former a word or sentence or paragraph can be deleted or rewritten very easily. Possibly writers realize that their documents can be changed easily with word processing and so produce text more quickly, relying on later revisions to perfect their ideas. While this certainly is a plausible explanation, numerous studies have failed to consistently support claims of increased revision with word processing (see Hawisher, 1989).

Further research should explore not only reasons for less planning with word processing, but also the impact of this decreased planning. Although most researchers agree that, in general, better writers plan more, the relationship of planning to text quality has not been established. It is not clear, for instance, if the differences in planning evidenced here would result in texts of lower judged quality.

Result 2: There was less conceptual planning and more sequential planning with word processing. Again, these results bear out reports of many writers and researchers that word processing encourages an over-attendance to low level concerns, tidying up and fiddling at a local word or sentence level (Bridwell-Bowles et al., 1987). Bangert-Downs (1993) has suggested that computers will have their greatest influence on writing by performing simple tasks (i.e., checking spelling, etc.) so that writers can "mindfully attend" (p. 70) to complex mental tasks. This notion that computers free writers of local constraints was certainly not borne out by the results of this study, where word processing seemed to increase writers' attention to low-level concerns.

Exactly why the word processor encouraged this attention to local concerns was not clear. Certainly word processing makes local word and sentence level changes very easy; text at the local level may have seemed more tangible, and computer systems more responsive to local changes, in the language of chapter 3 (this volume). There are few word processing programs which support and encourage an attention to large scale text issues, and in fact the limited view of one's text (i.e., size, as described in chapter 3) offered by most word processing systems may actually discourage attending to the whole text. Because it is difficult to see one's whole document with word processing, writers may have attended to what they could see on the screen.

Another factor contributing to the decrease in conceptual planning with word processing may have been that the initial planning periods were shorter; it may be that much of the conceptual planning that writers do—forming arguments and theses, determining structure, organization, and form—occurs during these initial planning periods.

Result 3: The effects of writing media were similar for both groups—experienced writers and student writers. One of the more interesting findings of this study was a lack of subject-by-condition interactions. Although some analyses showed the experienced writers planning significantly more (specifically, in total number of planning clauses), the effect of the word processing condition to repress planning in general, decreased initial and conceptual planning, and increase sequential planning was the same for each group. If the differences between the word processing conditions and the pen-and-paper condition were due to subjects' greater familiarity with pen-and-paper, we might expect to see fewer differences between conditions for the experienced writers, who were also more experienced with both computers in general and with this word processing program. However, this was not the case.

Although experience with word processing can be an important factor in how, and how well, writers use the technology, it may be naive to think that writers' concerns about the drawbacks of word processing and their continued use of pen-and-paper are simply a function of experience with the technology. The similar results for each group in this study certainly offer no support for this notion.

Result 4: There were vast differences in how writers used word processing and pen and paper together in the both condition. Maybe the most intriguing results of this study concern the way that writers responded to the both condition which allowed writers to use both word processing and pen and paper if they wished. The responses to this condition ranged from several writers who did not use pen-and-paper at all in this condition to one writer who wrote out her entire text in pen first, and then typed it into the machine. Interestingly, although several of the writers chose not to use pen and paper at all in this condition, none of them chose to work without the word processor.

CONVERGING PRODUCT AND PROCESS MEASURES: A DETAILED LOOK AT NOTE MAKING

This section describes a product analysis of writers' planning notes. Comparative numerical data of amount and types of notes made supplement the process analysis of think-aloud protocols presented earlier, and corroborate the results of the process analysis. In addition, detailed profiles of two writers and their notemaking activities are profiled. These profiles—constructed via converging process and product measures—provide a rich and complex comparison of the same writers engaged in very different writing activities and producing very different written notes. I use these profiles to hypothesize about why writers planning may be shortened and changed when they use computers.

For this analysis, only the notes of the experienced writers were examined. Because these writers planned more than did the student writers, and because they took more notes, these experienced writers' notes allowed for a more complete picture of notemaking and how it is manifest in different technological conditions. The term *notemaking* is used to refer to the creation and manipulation of planning notes prior to, and occasionally during, writing. The source for these notes is the writer's own thoughts and reflection; in this way, notemaking is distinguished from *note-taking*, in which a writer takes notes on an outside source such as a book or an observed event. Notes are at once the output of planning, a strategy for cognitive monitoring, and a writer's first attempts at visible language.

Research on writing processes (reviewed earlier) has identified the advantages of notemaking. Notes can provide an external memory for the considerable number of ideas that writers might generate in the course of planning their compositions—ideas that do not have to be held in conscious attention if they are written down as notes. Notes can also provide a way to work out relationships between ideas and to develop the structure of the argument.

Further, notes may provide a thumbnail sketch of the proposed composition—a briefer form of the whole that the composer might adjust or tinker with or totally revamp. Such tinkering can be quick and efficient with notes, whereas it might be time-consuming and cumbersome when done with an already-written text. Notemaking can do a great deal of conceptual work for writers, aiding them in activities like coming up with a topic, keeping track of ideas generated, exploring relationships between ideas, developing a structure for the written piece, and keeping on task. In summary, notes are an important cognitive management strategy, helping writers keep track of their ideas, their goals, and the structure of their developing text.

Although the word processor can aid some aspects of writing, there is some reason to expect that it could hinder or discourage planning and notemaking. First, because for many writers text production is quicker with a word processor, writers may be drawn into text production sooner—before they have had time to plan extensively or to make planning notes. In metacognitive terms, writers may be drawn into cognitive use and away from metacognitive awareness

(Durst, 1989). Second, small screen space may make it difficult to see large sections of the text at once and discourage whole-text planning, making it easier to tinker with the local text in view, rather than think about and plan for the text as a whole. And third, conventional word processors have few devices for the creation and manipulation of outlines, diagrams, or other kinds of structural notes that writers find useful.

The analysis of planning notes had two phases reflecting two slightly different goals: first, describing notemaking generally, and second, comparing notemaking across pen-and-paper and word processing conditions. I first examined the kinds and range of notes that writers made, regardless of writing medium used. The following is a detailed descriptive analysis of the kinds of notes these writers produced. I then turn to question of media-based differences in notemaking and use both descriptive and experimental methods to examine the notes writers made with pen and paper and with computer. I also present profiles of two writers and their notemaking in the two conditions; these profiles illuminate how notemaking was vastly different with different media. For each profile, written notes are supplemented with think-aloud protocols of the writers' composing sessions.

Types of Planning Notes

First, I examined and defined the range of notes made by these experienced writers. For this analysis, no distinction was made between pen-and-paper and word processing notes. A four-category scheme, developed for this analysis, accounted for over 95% of the notes. One half of the data was also coded by a second, independent rater and direct agreement was 92%, or .83 by Cohen's kappa. In general terms, virtually all the notes were accounted for by this four-part scheme, and writers could distinguish among the types of notes with a great deal of reliability. The four kinds of notes were content, structure, emphasis, and procedural.

Content Notes

These were the most commonly occurring notes. Content notes were typically brief, and they often occurred as a list of words without any clear relationship among them. Content notes were typically of two types: ideas for possible topics to write on and ideas for possible inclusion into the essay once a topic had been determined. Not only were content notes the most numerous, but they also seemed to be the first kind of note that the writers produced. Examination of the protocols revealed that creation of a content note was often accompanied by lengthy bursts of planning and that the note was a brief memory cue to what was often a very complex idea. The content notes revealed writers' cognitive awareness both of potentially valuable ideas and topics and of their own tendency to forget without external memory cues. Figure 4.2 presents some examples of content notes.

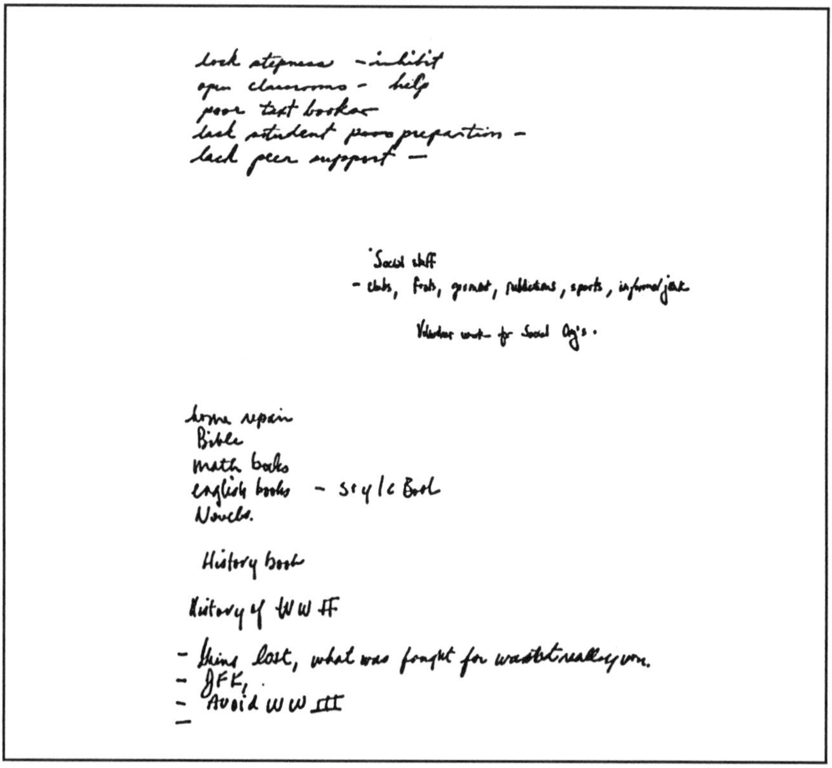

FIG. 4.2. Three examples of content notes.

Structure Notes

The second most numerous kind of note was the structure note. Structure notes could be content-less, such as "intro" or "point 1," but they were usually tied to content in one of two ways. Often the writer produced notes that combined content cues with a structure for the essay, as when a writer made a rough outline of the structure of the planned essay with content notes embedded in it. Less frequently, the writer took a list or string of content notes generated earlier and imposed a structure on it by adding numbers, letters, or arrows. In many cases, the same note functioned both as a content cue and as a placeholder in a structure for the planned essay. Structure notes provided a more or less detailed blueprint for the text. They show writers' metacognitive awareness of linguistic structures and their own plans for the text. Figure 4.3 shows examples of structure notes.

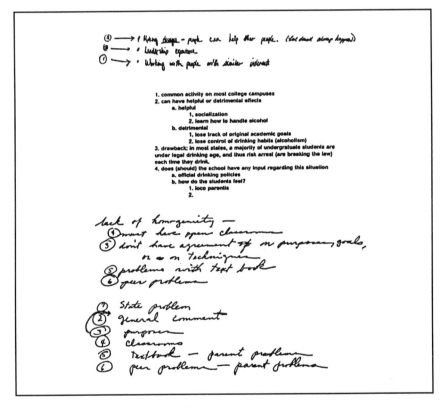

FIG. 4.3. Three examples of structure notes.

Emphasis Notes

The third kind of notes, emphasis notes, did not occur in isolation, but were added to content or structure notes. Typically, particularly interesting topics or

ideas that the writer wanted to emphasize, return to, or elaborate were highlighted with graphics such as circles, underlining, or stars.   In the word
processing conditions, emphasis was added with capitalization or asterisks.
Emphasis notes could emphasize potentially valuable ideas, or they could
reflect a plan to emphasize certain points.   Examples of emphasis notes are
shown in Figure 4.4.

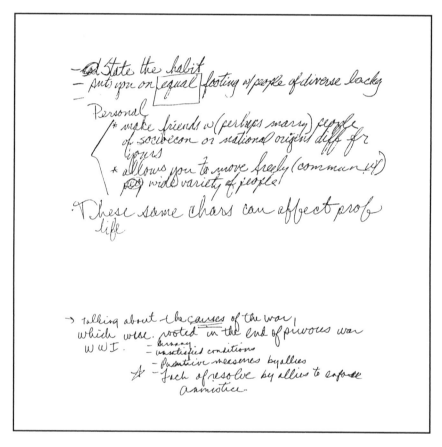

FIG. 4.4. Two examples of emphasis notes. Here, boxes, stars,
and underlining are used to add emphasis to content notes.

Procedural Notes

The fourth kind of notes, procedural notes, functioned as instructions that the writers wrote to themselves about how to proceed, or they were used to signal rhetorical goals, such as establishing purpose or setting up a particular persona. Examples included: "set the stage," "purpose," and "include examples." Although previous research (Burtis et al., 1983; Kaufer et al., 1986) has suggested the importance of procedural and rhetorical notes, procedural notes in this study were in fact quite rare—only four instances in 20 sets of notes. Therefore, in subsequent analyses, only content, structure, and emphasis notes were examined.

For writing that involves restructuring knowledge and transforming ideas in light of a particular writing purpose, all of these kinds of notes seem useful in composing. Writers could use lists to keep track of content items while they worked on retrieving and developing other ideas, and emphasis notes would be useful for noting particularly important or pivotal ideas that need further elaboration. Structure notes would help writers work out the relationship among ideas, as well as develop the structure of the proposed essay. Procedural notes would aid in keeping track of rhetorical goals and purposes.

One compelling argument for the advantages of notemaking lies in the fact that nine of ten writers made notes. That these experienced, competent writers—all of whom wrote daily in their work and a number of whom made their living by writing—made notes with no prompting to do so is highly suggestive that they believed notemaking to be a useful and advantageous writing activity.

Comparing Computer and Pen-and-Paper Notemaking

This section examines the following question: Are there differences between pen-and-paper and computer notemaking? This comparison will include analysis of the number of words of notes writers made in each condition, a comparison of the kinds of notes made in each condition, and a detailed description of two writers' planning and notemaking with pen-and-paper and with word processing.

One of the writers produced no notes in either condition, and thus was not included in this analysis. Therefore, the comparison of pen-and-paper and word processor notemaking was based on nine subjects. In the pen-and-paper condition, more notes were made, more writers made notes, and more notes per writer were made than in the word processing condition.   As shown in Table 4.6, a total of 907 notes were produced with pen-and-paper, whereas 524 notes were produced with word processor. All nine writers took notes with pen-and-paper, six of nine with word processor. The mean number of notes per writer was 100.7 in the pen-and-paper condition and 58.2 in the word processor condition. *T*-tests revealed that the differences between condition in the number of notes (measured as words) was short of significant. Further, of the six writers who made notes on the word processor, four produced more notes with it than they did with pen-and-paper. In sum, although more notes were made with pen-and-paper, the findings are neither entirely straightforward nor statistically significant.

Table 4.6

Number of Notes (in words) Made in Two Conditions

	Pen	Computer
Writer 1	93	—
Writer 2	99	128
Writer 3	79	85
Writer 4	60	75
Writer 5	78	44
Writer 6	271	—
Writer 7	36	—
Writer 8	54	110
Writer 9	137	68
Total words of notes	907	524
Mean words of notes	100.7	58.2
Writers making notes	9	6

Although the differences in the amount of notes made in the two conditions were not significant, it is possible that writers were making different kinds of notes with pen-and-paper than with word processing. This hypothesis was explored in the next analysis. The notes in each condition were coded as one of the four types of notes outlined earlier: content notes, structure notes, emphasis notes, or procedural notes. Because procedural notes were so rare—only three instances in 18 sets of notes—they were not included in the analysis. The presence or absence of the three remaining kinds of note for each writer in each condition was tallied and the resulting scores were submitted to a simple chi-square, adjusted for the small n by Yates' correction (see Table 4.7).

The results reflect, as expected, that more total words of notes were produced with pen-and-paper and that content notes were the most frequent kind of notes. All nine writers produced content notes with pen-and-paper, while six of them produced content notes with word processor. All of the writers also produced structure notes with pen and paper, but only five did so with word processor. The difference in emphasis notes was more striking: Six writers produced Emphasis notes in the pen-and-paper condition, but only one of them did when writing with word processor.

Table 4.7

Frequency and Chi-square Values for Notes

Produced in Two Conditions. ($N = 9$).

	Pen	Computer	x^2
Content notes	9	6	1.6 (NS)
Structure notes	9	5	3.0 ($p<.07$; NS)
Emphasis notes	6	1	5.1 ($p<.05$)

The chi-square value of 1.6 for content was not significant ($df = 1$), but a value of 3.0 for structure was close to significant ($df= 1$, $p <.07$), and the resulting value for emphasis, 5.14 ($df=1$, $p <.05$), was significant with a phi-coefficient showing a relationship of .534. It seems that these writers generated ideas, worked out relationships between ideas, set up points relative to one another, and sometimes even developed a structure for their proposed essay in the notes for the pen-and-paper essays but did so less often in the word processing condition.

Just as there were between writers in notemaking behavior, there were also differences in how individual writers made notes in the two conditions. Put another way, the notemaking of writers seemed to be affected by the medium—pen or word processor—with which they worked. This effect is illustrated here in detailed descriptions of two writers' notemaking and early writing sessions with pen-and-paper and with word processor. The first writer, Morgan, made extensive notes with pen-and-paper but did not make any notes with word processor. Don, the second writer, was one of the four writers who took more notes with word processing than with pen and paper. But there were differences in the kind and range of notes he made in the two conditions as well.

During Morgan's early writing session with pen and paper (see Figures 4.5 and 4.6), he generated 93 words of notes, including content notes, structure notes in the form of a numbered list and a tree diagram, emphasis notes (e.g., circles and underlining), and one procedural note about including anecdotes. Like the adult writers studied by Burtis et al. (1983), Morgan made notes that seemed to be tags to larger chunks of content.

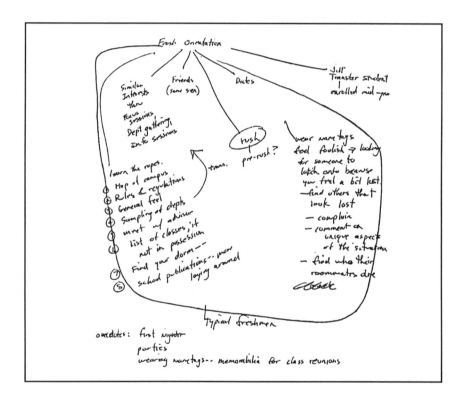

FIG. 4.5. Some of Morgan's pen-and-paper notes.

Reads prompt.

Limits topic.

"I don't know anything about [this university]. But I'm going to plan this as an undergraduate thing..."

Rereads prompt.

Begins generating ideas.

"Social groups—they get together. What else? Sit around and have bull sessions, go out and drink beer, athletics, drama, art. What is—oh, carnival. I don't know anything at all about that so it wouldn't be very useful. . . Trying to get a context for this. . "

Rereads prompt and continues generating ideas.

"Would be fun to do dating, but that's a real small group—only two people. What's the first thing—student orientation. It's probably the first thing they encounter, and it's very important."

Begins making notes of "class orientation." (C, S)

"So writing this down. Get some notes. Class orientation. OK, and the first thing I'm going to write her is Jill's name—because she wrote a paper for my class, and explained how tough it was, that she came in January rather than in the fall. Write that down—enrolled mid-year. What else happens? Well, friends—they also meet people with similar interests. Similar interests through what? You might call it focus sessions. Department gatherings, info sessions and well, you learn the ropes."

Begins numbered list of activities under "learn the ropes." (C, S)

Begins another list of notes on other side of the page.

"What else do they—sit around and run around and drink beer usually. Oh, you write name tags, right? And you're actually looking for someone to latch onto-because, because you feel a bit lost."

Continues notemaking, with ideas about rush and parties, and decides to include anecdotes (C, E, P)

Reviews notes, thinks about tone.

(FIG. 4.6, cont.)

"Let's see—do I want to do an outline? How does this flow? So many students encounter this stuff. Do I want to have this entertaining or do I want to have it serious. I really don't want to write it seriously, that would be terrible. Who would want to read this? Let's start this."
Begins writing.

FIG. 4.6. A detailed outline of Morgan's early writing session with pen-and-paper. Letters in parentheses indicate the kinds of notes he made at various points: C = content notes, S = structure notes, E = emphasis notes, P = procedural notes. Quotations are excerpts from the think-aloud protocol. Underlining indicates a note was written.

As shown in Figure 4.7, Morgan's early writing session with the word processor was very different. First, it is much shorter—only about one minute, 30 seconds versus the five minutes, 20 seconds spent planning before writing in the pen-and-paper condition. (In the earlier study [Haas, 1989b] initial planning periods before beginning to write were significantly shorter with word processor.) Second, he generated many fewer ideas and comes up with only three possible topics, none of which he wrote down. He then decided to "take a stand." There is much less evidence of planning and monitoring strategies than in his early pen-and-paper writing session. Finally, while he took a page of notes with pen-and-paper, Morgan took no notes for his essay written with word processor.

In summary, Morgan's early writing sessions were quite different: With pen and paper, he did a great deal of initial planning and took 93 words of notes, whereas his initial planning with word processing was brief, and he made no word processing notes. His initial planning with pen-and-paper was richer and more extensive, and he took a number of various kinds of notes with this medium.

Reads prompt.

Creates computer "file."

"Edit morgan-dot-see."

Rereads prompt.

Brainstorms possible ideas and approach.

"How about, that the GPA is the most important indicator of quality of life. . I suppose I could do female-male relationships. That might be an interesting one to do. I could compare colleges—or St. John's with a coed institution. I have to explain or take a position. I'll probably take a position."

Begins writing.

[No notes taken.]

FIG. 4.7. A detailed outline of Morgan's early writing session with word processor. Quotations indicate excerpts from think-aloud protocol.

There were a number of writers like Morgan—writers who planned extensively and took notes with pen-and-paper but whose word processing notemaking was sparse, or nonexistent (See Table 4.6). But there were also a number of writers who did make notes with word processing, and Don was one of the writers who made more word processing notes than pen-and-paper notes. Don's pen-and-paper notes, shown in Figure 4.8, had the diagrammatic, spatial quality of some of the other writers' notes. He set up columns to generate topics and content, used arrows to show relationships, and constructed a brief outline of his proposed essay. As seen in the detailed description of his early writing session (Figure 4.9), Don, like Morgan, began by generating brief notes on content and later moved on to an outline. There was ample evidence, too, of Don evaluating and monitoring content, structure, and his own process.

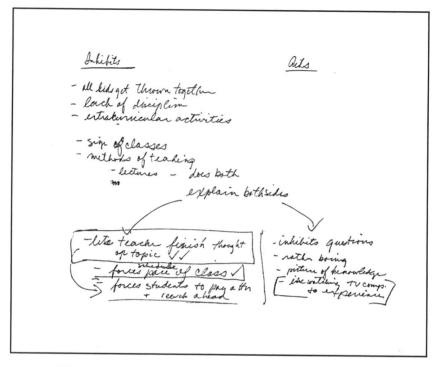

FIG. 4.8. Some of Don's pen-and-paper notes.

Reads prompt.

Begins taking notes under two headings, labeled "inhibits" and "aids." (C, S, P)

"It inhibits when all the kids get thrown together, and there's a lack of discipline. Aids learning. Let's see. I wonder about some of the extracurriculars, extracurricular activities. I don't know whether those inhibit or aid. . .I'm thinking of lectures which either help or inhibit in a big way. Lectures—I guess that's a pretty common practice. How it inhibits or aids learning. Probably does both. So I'm going to explain both sides."

Begins more structured outline about lectures (C, S, E)

"So I'm probably going to explain both sides. I'm going to start outlining that. Well, it inhibits questions, but it lets the teacher finish the thought or topic. So I guess it forces the pace of the class. . .I'm thinking it inhibits questions—it's kind of boring sometimes, and students left with a kind of a picture of knowledge rather than a well-modeled understanding of it."

Decides on approach to the topic.

(FIG. 4.9, cont.)

> "I really don't feel I can settle the question of aids or inhibits. I can just say it does both, because I'd rather not take a position about it. So I'll just explain it."
> Begins writing.

FIG. 4.9. A detailed outline of Don's early writing session with pen-and-paper. Letters in parentheses indicate the kinds of notes he made at various points: C = content notes, S = structure notes, E = emphasis notes, P = procedural notes. Quotations are excerpts from the think-aloud protocol. Underlining indicates a note was written.

Don's word processor notes are shown in Figure 4.10. These notes are different in a number of ways from his pen-and-paper notes. Although Don had slightly more words of notes with word processing, these notes had none of the diagrammatic quality of the other notes this study has examined. There is little relationship shown among ideas (except possibly by proximity). Don's word processor notes were all content notes; there were no notes indicating structure or emphasis, nor were there procedural notes written to himself. The word processing notes were a sort of stream-of-consciousness style, with little order imposed.

Perhaps most significantly, whereas the pen-and-paper notes were brief tags to larger chunks of information, the word processing notes appeared more text-like than note-like, an intriguing parallel to the notemaking behavior of the young children studied by Burtis et al. (1983). The fourth group of notes was almost able to stand as a paragraph of text. Figure 4.11, the detailed description of Don's early writing session, showed that he was writing many of his thoughts down completely, not making notes by gisting as many writers, including Don himself, did in the pen-and-paper writing session.

Religious values
Social values--tolerance and patience, openness to other
peoples views and lifestyles.

Study habits--perhaps the habit of doing their best under
pressure and being satisfied with it.
Ties in with being patient.

Being thorough and more deeply analytical in their work.
Really learning to think critically in their field of study, and
to apply that ability to other subject areas.

Tolerating supervisors (professors and teachers) who are
sometimes eccentric or difficult to work with. You have to
acquire the habit of gettiing along and getting work done
sometimes in spite of the people you work with. There's
always the joke about knowing and doing what the teacher
wants.

Fundamental trust in other people with different view

FIG. 4.10. Don's notes made with word processor.

Reads prompt.

Begins taking notes. (C)

"I'm wondering about religious values, but that might be something that gets broken down rather than acquired during college. Also some social values, perhaps tolerance and patience, and even more than that I can encompass openness to other people's views and lifestyles."

Continues notemaking and develops ideas of working under pressure and tolerance. (C)

"Habits, like study habits. Perhaps the habit of doing their best under pressure and being satisfied. That's a pretty good one; that ties in with patience, being patient. Also being thorough and more deeply analytical in your work, really learning to think critically in their study and to apply that ability to other subject areas. You

(FIG. 4.11, cont.)

> can also acquire and ability of <u>tolerating supervisors</u> or in this case, <u>professors and teachers who are sometimes eccentric or difficult to work with.</u> So you have to, <u>you have to acquire the habit of getting along and getting work done sometimes in spite of the people you work with.</u> <u>There's always the joke about</u> doing what the teacher—about <u>knowing and doing what the teacher wants.</u>"
> Decides on approach.
> "I think I'm in good enough shape to start right now. I think again I don't need to take a position, I just need to explain what I mean by the assertions that I'm making."
> Begins writing.

FIG. 4.11. A detailed outline of Don's early writing session with word processor. Letters in parentheses indicate the kinds of notes he made at various points: C = content notes, S = structure notes, E = emphasis notes, P = procedural notes. Quotations are excerpts from the think-aloud protocol. Underlining indicates a note was written.

The differences between Don's word processing and pen-and-paper notemaking could be summarized in this way: With word processing he produced more word of notes, but they were all content notes. With pen and paper, he made structure, emphasis, and procedural notes as well. The pen-and-paper notes showed relationships among ideas graphically, and whereas the pen-and-paper notes were brief and gist-like, the word processor notes appeared much like written text. Don was not alone in this behavior; a number of the other writers began their word processing writing session by making notes—or by saying they were going to— but quickly fell into producing text instead. Another writer initially set up a separate file for his notes, but after writing several complete sentences of text in the notes file, he said "Oh, why don't I just write it?" He then proceeded to write his essay in the notes file and in the end forgot to rename it. The entire essay was written in a file called "notes."

Discussion of Notemaking

The profiles of Morgan and Don are useful in explaining the results of the process portion of this study (i.e., that there was less planning with word processing and that planning tended to be more local than pen-and-paper planning). Certainly in both cases these writers began writing sooner in the computer conditions, possibly cutting short their planning times. In a sense, the computer systems used here seemed to invite writers to begin writing connected and intact prose sooner than they might have with pen-and-paper. Further, the kinds of notes that Morgan and Don made with the computer were exclusively content notes, rather than more conceptually based structure or emphasis notes. This parallels the findings in the process analysis, where writers focused on local textual concerns when writing with computers.

In a very real sense, in these profiles of Morgan and Don we see two writers doing, for the most part, what the available technology allows them to do. For example, text production is easy and quick with word processing, and, consequently, both writers (and the other 18 writers studied in the writing process analysis above) began writing sooner when using a computer. Conversely, diagrammatic structure and emphasis notes tend to be easier to create using a pen and, again, writers took advantage of this ease to make more of those kinds of notes when using pen and paper.

CONCLUSION

In one sense, the results reported here—that the planning processes of writers are different with computers than with pen and paper—would not be surprising to writers who have used both media. Many of them, like the ones whose interviews I described in chapter 3 (this volume), already have a sense that writing with pen and paper and writing with computers are very different activities. However, neither these anecdotal reports nor the empirical results presented here are predicted by current theories of writing (see chapter 2, this volume).

Although, the question of the relationship between the material and the mental is one that, within philosophy, continues to be wrestled with by pragmatists such as Putnam (1981) and Rorty (1982), phenomenologists like Merleau-Ponty (1965), and poststructuralists like Foucault (1977), writing theory and research has not for the most part addressed this question directly. The result has been an implicit acceptance of the notion of technological transparency—an assumption that the technologies of writing have no impact on the mental processes or cultural functions of writing and that writing is writing is writing, regardless of the writing medium. The results of the planning study reported here not only call into profound question the transparent technology assumption, but also illustrate the almost complete lack of theoretical grounding that could predict or explain such results.

The analysis of planning notes, particularly the profiles of Morgan and Don, allows at least a tentative, plausible connection between technology and thinking. The computer system used here facilitated certain kinds of writing activities—for example, the production of intact prose. This increased facility is probably due to the greater responsiveness (see chapter 3, this volume) of the high-speed system used by these writers. Similarly, the greater tangibility (and possibly legibility) of pen and paper made the creation of diagrammatic, conceptual notes easier when writers used that medium. Because the technologies allowed or even invited certain kinds of notemaking activities, they also, then, allowed or invited the thinking that is required by those activities. By supporting one kind of physical writing activity rather than another, technologies can affect writers' thinking processes in very real ways. I return in my conclusion (Chapter 9) to an examination of how a theory of technology could explain how material technologies impact on mental activity.

ACKNOWLEDGMENTS

Parts of this chapter were published previously as "How the writing medium shapes the writing process: Effects of word processing on planning" *Research in the Teaching of English 23* (2), pp. 181-206, copyright 1989 by National Council of Teachers of English and used by permission; and "Composing in technological contexts: A study of notemaking," *Written Communication 7* (4), pp. 512-547, copyright 1990 by Sage Publications and used by permission.

5

TEXT SENSE AND WRITERS' MATERIALLY BASED REPRESENTATIONS OF TEXT

In chapter 4 (this volume), we saw how computer technologies can affect thinking processes. In the study presented there, writers using word processing planned less, and planned at a more local level, than when they used pen and paper for writing. This chapter examines writers' text sense problems and argues that writers' representations of meaning for their own texts are materially based. It also examines what writers mean when they speak of "having a sense of the text" and what circumstances lead to the construction of text sense (and what circumstances seem to impede it). Finally, this chapter also presents an empirical study of writers' sense of the text and a detailed description of writers' physical interactions with text which may contribute to text sense.

In fields from cognitive science to literary theory, it has become commonplace to say that reading is a constructive process. Readers build or construct representations of a text's semantic content (Rumelhart & Ortony, 1977; Vipond, Hunt, Jewett, & Reither, 1990), rhetorical context (Brent, 1992; Haas, 1994; Haas & Flower, 1988; van Dijk, 1987), and structure (Horowitz, 1987; Kintsch & van Dijk, 1978). Readers construct these representations—or what is more elusively and prosaically called "meaning"—from textual and contextual cues, as well as from their own experiences as readers and as human beings (Beach, 1990). These representations allow readers to predict, infer, instantiate, and, in general, construct representations of meaning. (For an overview of constructivist research in reading, see Spivey, 1987; for discussions of the parallels between theories of reading in diverse disciplines, see Brent, 1992; Hunt, 1990.)

Writers also build representations of meaning. A representation of a secondary source text is crucial in reading-to-write and writing-to-learn tasks.

Writing about a text may influence one's understanding of that text, and consequently what is learned from the text (Newell & Winograd, 1989). However, there is another text that writers read and evaluate and use, and that is their own text—the text that they are in the process of producing. For instance, children apparently learn much about reading by creating their own written texts and then rereading them (Dyson, 1988; Langer, 1986). The text produced so far is a powerful guiding force in the composing process theory put forth by Flower and Hayes (1981a), with the extant text itself becoming an important part of the writing environment. The existing text may serve a heuristic function in the invention of new ideas: Writers' rereading of their texts may serve as both a rehearsal of new ideas and a taking stock of existing ones. In addition, writers must critically reread their texts (Hayes, Flower, Schriver, Stratmen, & Carey, 1986; Bereiter & Scardamalia, 1987) in order to revise and improve them.

Clearly, writers interact constantly, closely, and in complex ways with their own written texts. Through these interactions, they develop some understanding—some representation—of the text they have created or are creating. This chapter argues that one of the things that writers come to during the course of text production is an understanding of the meaning and structure of their own written arguments; I call this understanding or representation of one's own text *a sense of the text*. Writers' representations of the meaning and structure of their written texts exist as separate and distinct from the actual material artifact that writers produce, but this artifact is intrinsically tied to the material conditions of text production. Specifically, in an empirical study presented later in this chapter, different material conditions lead to differences in constructed meaning for writers' own texts. Later in this chapter, I present detailed descriptions of two writers' physical interactions with their texts and discuss how these physical interactions are, on the one hand, shaped by material technology and how, on the other, they contribute to a sense of the text.

TEXT SENSE PROBLEMS OF COMPUTER WRITERS

As is often the case, new situations—in this case new technological contexts and situations for writing—bring to the fore aspects of writing that may have been there all along, but that have not been previously noticed. The notion of a sense of the text—something with which writers have presumably been operating all along—becomes obvious in such a new situation or context: the changed technological context of composing with word processing.

The phrase "a sense of the text" comes from writers themselves. In the interview studies described earlier (see chapter 3, this volume), writers told of their use of computers for writing, and most writers were positive and enthusiastic about the technologizing of their own writing processes. However, most of the writers mentioned problems as well, including the reading problems described in chapter 3.[1] One of the reading problems that writers frequently mentioned was getting a sense of the text on-line; virtually every writer who mentioned text sense problems reported generating a hard copy printout of their texts in order to compensate for this problem. They often said things like, "I need to generate a hard copy to skim over—just to see where I'm going," "It's hard to get the center of gravity of the piece," or "I just don't have a sense of the text when I write on-line" (Haas, 1989c; Haas & Hayes, 1986).

What is a sense of the text? *Text sense* is a mental representation of the structure and meaning of a writer's own text. It is primarily propositional in content, but includes spatial and temporal aspects as well. Although text sense—as an internal construction—is distinct from the written textual artifact, it is tied intimately to that artifact. Text sense is constructed in tandem with the written text and seems to include both a spatial memory of the written text and an episodic memory of its construction.

When writers talk about text sense they allude to the idea that the written textual artifact should "match" writers' own intention—what Witte (1985) calls matching of the projected text, or pretext, to the written text. This kind of matching is necessary in order for writers to determine if the text needs reorganizations or other revisions. In addition, a sense of the text seems to be based on the ability to get a kind of distance, to step back and read the way an intended audience might. To detect a mismatch between intended text and actual text, a writer must have a representation not only of his or her intended or projected text, but also a representation of the actual text. This latter representation would seem to rely more on spatial cues and writers' physical interactions with their texts. If reading to get a sense of the text is important for representing a text to oneself, it is much more closely tied to the compositional or meaning-making aspect of writing than are proofreading and checking format (see chapter 3, this volume) and therefore may be a more important problem for computer writers than are other computer reading problems. In general, the text sense problem seems to be a complex constructive reading problem—a problem of reading to construct, or reconstruct, the macrostructure of meaning in one's own text.

Many writers talked about "distance" in conjunction with the text sense problem, and this suggests a spatial component. One way in which writers talked about distance was in terms of objectivity. Some writers reported that they needed to read their texts from hard copy to "get some objectivity." This may be related to the display problems that contribute to proofreading and other reading problems (i.e., poor resolution may make reading for fine features like letters difficult). In addition, many of the writers interviewed mentioned their need to get away from their workspace, to get some distance from the text both literally and figuratively, in order to establish objectivity with their writing. Paradoxically, other writers complained that they felt too much distance from their computer texts: "I just don't feel that I know my text as well when it's on the screen." They mentioned immediacy and intimacy as qualities that were missing when they read their own texts on a computer screen.

Generally, writers were vague—and even somewhat puzzled—about the text sense problem. It clearly was not a problem they had expected or for which they had an explanation. The presence of this problem is intriguing, however, because it suggests that a writer's reading of his or her own text, the representation of that text, and the assessment of its value are complex activities, involving not only conscious attention to intention and audience but also a representation of the text as a spatial and physical object.

Interestingly, the metaphors used by writers underscored these spatial and temporal aspects of text sense. The writers interviewed struggled to name and describe the complex notion of text sense. This complexity is reflected in the fact that the writers often used metaphors, and these metaphors were often of material objects—spatial objects, living and growing objects, objects moving through time and space. Figure 5.1 gives some examples of these metaphorical references.

Spatial Objects

"I have to print it to *get a perspective* on it."

"Seeing it on the screen isn't really *seeing it.*"

"It's hard getting your *center of gravity* in the writing."

"It doesn't really seem *like a paper* 'til it's on paper."

"[Printing it] makes it more *real,* you know—*substantial, concrete.*"

Living Objects

"My text is *hard to pin down* on-line."

"[With the computer, the text] *gels* too soon—I need it to *stay fluid* for longer."

"I don't have the *intimacy* I need with my text on the computer."

"I get a printout just to see that *it's developing right.*"

Moving Objects

"When I write on the computer, I have a hard time *knowing where I am.*"

"I can't get any *distance* from it when it's here" [points to the screen].

"I need to see if it's still *on track.*"

FIG. 5.1. Text as object: Metaphors writers use to describe the text sense problem. (Emphasis added.)

The spatial metaphors describe the text as something one sees or views, or as something that one holds in one's hands. The text as living object is capable of development, or of intimacy, or is described with "protoplasmic" metaphors (e.g., gel, fluid, hard to pin down). The moving object metaphors describe the text as distant or on track. One writer described herself as moving in the text—"I have a hard time knowing where I am."

How do writers use text sense? What does it do for them? To revise, writers must have some notion of the text's weaknesses, faults, or blanks. In addition, writers may need a representation of their own text in order to take a reader's point of view, gauge intended effects, and determine if the text in fact meets the writer's goals. For this to occur, writers must not only have some notion of what they wish to do (their goals) but also what they have in fact done (a representation of their text). Finally, representing their texts to themselves may be important for writers to learn or discover new ideas while writing. It may be that in the construction of internal representations of their texts—even more so than in the transcribing of a written artifact—writers learn through composing.

In the interviews with computer writers, the text sense problem did not seem to be constant across writing tasks. Rather, writers mentioned it most frequently in conjunction with the kind of writing situations that Bereiter and Scardamalia (1987) labeled compositional tasks (i.e., tasks in which the structure of information in the writer's memory does not easily map onto the finished text and tasks that require the forging of new connections and links in the writer's knowledge). For instance, one writer said, "It was easy to do my [doctoral] exams on the computer because I really knew that stuff, and I had a good idea from [advisor] what the questions would be." However, in texts where writers form and develop new ideas, getting a sense of the text—that is, adequately representing the text to themselves—may be more difficult. One writer said that writing letters of recommendation for students, a task he does frequently, was easy to do on-line without hard copy. However, he found that writing a letter of application for a summer scholars' program—a task of the same length, but one that was much less well rehearsed and arguably more important to him—was impossible to do without frequent hard copy reading and editing.

In addition, the text sense problem occurs most frequently in long writing tasks, and rarely occurs with a document only one or two screens long. This phenomenon makes sense from a cognitive point of view: As the text gets longer and more ideas are introduced and developed, it becomes more difficult to hold an adequate representation in memory of that text, which is out of sight. Clearly, size (see chapter 3, this volume) is an important variable in writers' text sense problems.

Other factors of on-line writing may contribute to text sense problems. Because for many writers text production is faster on-line and because there is no need to recopy after changes, writers may not spend so much time producing and reproducing their texts as before. Consequently, they may not devote so much time to fixing the text in spatial and episodic memory. The writing and recopying done by hand, however tedious, may serve a rehearsal function, helping writers to know their own texts better. In this way, increased responsiveness of computer systems (as described in chapter 3, this volume) may actually hinder the construction of a sense of the text. In addition, as reported in chapter 3, readers' spatial memory is constrained by computer displays, and writers may have similar kinds of problems recalling the spatial structure of text. The fact that scrolling text does not have a constant physical configuration may contribute to computer writers' problems representing their texts to themselves. This suggests that physical and spatial aspects of text (the text's tangibility, as described in chapter 3, this volume) may provide cues to writers, helping them represent structure, meaning, and intent.

Many current word processing systems have outline programs or other overview features that writers can use to keep track of the structure of their computer written texts. (See Eklundh, 1991, for an analysis of these kinds of programs.) Although such overview programs are useful for writing (especially writing that is highly structured) and for the generating tables of contents and other organization aids, it is not clear whether they would alleviate writers' text sense problems. First, such overview programs rely on actual text (usually headings and subheadings) typed in by writers themselves. Such programs do not give a sense of the implicit argument or function of the sections of text, unless writers type this in also. Second, and more important, the complex sense of text that writers use metaphors to describe (see above) would seem to extend beyond a mere representation of text parts.

A STUDY OF WRITERS' SENSE OF TEXT

So far, in describing computer writers' text sense problems, I have relied mostly on what writers have told me in interviews. The following study does not draw on writers' reported experiences—as valuable as those can be. Rather, I tried to determine whether writers really do have some eroded sense of text when they compose on line. Although a writer's sense of text, or internal representation of text, is undoubtedly a complex cognitive structure (Flower & Hayes, 1984), a simple way to examine this phenomenon would be to have writers recall the topical structure (i.e., the main points) of their essays. If writers do indeed have an eroded sense of text when composing on-line, as they often report, then this text sense problem might show up as a less accurate recall of the main points of the essays composed on-line.

Task

This study was an extension of the planning study described in chapter 4 (this volume). The study employed a within-subjects design. Ten experienced writers completed two-part tasks in both word processing and pen-and-paper conditions. The both condition (see chapter 4, this volume) was not examined in this study.

Part One

Writers first composed persuasive essays on topics about schooling and education, as described in chapter 4. For more information on the composition part of this study, see chapter 4.

Part Two

Two weeks after the composing sessions, writers completed a recall task. In the same room where they had written the original texts, they were presented with the actual stimulus materials for the essays they had written previously (topics and prompts). They were then asked to recall the major points or ideas of their essays in order and in as much detail as possible. Writers completed the recall task in the same order as they had completed the composition task. In other words, if they had written the pen-and-paper essay first, they were asked to recall that essay first.

Participants and Computer System

The subjects were 10 experienced writers who wrote daily on the job and who were either published professional or academic writers, or were recommended by their supervisors as better-than-average writers. The study was conducted using the Andrew system, an educational computing system being jointly developed by IBM and CMU (Morris et al., 1986). All writers had been using this computing system for a minimum of 6 months. Each writer also success-fully completed a pretest of facility with both the computing system and the word processing program that were used in the study (for more details, see chapter 4, this volume).

Analysis

The scoring of the accuracy of the recalls was done by the writers themselves; that is, after completing the recall, each writer was shown his or her essay and asked to indicate the correctness of what they remembered. In other words, each writer did his or her own scoring by indicating the accuracy of their recalls. This procedure made sense because I was interested in the writers' *own* sense of text, rather than in how an outside reader would objectively score the recalls. For each point in the essay, writers gave a letter score for their recall of that point. The scoring rubric is shown in Figure 5.2. Measures were taken of both time to recall and accuracy of the recall. Due to an error in conducting one subject's recall session, the final number of subjects was reduced to nine.

Recall accuracy scores were represented as proportions of total points in the essays (which varied across writers). Accuracy scores were normalized for slight order effects. Points recalled out of order ("O") occurred in less than half of the recalls; points recalled in too little detail ("D") and points listed in the recall but not in the text ("N") occurred even more infrequently. Therefore, these three categories were omitted from the analysis, and only a proportion of total points that were correctly recalled in order ("C" below) and the proportion of points that were not recalled at all, or forgotten ("X" below), were analyzed. These were the two extremes on the scoring rubric in Figure 5.2.

"C"	"O"	"D"	"N"	"X"
correctly recalled	recalled out of order	recalled in too little detail	listed in recall but not in text	not recalled at all

FIG. 5.2. Scale of responses for scoring recalls.

Results

There were no differences across conditions in recall times, but there were differences in the accuracy of the recalls, as shown in Table 5.1. First, the mean number of main points in the essays—as judged by the writers themselves—was similar across conditions: 6.9 main ideas in the pen-and-paper condition and 6.6 in the computer condition. However, eight of the nine writers correctly recalled more of the points ("C" in Figure 5.2) in their pen-and-paper essays than they did the points in their word processing essays, and the mean difference between each writer's two recall scores was 1.9. Proportionately, writers recalled more of the main points of the texts they had composed with pen and paper than of the texts written with word processing: A proportion of .61 ideas were recalled in the pen-and-paper condition, but only .39 of the ideas were correctly recalled in the computer condition. These differences were significant by simple T test ($p<.05$).

At the other end of the scale, the analysis of points not recalled at all ("X" in Figure 5.2) showed that seven of nine writers forgot more points in the word processing condition than in the pen-and-paper condition, and the mean difference between each writer's two recall scores on this measure was 1.2. Overall, the proportion of points not recalled at all was greater in the word processing condition: .37, versus .20 forgotten in the pen-and-paper condition. However, these differences were short of significant.

Table 5.1
**Results. Mean Number of Points, Numbers of Writers, Differences,
and Proportions of Points Recalled and Not Recalled. N = 9.**

	Pen and paper	Word processing
Total points in essay	6.9	6.6
Points recalled correctly ("C")		
Number of writers recalling more points	8	1
Mean difference between conditions		+1.9
Mean proportion of points recalled*	.61	.39
Points not recalled at all ("X")		
Number of writers forgetting more points	2	7

(TABLE 5.1, cont.)

Mean difference between conditions		+1.2
Mean proportion of points not recalled**	.20	.37

*Differences on this measure significant (*p*<.05).
**Not significant.

Discussion of Recall Study

These results—showing poorer recall when writers were composing on-line—add credence to writers' reported text sense problems and suggest that writers may indeed have a less accurate representation of their own written texts when composing with computers. Although the study was small, the results (for points recalled correctly) were significant. These results, coupled with writers' repeated reports of text sense problems, suggest both that text sense is a psychologically real phenomenon and that the writing medium can influence writers' sense of the meaning and structure of their own texts.

One explanation for the poorer sense of text with word processing may be in how the texts were produced. In the study reported in chapter 4 (this volume) of these same writers' planning processes, when composing pen and paper texts—the texts that they subsequently recalled more accurately—writers planned significantly more than when writing with word processing (Haas, 1989a). A close examination of the composing performance of the nine writers studied here, and a comparison of their planning behavior and text sense scores, are enlightening. All nine of these writers planned more when composing their pen-and-paper essays, and eight of these nine recalled more of the points of those essays. On the other hand, seven of the nine writers forgot more of the main points of their computer essays, the same essays in which all nine planned less. (Appendix A shows a comparison of amount of planning and text sense scores for these nine writers.) In a very real sense, planning may represent a rehearsal of the ideas that the writer is creating, allowing for a greater sense of text. This underscores the way in which seemingly diverse aspects of writing—planning and evaluating—may in fact be intrinsically related.

Writers' representations of their texts' semantic content may also be tied to spatial structures, including page layout, paragraph shape, or size of manuscript. Spatial location does not remain constant on a computer screen (because of scrolling), and the computer text is two dimensional, not having the additional spatial cues of the print text's physical pages. Further, the way that writers interact with computer texts—via keyboard or mouse—is much less direct than the physical manipulation of the text that is possible with printed texts. Writers working with hard copies of their texts, on the other hand, may draw heavily on spatial cues in their text (e.g., bracketing paragraphs, turning down page corners, flipping through manuscript pages). The next section describes an analysis of two writers' physical interactions with texts as they composed with pen and paper and with word processing. These detailed descriptions show some of the ways that writers' interactions with their texts and tools differ when they are using different media.

THE PRESENCE OF THE TEXT:
PHYSICAL INTERACTIONS WITH TEXTS AND TOOLS

These descriptions of writers' physical interactions with material tools and texts were constructed by analyzing videotapes of two writers—one student writer and one experienced writer—who participated in the study described in more detail in chapter 4 (this volume). Using analytic induction, I first viewed the videotapes several times and wrote detailed chronological descriptions of writers' activities. Using these descriptions, a coding scheme of physical interactions with text was developed. The physical interactions found with some regularity across writers included: distancing moves, pointing, moves to change perspective, and tactile manipulations of text. The following section introduces each of the writers and characterizes in a general way how they interacted physically with their texts. It then describes each of the four types of physical interaction and presents some numerical data showing differences in one of the interactions, distancing moves.

Writer Profiles

Belle

Belle was an 18-year-old college freshman when the study was conducted. Although Belle was majoring in biology, she said she enjoyed writing and that she enjoyed it even more when she could use a computer. She received a B+ for her freshman composition course, a course in which the Andrew system was used for writing. She had been using a computer for writing since her sophomore year in high school, and she had been using the Andrew system for writing for about 6 months. She seemed equally facile with both media, reflected in the fact that she composed at virtually the same rate (12.5 words per minute) in both conditions. With pen and paper, Belle wrote an essay that was 500 words long. Her computer essay was 438 words long.

In general, Belle was a physically active writer; that is, she was almost constantly moving during writing—shifting in her chair, rocking back and forth, fiddling with a pencil or moving the mouse, tapping the keyboard or the writing pad. Her physical interactions remained at a fairly constant level throughout the writing sessions. Although they often accompanied planning or rereading (as described later) they also occurred regularly at other times.

Patsy

Patsy was a 43-year-old graduate student completing her dissertation at the time of the study. Like Belle, she enjoyed writing and had been employed as a teacher of writing during her tenure as a graduate student. She had been using a computer to write for about 3 years at the time of the study and had been using the Andrew system for about 18 months. Patsy was a hunt-and-peck typist, often using only one hand for typing, when she used the computer. Even so, she produced text rapidly, typing at the rate of 14 words per minute, when using the computer (the ten experienced writers as a whole averaged 11.6) and 11.2 words per minute when writing with pen and paper. Patsy's computer essay was 510 words long, and her pen-and-paper essay was 681 words long.

Patsy was a much more sedate writer than was Belle. That is, she often sat quite still as she wrote, moving only her arms and head. When she did engage in physical interactions with the text, she tended to do so in spurts. These intensely active periods, which were interspersed with longer, relatively still periods, tended to occur at major junctures of Patsy's writing process: after completing her notes and moving into text production, during the planning and executing of a major text reorganization, and as a final editing of the text began.

Types of Physical Interactions

Although there were some differences in frequency, both writers exhibited all four types of physical interaction. In general, despite differences in age, discipline, and status, the similarities in Patsy's and Belle's interactions with their texts were remarkable.

Distancing Moves

Distancing moves are interactions in which writers either move closer to the text or back away from it. For instance, when writing with a pen, a writer might move in on the text, hunching over it as she writes; or, a computer writer might sit back from the screen to reread the text. Distancing moves are those in which, for the most part, only the physical distance between the writer's face and the text changes. (Other moves, in which the angle or perspective that the writer has on the text changes, are described later.) In addition, only moves in which the distance between the writer's face and the text changed by more than about four inches were included in this analysis. I combined moves toward and away from the text after noting that for these writers, the two moves often seemed to accomplish the same purpose; that is, when they got to a "stuck place" and needed to plan or evaluate, these writers both often moved toward the text, but almost as often, they moved away from it. Similarly, sometimes the writers moved in to reread, and sometimes they moved out. Occasionally, a writer using a computer would make a rather large distancing move toward the text in the process of doing surface-level editing. These moves might have been so that the writer could clearly see where to place the cursor.

Distancing moves occurred with a great deal of frequency in both computer and pen-and-paper conditions. Over three-quarters of the time, these distancing moves occurred when writers were shifting from one writing activity to another; in particular, these moves often accompanied writers' planning of new text or their rereading of existing text. More information on numbers of distancing moves is provided later.

Pointing

Writers used both pen and mouse cursor for pointing, and pointing seemed to be used for two purposes: as a placeholder or memory aid and as a guide in rapid reading. When planning a reorganization, a writer might place the point of the pen at a particular place in the text and hold it while moving to the new place in the text where an insertion is contemplated. The mouse cursor can be used in a similar way. Pointing (using either cursor or pen) was also done when writers were rereading their texts, especially when they were reading or skimming quickly. Pointing while reorganizing was somewhat infrequent (occurring only five times in the four writing sessions), and pointing for rereading occurred a bit more often (eight times in four writing sessions). Although it appeared that pointing occurred more frequently in pen-and-paper conditions, it was not always possible to see the cursor on the videotape; therefore, pointing in computer conditions may have occurred more often. In any case, these moves were rather infrequent.

Moves to Change Perspective

Distancing moves and pointing occurred in both computer and pen-and-paper conditions, whereas moves to change perspective occurred only when writers used pen and paper. A move to change perspective is literally that: a move the writer makes to change the angle from which he or she views the text. These moves occurred approximately five times per pen-and-paper writing session, and the two writers' use of this move was similar. When writing with computers, writers kept their faces straight in front of the screen, seldom viewing the text from an angle. Given that computer screens are two dimensional, this kind of reading at an angle may be difficult when writers use computers. In addition, writers would have to lean around the keyboard to view their texts from an angle. It may be that whatever writers gain from viewing text from an angle is not worth the discomfort and inconvenience of working around the keyboard.

It is unclear what writers would gain by looking at their texts from an angle, and these moves did not seem to occur regularly with changes in writing activities (i.e., moving from planning to text production, or from text production to rereading). Therefore, the changed perspective may be an indirect result of the move, not the reason for it. In other words, writers may move around and reposition their bodies in order to find a more comfortable writing position. Sometimes these types of moves would result in a changed visual perspective on the text. In the three-dimensional world of pen-and-paper writing, these kinds of moves are allowed; but when composing with computers, writers are somewhat limited in the bodily positions they can take and still view the screen adequately. Indeed, the videotapes showed writers using computers to be much more stationary, whereas writers using pen and paper often appeared to be moving around a great deal. This limitation in allowable bodily positions may explain anecdotal reports that people become uncomfortable and stiff when working at computers.

Tactile Manipulations of Text

Tactile manipulations of text also only occurred when writers were using pen and paper and again this has to do with the two-dimensional nature of computer writing. Tactile manipulations of text included holding the text in the writer's hands, spreading pages out, stacking pages together, and flipping through the stacked manuscript. The only comparable activity for computer writers would include touching the screen—an activity in which neither of these writers engaged. Sometimes these tactile manipulations had an obvious purpose, as when the writer picked up the text in order to sit back and read it, or when he or she shuffled through several pages to find a section he or she wants to revise. Other times, however, writers' tactile manipulation of text had no clear purpose: Writers might spread pages out, or stack them up, in a rather distracted manner. In these cases, the physical manipulation of text may have provided a way for the writers to take time out—a few seconds in which to collect their thoughts but still be engaged (in a physical way, at least) with the text.

Frequency of Distancing Moves

Distancing moves occurred rather frequently in these writing sessions, and they occurred with both computer and pen-and-paper writing. However, there were more distancing moves when Belle and Patsy used pen and paper than when they used computers. Belle made 19 distancing moves when writing with the computer, and 30 when writing with pen and paper. On average, Belle made .51 distancing moves per minute when using the computer and .75 per minute when using pen and paper (50% more when she used pen and paper). The differences were similar for Patsy: She made 18 distancing moves with the computer and 40 with pen and paper. These differences are similar in proportion to Belle's: .41 moves per minute with computer and .63 moves per minute with pen and paper (again, about 50% more with the latter). Note that Belle's rates were slightly higher in each category, reflecting the fact that she was a more physically active writer. As noted earlier, writers often used distancing moves when they were shifting to planning or when they began to reread. Thirty of Belle's 40 distancing moves occurred either as she began to plan or as she began to reread; 43 of Patsy's 58 moves similarly occurred as planning or rereading began.

Discussion of Physical Interactions

This analysis revealed four primary ways that writers interacted with the physical text: distancing moves, pointing, moves to change perspective, and tactile manipulations of texts and tools. These moves occurred in the composing behavior of both writers profiled here, and they often seemed to occur in periods of intense planning, or when writers were moving from one writing activity to another. For Belle and Patsy, the three-dimensional world of pen-and-paper writing supported more interactions between writer and text.

　　Although these results might be interesting to computer interface designers (i.e., new computer features could be designed to support the kinds of interactions that writers can do with pen and paper, but cannot do with computers), my purposes here are different. This analysis of physical interactions may suggest why computer writers' sense of their own text is poorer. Because computer writers are interacting with their text in two dimensions only, they cannot manipulate the text spatially in the same way that writers can when they use pen and paper. These physical interactions with text—which may be greater in both number and variety with pen and paper—may lead to a more well-developed sense of the meaning and structure of writers' own texts. The fact that the physical interactions also often occurred during planning sessions may further support the notion that text sense and planning are related phenomena.

CONCLUSIONS

This chapter described writers' reported text sense problems and examined what text sense is, what it does for writers, and what factors of computer writing seem to impede its construction. The empirical study presented in this chapter supports the psychological reality of writers reports of text sense problems when they use computers for writing, and suggests as well that text sense may be tied to planning processes.

Critical to this book's larger argument about the relationship of material tools and writing is the detailed description of writers' physical interactions with texts and tools. In this analysis, the interactions of the two writers examined in detail were surprisingly similar, despite differences in age, status, experience, and composing style. Further, and most important, these two writers' physical interactions with their texts were limited in a similar way when they moved from the three-dimensional world of pen and paper to the two-dimensional world of computer writing. It may be that these physical interactions provide a link—via bodily interactions—between the material tools and artifacts of text production and the mental processes and representations of writers. That is, through their physical interactions with the material tools and texts of literacy, writers' thinking is shaped by culturally-made technologies.

FOOTNOTES

[1]Many of the writers were also concerned that they focused on surface-level concerns at the expense of more global problems when they used computers for writing, a concern at least partially borne out by the results of the planning study presented in chapter 4 (this volume).

III

THE SOCIAL AND CULTURAL CONSTRUCTION

OF LITERACY TOOLS

6

Social Dynamics, or Scientific Truth, or Sheer Human Cussedness: Design Decisions in the Evolution of a User Interface

In Part Two of this volume, I argued that technology can effect writing at the level of individual cognition. Part Three turns to an examination of how writing technologies are culturally made. Chapter 7 details how computer technology is constructed within and through the discourse of scholars in English Studies, whereas this chapter presents a longitudinal study of technology development. In particular, this chapter examines technology-in-development by tracking the evolution of one particular educational computing system in the late 1980s. This case-study of technology development within an academic setting is used to argue that today's literacy technologies are neither inevitable nor self-determining. Further, I illustrate how particular features of these technological systems may be the result of a complex combination of very human factors—including the dynamics, methods, and "cussedness," to which the chapter title refers.   When we look into the "black box" (Latour, 1985) of computer technology by examining how that technology came to be, the powerful cultural myths of technological transparency and self-determination are brought into question (chapter 8, examines the history of technology in a slightly different way).

THE CULTURAL CONSTRUCTION OF PSYCHOLOGICAL TOOLS

The chapters in Part Two showed how writing technologies affect the thinking processes of individual adult writers in subtle, but measurable and somewhat regular ways. Specifically, material tools and artifacts made a difference in the cognitive processes involved in text production (i.e., in two key aspects of composing—planning and reading—writers using computers had measurably different composing processes). In the study presented in chapter 4, writers using computers planned their texts significantly less than they did when using pen and paper, and their planning when using computers was mostly at the local, rather than the conceptual level. Similarly, as shown in chapter 3, technological variables made a difference in how successfully and quickly people were able to do specific writing-related reading tasks: recalling and retrieving information and reading-to-revise. Finally, as chapter 5 illustrated, material tools and artifacts made a difference in the knowledge structures that writers created in the course of text production.

As we saw in chapter 2, for Vygotsky (1981b, 1986), writing is a psychological tool that provides the mediational means for certain kinds of thought. The results of the studies presented in Part Two can be viewed from within a Vygotskian framework as suggesting that writing-with-pen and writing-with-computer function as slightly different psychological tools. These differences may be quite subtle, and they should not be interpreted as supporting the notion that the use of computer technology will constitute a rupture in human thinking, or that it will universally and immediately transform writing. In their broad outlines, writing-with-computer and writing-with-pen still have very much in common. At the same time, different writing tools do seem to have real, if subtle, effects on the mental processes of text production.

Vygotsky was, of course, interested in cultural systems as much as in individual behavior. In *The Instrumental Method in Psychology* (1981b), he wrote at length about psychological tools and signs. Here he makes the point that psychological tools are neither organic nor individual, but rather social. That is, individual human beings do not invent or create psychological tools or sign systems; they appropriate them from the surrounding cultural milieu. Clearly, individuals do not invent or make literacy tools and sign systems for themselves from scratch (the Brontë children providing a noted exception). Rather, writers adopt, and sometimes modify, the psychological tools of their culture. As argued in chapter 1 (this volume), writing and its technologies are always material tools and, as such, are culturally created tools. This is true for writing generally, and it is true for computer writing systems as well.

Seeing computer writing tools, which are material objects, as culturally created means looking behind, underneath, or inside the box on the desk to the genealogy of particular writing systems at particular historical junctures. Computer writing tools have a history in at least two senses. First, writing technologies, like all modern material tools, are built on layer upon layer of other technologies. That is, computer literacy technologies are built upon the Roman alphabet and writing in its most general sense, as well as many of the conventional notions of directionality and form that come from print, and even manuscript, technologies (e.g., the idea of scrolling as text movement; the notion that forward movement in a text is down and to the right; the conventions of display size and italic, bold, and underlining). Chapter 8 discusses some of the features that computer writing systems borrow from earlier systems in greater detail.

Further, computer writing tools have a history in that they are the product of actual human design decisions: These machines are actually made by somebody. From the user's point of view, of course, this construction of technological artifacts may be far from obvious. Indeed, if a system is well designed, its features should appear transparent to the user. In this book *Programming as if People Mattered* (1991), Nathaniel Borenstein argues that a well-designed computer system should be "so well suited to its intended use that the end user will never once stop to think about" those who designed it. Computer designers, according to Borenstein (who is himself a systems designer with a Ph.D. in Computer Science), must try to "make their own work invisible and their own significance largely lost in anonymity" (p. 178).

However, the invisibility of the computer's features and the anonymity of the designers, while it may be important for easy learning and use of the system, can be dangerously seductive for those interested in critically examining technology. The naturalness of a well-designed computer interface may suggest an inevitability that masks the human decisions that have created the technological artifact. Careful studies of technology development can get behind the mask of inevitability.

In particular, as reports of system design have suggested (Kidder, 1981; Lundstrom, 1987), almost every feature of a computer system (even, or maybe especially, those that eventually seem most transparent to users) has been contested, and may continue to be for contested long periods of time. For instance, a user might look at a scroll bar and think, "Well, yes, how else could a scroll bar work?" The answer is that there are any number of ways a scroll bar could work, can work, and probably has worked. The fact that users see one version and not another is not simply because the version in use is "better." As Borenstein (1991) argues, the notion of better or best interface features is always fraught with questions of "better for whom?" and "better under what circumstances?" Rather, the decision to deploy a particular version of any computer feature is usually the end result of a series of highly contested decisions—decisions based on politics (the status of the designer or designers working on the scroll bar), history (is there already an existing, widely used version?), logistical concerns (how many "man" hours would it take to redesign it?), as well as implicit theories about how such devices should work (what does a hypothetical "reasonable person" need to do with a scroll bar?).

Computer writing systems, like all writing tools, work one way and not another because of institutional history and politics, underlying theories of technology and writing, and human decision making within a social context. Computer tools are not self-determining, nor is their design inevitable. These kinds of beliefs about technology are part of what stand in the way of a truly interdisciplinary, critical inquiry about technology, as discussed in chapter 3 (this volume). To paraphrase Vygotsky, to understand an artifact, we must understand the history of that artifact. The study described herein was designed to illuminate the institutional history of a small part of one technologically-ambitious educational computing system under development in the late 1980s.

The features whose five-year history is traced in the following sections are features of the user interface—that part of the computer that is visible and responsive to users and through which they interact with the central processing unit (CPU) of the computer. The user interface includes keyboard and screen, as well as particular software features (e.g., icons, menus, keystrokes) by which users create documents, manage files, and send messages. According to Borenstein (1991), it was only in the second stage of the computer revolution (beginning in the 1970s) that the design of a user interface became an issue within computer science. Earlier computers had been created for an elite of specialized, highly technical users. Borenstein describes these early machines as "tyrants" (p. 5), and the huge technical difficulties of getting them to run at all overshadowed any concern with how people used them, or learned to use them. However, "when computers met the common man [sic]" (Borenstein,

1991, p. 5), beginning in the late 1970s, the flexibility or friendliness of computer systems gained importance, both within technical fields and in the marketplace.

Clearly, it is the user interface—not the "guts" or CPU of a system—that most lay people recognize as "the computer." The icons and mouse of the Macintosh, or the keys and screen of the IBM-PC *are* these systems for most of their users. Further, user interface features are critical for writers. Most writers do not know or care how their particular personal computer stores information or how files are retrieved (as long as these functions proceed smoothly). Users do care about the devices they use to enter text, the way the text is displayed, how they format and edit text, and how they move through a document. These concerns are all matters of user interface design and in the following sections I trace the history of the design of two interface features that are critical for writers: a scroll bar and a set of menus.

THE ANDREW PROJECT

The Andrew Project (Morris, Satyanarayanan, Conner, Howard, Rosenthal, & Smith, 1986) was an ambitious attempt to develop and deploy a prototype educational computing system for the Carnegie Mellon University campus in the mid- to late-1980s. The Andrew Project was housed in the Information Technology Center (ITC) at Carnegie Mellon and was jointly funded by IBM and CMU. The project had three main parts: (a) the Andrew File System (Howard, 1988), a large, distributed network file system; (b) the Andrew Message System (Borenstein & Thyberg, 1991), a multimedia electronic mail and bulletin board system; and (c) the Andrew Toolkit (Palay, Hansen, Kazar, Sherman, Wadlow, Neuendorffer, Stern, Bader, & Peters, 1988), a programming library that supported interface software development in a number of applications. The user interface features with which this chapter is concerned are part of the Toolkit, although they appear in the interface of the Message System as well. The Andrew system was used by writers and readers in the studies described in chapters 3, 4, and 5 (this volume), and the user interface features relevant to those empirical studies are described in some detail in chapters 3 and 4; illustrations of the system are provided in chapter 4.

A team of about 35 people—primarily computer scientists and engineers, but including writers, human factors researchers, graphic designers, and social scientists—worked at the ITC on the project from its inception in 1983 through

1991. The initial goal of the project was to build a workable computing and communication system, deployed to and used by the campus at large, within five years. For the bulk of the project, from 1983 to 1988, James Morris was the director of the ITC and the leader of the project; the upper management also included an associate director assigned to the site from IBM. The organization under Morris was loosely structured into small work groups under formal or informal managers. These groups, some of which were more cohesive and focused than others, were responsible for the development of various aspects of the system. The groups included, at various times, one or more file system groups, a mail group, a hardware maintenance group, networking groups, and a user interface group. Membership in groups was somewhat fluid, with changes made on the basis of project needs or personal preference. In addition to a regular staff of computer scientists and computer engineers, Morris also brought in part- and full-time consultants from graphic design, English, psychology, and other social sciences.

The users and potential users of the system were diverse and varied. The audience for Andrew included developers both within the ITC and from the campus at large, administrators within the university and liaisons from IBM, students of all ages and levels of experience, and faculty and staff from the humanities and the arts, as well as science and engineering. Some of these user groups—particularly the developers of the system and contacts at IBM—were vocal in their complaints and preferences about the system and had access to people who could act on their suggestions and criticisms. Consequently, these groups had a direct and important impact on the development efforts. Other groups, including nontechnical students, often had only indirect or theoretical impact on design decisions. That is, although novice user groups, like students, were often invoked in discussions of the user interface, only occasionally were they brought in to actually use the system, at least in the early phases of the project. Later, a deployment of the system to the university community at large brought students of various types and levels of expertise into contact with the system, and bulletin board systems were set up to collect bug reports and other feedback from users all over campus. However, at this point, most of the basic user interface decisions (including the ones described in this chapter) had been made.

METHODS AND PROCEDURES

This report is based, in substantial part, on my own experiences as a consultant to the ITC during the development of Andrew, as a member of the User Interface Group from 1984 to 1988, and again in 1990, and as an active participant in many of the decisions described in subsequent sections. In addition, eleven other participants were interviewed in detail, some over the course of several hours, about the evolution of the user interface and about their roles in interface design decisions, particularly decisions about the scroll bar and menus. The participants in the interviews included four developers (all computer scientists) who were members of the User Interface Group, four developers (all computer scientists) who were outside this group but who were directly involved in decisions about or implementations of the features described here, the director of the ITC, and two User Interface Group consultants—a writer and a graphic designer—who contributed to the design and redesign of the scroll bar and menus. All of the interview subjects were given copies of early drafts of this chapter for comments and suggestions. In several cases, this resulted in another lengthy conversation about the design process, which, in turn, provided further data.

I also examined bulletin board discussions devoted to user interface issues in general, and the scroll bar and menus in particular; selected e-mail between members of the User Interface Group, including lengthy correspondence about the scroll bar and menus; and documentation and other correspondence having to do with these features. (Permission was granted by all electronic correspondents to examine these materials.) I also collected periodic screen snapshots showing the evolution of the scroll bar and menus (and several other interface features not discussed here) through design changes over the course of about three years.

It is important to realize that this chapter presents a reminiscence as much as a research report; I was actively involved in the decisions described here, and I was very much an interested party in the resolution of contested features of the interface. Therefore, I do not claim to have had scientific "objectivity" in my reporting of the evolution of the Andrew interface—if such objectivity were even possible. My major claim in this chapter is that computers, computer systems, and computer features have a history. The history of the scroll bar and the menus presented here, while I believe it is accurate, does not in fact have to be the "correct" history in order to support my larger point.

Further, the narrative of the evolution of interface features constructed here is just that: a construction. Interview participants were seldom in complete agreement about just what had happened with a particular feature, even if the decision was only a few weeks or days old. Sometimes I received almost completely contradictory information from two seemingly reliable sources. When I shared drafts of this report with developers and other participants, no one participant was in complete agreement with the narrative I had constructed. Participants' disagreements, however, were mostly about such things as the order in which events occurred, who exactly was involved in particular decisions, or who did the work to make a particular feature functional. Participants generally did not counter my larger claims that technologies are constructed, and that politics, theories of technology, and opportunism shaped the development of the Andrew user interface. Again, the fact that participants did not agree on what should stand as the official or essential history of these interface features does not negate the larger point that they *have* a history. Indeed, the kinds of political concerns that motivate the construction of a computer system may well influence the construction of its history as well.

THE EVOLUTION OF TWO INTERFACE FEATURES: SCROLL BAR AND MENUS

Between early 1985 and early 1986, the Andrew system went through substantive changes. These changes were doubly motivated by an imminent release of the system to the Carnegie Mellon campu, and by an impending announcement from IBM about the RT—the advanced workstation on which Andrew was to run. Improvements were made across the board—in performance, in networking, in support and documentation. Many important changes were also made to the user interface; the changes made specifically to the scroll bar and the menus are detailed here. Of the several changes made to the user interface, these two are in many ways representative. First, they were changes that were very obvious to users both inside and outside the development group. Second, they were changes on which a number of people advised. Finally, the decision making behind these changes revealed a range of ways in which decisions were made and the range of factors that impinged on those decisions.

The User Interface Group's Wish List

The User Interface Group (UIG) was probably the largest work group at the ITC in 1985-1986. It was also the most fluid, with members coming and going from the group on a regular basis. For the first several years of the project, the group had discussion leaders (including, at different times, the director and associate director), but no formal manager. The group was also the most interdisciplinary, with members responsible for research and testing, writing and documentation, and graphic design, as well as, of course, systems designers. In the early years of the project, this group had less clear consensus and direction than did other groups. One system designer who worked on the project thought this had to do with the inherently problematic nature of interface design, specifically, that it is much less clear cut and well defined than some other aspects of systems design.

As the campus deployment and announcement of the RT approached, the UIG (like other groups at the ITC) stepped up efforts to make significant changes to the system and began meeting more regularly than they had in the year or so previously. In addition, it was about at this point that Morris assigned a formal manager to the group. At least three different managers headed the UIG over the course of 1985-1987.

A small but vocal minority of the members of the User Interface Group were not computer scientists by training. They had been recruited from around the campus to produce documentation and training materials, to advise on visual aspects of interface decisions, and to conduct user studies. Their number ranged from three to six over the years 1985 to 1987. These "user advocates," as they characterized themselves, saw their role as advocating the needs of novice, nontechnical users. They included professors and graduate students from humanities departments on campus, and many of them were in regular contact with students through teaching and advising in their own departments. One of the user consultants used an early version of the system in a writing class she was teaching.

The status of the user advocates was rather low relative to the rest of the UIG, most of whom were systems designers trained in computer science or electrical engineering. Several factors contributed to the user advocates lower status: First, most members of the group were part-time workers who were contracted as consultants, rather than regular employees. Only one member of the group had a Ph.D., whereas most of the systems designers in the ITC had a doctorate. Further, the user advocates were from disciplines within the humanities, rather than from technical fields. Finally, all but one of the user advocates was female, whereas the systems designers within the ITC were almost all male; at no time during the period 1985-1987 were there more than three female programmers or designers (out of a total of about 25).

Around mid-1985, several of the user advocates became involved in user testing, either informally through observations (like the professor who taught using the Andrew system) or formally through empirical studies of user interface features. Through this testing, the user advocates began to recognize numerous problems with the system, and they began making frequent recommendations—some small or trivial, others more profound and sweeping—about needed improvements to the system. One computer scientist in the UIG recalled that it seemed that huge lists of problems were brought forth at every meeting: "There was no satisfying them—they kept finding more and more problems."

In response to what seemed to some as the endless list of complaints brought forth by the user advocates, and to the growing impatience and reluctance of the developers in the group to take these complaints seriously, the director suggested—somewhat facetiously at first—that the user advocates be allowed "three wishes" for the immediate improvement of the Andrew interface. This suggestion was taken up, and the result was a "wish list" of interface changes that was submitted to the director and subsequently distributed to the group. This wish list included attention to the scroll bar and to the menus, among other things. Not surprisingly to many of the systems designers in the UIG, who were by this time "mostly fed up with" the complaints of the user advocates, the list contained more than three items. However, because it was the director of the ITC who had requested the list, and because he seemed to take it seriously and agree with much of it, the systems designers in the UIG began to address these problems in earnest.

The following sections describe and illustrate the initial and revised scroll bar and menus, and discuss the evolution of these features. For each of these features, the following issues are discussed: some of the impetus for change and who took leadership roles, the number and kind of people involved in the changes and their implementation, consensus about and acceptance of the changes at the time, and the kind of agreement after the fact among participants about what had actually occurred in the development of these two features.

The Scroll Bar Wars

Description of Changes to the Scroll Bar

The Andrew scroll bar had two functions: It was used to move through a document, and it functioned as a visual indicator to show which part of the document was currently displayed and the approximate length of the document. The first version of the scroll bar was a white box with a black line indicating the part of the document currently in view. The location of the text caret in the document was indicated by a black circle within the scroll bar; this circle would enlarge when a part of the text was selected.

The scroll bar could be used in two different ways, each of which utilized a different cursor. The first function, thumbing, utilized the right pointing triangle cursor to move quickly to a general part of the document. The user would point this cursor at the area of the scroll bar representing the section of the document he or she wished to see. The second function, scrolling proper, utilizing the up-and-down arrow cursor, allowed for more precise movements. When this cursor was placed next to a particular line of text, that line would move to the top or bottom of the screen, depending on which mouse button was used.

Figure 6.1 shows an early Andrew screen with several scroll bars labeled A, B, C, D, and E. In Scroll Bar A, the black line extending the length of the scroll bar shows that the entire document (in this case, mail captions) is in view; the circle at the top of the scroll bar shows that the caret or selection is at the beginning. Scroll Bar B, in the body of the message, shows that approximately one third—the middle one third—of the document is in view. Scroll Bar C, in the Edit Text window above the mail program, indicates a very long document—here the line indicating the portion of the text in view has shrunk to a small dot. In this document, too, the caret is at the beginning, shown by the black circle. Similarly, Scroll Bar D is in a window with a long document, but here the typing caret is at the end of the document (because the black circle is at the bottom of the scroll bar). Scroll Bar E, also in an Edit Text window, shows that some text is selected by the elongated circle instead of the usual small circle indicating the cursor. Here, about half of the text that is in view is selected, and this is reflected in the scroll bar.

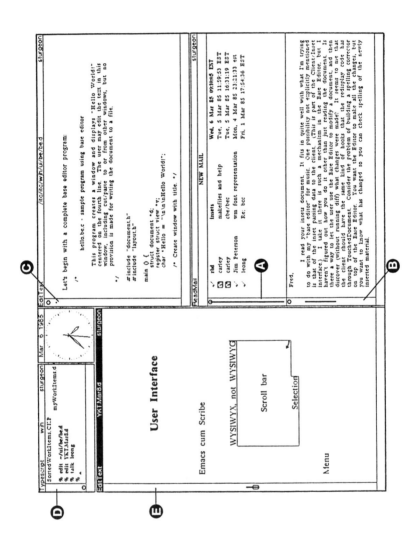

FIG. 6.1. Early Andrew screen with original scroll bars A, B, C, D, and E.

Beginning in mid-1985, significant changes were made in the visual appearance of the scroll bar and smaller, but still important, changes to its functionality. The revised version of the scroll bar is shown in Figure 6.2. The new scroll bar was gray with a white bar indicating the portion of the document in view. The cursor location was still shown, but now with a small black bar that expanded to a rectangle when something was selected. New features in this scroll bar included lighter gray "end zones" at the top and bottom of the scroll bar, representing the beginning and end of the document. This revised scroll bar used only one cursor—the up-and-down arrow cursor. Fine, precise movements were still made by positioning this arrow next to a particular line of text and pressing the right or left mouse button to move up or down in the document. Large movements could be accomplished in two ways: One could move to the beginning or end of the document by placing the cursor in the top or bottom end zone. Placing the cursor inside the white portion of the scroll bar, holding down the left mouse button, and moving the mouse up or down resulted in the white portion sliding up or down the scroll bar. Releasing the mouse button brought the corresponding part of the document into view. The following section details how these changes came about.

typescript | **blythedale**

```
(blythedale.andrew.cmu.edu)% cd
(blythedale.andrew.cmu.edu)% messages
Starting messages (Version 7.14, ATK 14.8); please
wait...
(blythedale.andrew.cmu.edu)% finger sidebotham     In real
Login name: bob          life: Bob Sidebotham          Shell:
Directory: /afs/andrew.cmu.edu/usr1/bob    /bin/csh
Address mail to:
bob@andrew.cmu.edu        Affiliation: Information
Technology Center
Account used on Mon Apr 30 22:40 (8 days 11 hours
ago).
No new mail, last read Mon May 7 10:20 (4 minutes 35
seconds ago).
No Plan.
(blythedale.andrew.cmu.edu)%_
```

console | **Monitor** | **blythedale** | Monday 5/7/90

Load   Monitor

```
Butler: Looking for left over processes. (10:15:16 AM)
Butler: Cleaning out /tmp. (10:15:16 AM)
Butler: Cleaning out /usr/tmp. (10:15:16 AM)
Butler: Butler exiting. (10:15:36 AM)
```

messages | **9 Changed Folders** | **blythedale**

```
mail (Mail: 0 new of 187)
official.andrew (Has New Message)
official.cmu-news (Has New Message)
cmu.market (Has New Message)

✓ 3-May-90 Re: protocol analysis - Severinsson - Eklundh@nada (442)
  3-May-90 "Computers and Composition .. - "Composition Digest @vma (32643)
  4-May-90 "Computers and Composition .. - "Composition Digest @vma (19341)
  5-May-90 "Computers and Composition .. - "Composition Digest @vma (24288)
  6-May-90 Computers and Composition D.. - "Composition Digest @vma (19279)

Date: Wed, 2 May 90 08:30:23 -0400 (EDT)
From: Nathaniel Borenstein <nsb@thumper.bellcore.com>
To: Chris Haas <ch+@andrew.cmu.edu>
Subject: Re: Book

Well, I hope you enjoy it, and I look forward to any comments you might
have -- it is still definitely very rough around the edges, at the very
least.

Checkpointing message server state.. done.
```

messages-send | **Sent/Posted** | **blythedale**

```
To: Nathaniel Borenstein <nsb@thumper.bellcore.com>          Won't Keep Copy
Subject: Re: Book                                            Won't Clear
In-Reply-To: <ka Dh - TCOM2Yr4g7lK@thumper.bellcore.com>     Won't Hide
References: <sa AoJCyODVsROSsolM@andrew.cmu.edu>,             Won't Sign
  <EaAoVgW0M2YtACXKcC@thumper.bellcore.com>,                 Reset

Hi Nathaniel -- I'm enjoying the book. Almost finished.

A woman from Cornell who is on a Dana Fellowship here (Nancy Kaplan) is writing an interesting
piece of why educational software fails. Her thesis (I think) is that the organizational structures of
universities are not set up to foster or maintain good educ. software. She's using some pieces of great
educational promise (Kaufer and Neuwirth's Comments and Notes) and arguing that the capitalist
mentality of an institution like CMU is not set up to foster the essentially cooperative climate that
educ. software needs.

Anyway, I think her thinking could benefit greatly from reading People are Perverse. Would you
mind if I copied it (or selected chapters) for her?

ch
```

FIG. 6.2. Andrew screen with revised scroll bars.

Narrative of Changes to the Scroll Bar

The changes in the scroll bar were not brought about by a groundswell of dissatisfaction with the existing scroll bar, and during the initial changes there was little consensus. On the contrary, most members of the ITC, having used no other scroll bar, "basically thought it was fine," according to one member of the UIG. The impetus for change in this case came from the user advocates who were involved in user testing. Teaching new and novice users to use the scroll bar had proven to be quite difficult and time-consuming. Because the two functions of the scroll bar (thumbing and scrolling) used the same narrow space, users often did one when they wanted to do the other, according to a writer who had been testing her documentation with undergraduates. She also felt that the black line representing the current view of the document was "not intuitive," especially because this line grew shorter as the document grew longer. Consequently, scroll bar improvements became one of the user advocates' three wishes.

The redesign of the scroll bar was the result of a small committee's efforts. About five members of the UIG—including at different times two or three developers and three user advocates (a graphic designer, and two members who had done user testing)—volunteered to come up with an improved scroll bar. Because at this point, many of the developers considered the scroll bar a "nonproblem," as one of them put it, the UIG as a whole seemed content to let this small group go off and work on a redesign. The relative calmness with which the scroll bar redesign began, however, gave way to turmoil and strident disagreements before the final decision was made on a scroll bar redesign, about three months later.

After about two weeks' work, interviewing users both inside and outside the ITC, the committee came up with at least two slightly different versions (pen-and-paper mockups) of a new scroll bar. Both versions borrowed some of their looks from the Macintosh scroll bar, but duplicated most of the functionality of the original Andrew scroll bar. These versions were then introduced to and critiqued by the entire UIG. Some members made suggestions, which resulted in a third redesign put forth by the committee.

By this point, word was getting around the ITC that the scroll bar was being redesigned. Suddenly it became clear that a major feature of the system was about to change, and it was to change to a version (one of three) that the nontechnical, user advocates had had a strong role in designing. Rather quickly, in fact over one weekend, a number of rival scroll bar designs were put forth, both by members of the UIG and by members of other design groups within the ITC. It was at this point, according to one observer, that "the scroll bar wars ensued."[1] To call these discussions about scroll bar design "wars" is somewhat exaggerated, but for several weeks there were heated discussions between several factions about the looks and needed functionality of the new scroll bar. These discussions took place in UIG meetings, but they also took up a substantial amount of time in weekly meetings of the whole ITC, and, of course, they spilled into hallway and kitchen discussions as well. As one developer recalled, "It was as if everybody had to get on board, to get their two cents in about the redesign, even if they didn't have anything really interesting to offer."

Controversy, of course, is not unusual in engineering settings like the ITC, where engineers and others are working together to design artifacts that work. In this case, however, the vehemence with which various parties argued their positions may not have completely been a question of design issues *per se*. Many rival scroll bars were quite similar, and in conversations several years later, few of the developers could remember the details of the differences between various versions. Many could not even recall the functionality or appearance of the versions they themselves had put forth.

The scroll bar wars ensued, in part, because of the ambiguous political status of the group responsible for the initial revision, particularly the user advocates. Up until this point, the user advocates had been viewed by most of the designers in the ITC as consultants, troubleshooters, or support staff. They were, for the most part, "out of the design loop—or at least that's how they were perceived," as one developer put it. However, with the campus deployment approaching, Morris (the director of the ITC) began to publicly ask for and listen to the advice of the user advocates. He had requested the three wishes for improvement of the user interface, and he had distributed a copy of this wish list to designers working on user interface issues. No one could recall Morris ever taking a public stand on a particular version of the scroll bar. Indeed, he had the reputation of an interested, but hands-off manager. As one designer put it, "Morris would just wander into your office, ask a bunch of hard questions, and wander out again. But somehow he motivated people to get the work done."

In this case, however, Morris changed the status of the user advocates through his public attention to their concerns. This made it difficult for designers—within the UIG or within the ITC as a whole—to publicly dismiss the versions of the scroll bar that the user advocates had helped design. But it was also difficult, several of them admitted later, to just "roll over" and let the design of the subcommittee, including user advocates, carry the day. Hence, there was a proliferation of rival designs from all parts of the ITC, designs that in many cases were only different in subtle or superficial ways from the three versions the committee had proposed.

The final deployed scroll bar—shown in Figure 6.2—combined features from several competitors in the scroll bar wars. In fact, by 1990, no one could recall (or agree on) which features were suggested by the small committee, which came from critiques of their work by the larger UIG, and which were elements of rival scroll bars. The implementation of the new scroll bar was completed over one weekend by a UIG developer after that group decided on a final version (see Figure 6.2).

One decision made by the developer who implemented the scroll bar caused a minor furor, and this illustrates some competing theories of software design. It was taken for granted by most members of the ITC that what the UIG was designing was a "default" interface; that is, an interface that most users, particularly novices, would see. There was also an assumption, however, that expert users (i.e., computer scientists and other highly technical users) should be able to "customize" the interface that they saw on their particular machines. Therefore, when a user interface decision was made—to go with a particular system monitor, for example, or a particular clock design as the default—most expert users within the ITC assumed that they would be able to access and use any number of versions of monitors or clocks that had been in operation previously. For many designers within the ITC, the notion of customization was an almost sacred concept: Most believed that users (usually taken to mean expert users) should always have options for how particular features within the system looked and behaved. Therefore, while certain defaults were suggested and implemented across the user interface, expert users for the most part retained the ability to override those defaults, with more or less effort. One designer described this as the "free market" in operation; if a new feature really was an improvement, then people would "buy it" by using it and discarding old versions.

The scroll bar, however, broke this free market rule. The developer who eventually implemented the scroll bar said that, in contrast to most of his colleagues for whom customization was a sacred concept, he believed that "design is making a decision; design isn't leaving all the options open." He was one of the few advocates of disallowing preference customization of interface features. Therefore, "when I did it, I just threw out all the other [scroll bar alternatives]—they're gone." Therefore, when people came into work the following Monday morning, they saw the new scroll bar—and only the new scroll bar. By this time, most people had resigned themselves to the new scroll bar, at least as a system default. But by midmorning it was becoming clear that old versions of the scroll bar were not available, and many people within the ITC were disgruntled at this affront to customization, that is, to experts' ability to use any version of the scroll bar that they happened to prefer. This meant that the new scroll bar was not, for many expert users, the free market choice that many believed it should be. However, in interviews after this period, most agreed that once people got used to it, the new scroll bar was a marked improvement over its predecessors.

The Menus Fiasco

Description of Changes to the Menus

In its earliest versions, Andrew employed hierarchical menus in which selecting certain menu items invoked submenus. Figures 6.3a, 6.3b, 6.3c, and 6.3d show examples of these hierarchical menus. There were no constraints for size built into this system, so menus could have both an infinite number of items and infinite levels of submenus. The cursor in these menus was the "pointing finger cursor" and a preference option allowed for a feature which reselected the last selected menu item when the menus were invoked.

There were several problems associated with these menus. These problems included unwieldiness as menus items in various applications grew and unpredictability in placement of the submenus. Figures 6.3a and 6.3b illustrate this latter problem: In Figure 6.3b, the menus were invoked too close to the right edge of the screen for the submenu to be placed to the right as it normally would be (and as is shown in Figure 6.3a). Therefore, the submenu comes up backwards or on the left rather than on the right as would usually be the case. Figure 6.3c illustrates another problem: the middle pointing finger cursor which some users on the Carnegie Mellon campus found offensive. Figure 6.3d shows the selection menus (a supplementary set of menus which include style and editing commands) in the original hierarchical menu scheme.

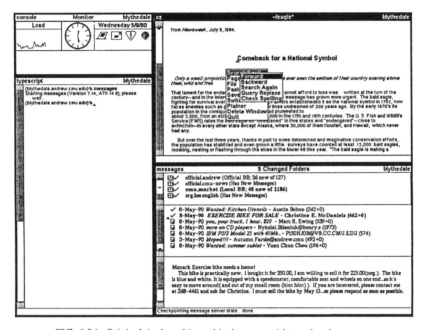

FIG. 6.3A. Original Andrew hierarchical menus with two levels.

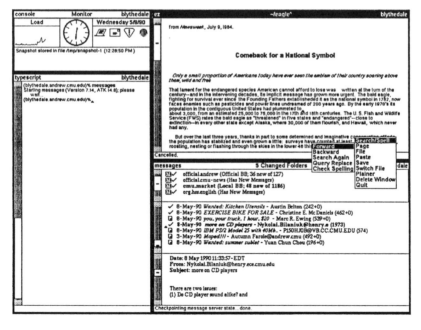

FIG. 6.3B. Original Andrew hierarchical menus, shown with second level "backwards."

FIG. 6.3C. Close-up of hierarchical menus with "pointing-finger" cursor.

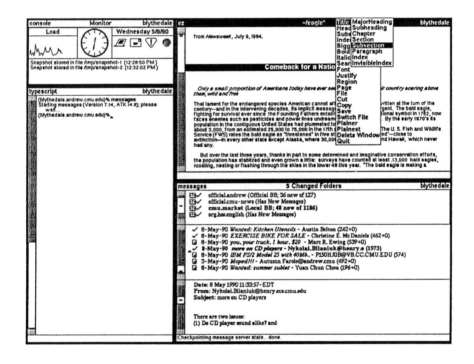

FIG. 6.3D. Original Andrew hierarchical selection menus.

The Andrew menus went through several iterations, over the course of more than a year; only the version of the menus that was finally deployed on the campus community are described here. Figures 6.4a and 6.4b shows these menus; Figure 6.4a shows the search menu card and Figure 6.4b shows the selection menus. These revised menus used a "stack of cards" metaphor to organize the commands on the menus; henceforth, I will refer to these revised menus as stack of cards menus. The stack of cards design immediately constrained the number of levels which the menus could accommodate to two. Commands were grouped on different cards and titles indicated the general nature of the items on a card. While holding down the mouse button(s) which invoke menus, the user moved the cursor to the left to select a particular card and then up or down to select an item on that card. Once the user moved to cards in the back, the front card or cards become gray (see Figures 6.4a and 6.4b); by moving back to the right the user can reactivate these cards. A "mouse hole" on the front card allowed the user to quickly reselect the last selected item. These revised menus used a straight right-pointing cursor.

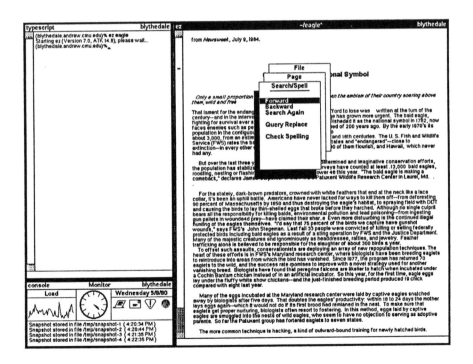

FIG. 6.4A. Revised "stack of cards" menus.

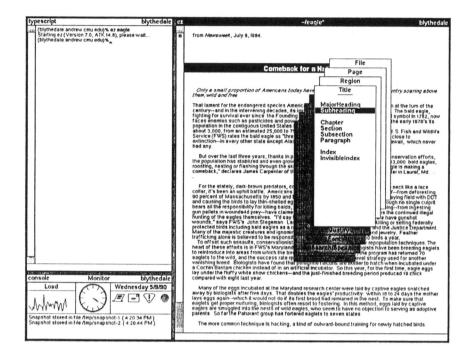

FIG. 6.4B. Revised "stack of cards"

Narrative of Changes to the Menus

In contrast to the scroll bar development efforts which involved short periods
of rather intense work, the changes to the menus "dragged on forever," as one
developer outside the User Interface Group put it. There had been a fair amount
of grumbling all along about the hierarchical menus, for many of the reasons
described above: their unweildiness, the pointing-finger cursor, the large
amount of space that they took up. This grumbling had not, however, taken on
any specific focus, and menu concerns were not part of the user advocates wish
list, nor were they taken up in any concerted way by the User Interface Group.
Rather, a designer who was not part of the User Interface Group said that he "got
really frustrated with the [original] menus" and since it was currently a slow
time in his own work, decided to try his hand at an improvement to the user
interface. Several interview participants commented on this: They thought it

underscored the fluidity of the organizational structure of the ITC that a developer essentially out of the user interface loop could be responsible for the beginnings of a major change to that interface. Most people agreed that this was a good thing: "Really there was an openness to ideas—not that people just readily accepted [the new menus] but it was seen as OK to be spending some of your time on other stuff. It essentially meant a big change for the better for Andrew."

The idea behind the stack of cards menus which were released internally at the ITC was that menus would always look the same—they would always have the same basic size and shape. The developer who had implemented the system said that he had been influenced by talk he had heard from some of the user advocates—that users should develop automaticity with computer interactions whenever possible. The stack of cards menus were an attempt to give users an opportunity to develop this automaticity. There had been some suggestion, primarily from nontechnical user advocates, that the menus might mock Macintosh menus and be available only in the titlebar of an application. This idea was quickly dismissed, however, when several senior designers pointed out that such a change would be incredibly costly, involving basically the development of an entirely new window manager. One of these designers said, "They [user advocates] basically aren't aware that some of the stuff they ask for would literally take thousands of man hours to do. This is not a perfect world; we have a bottom line—and only so many people."

The revised design, the stack of cards menus, met with mixed reviews at first. Some people liked the change—or liked what they saw as the potential for improvement in the design—but others were skeptical. The problems with the stack of cards menus included the lack of functionality in moving back through a stack once one had passed through it, the lack of speed, and, because a feature had been added which automatically mapped old menus items onto the stack of cards scheme, sometimes very long, inconsistent, or nonsensical menu item names. In response to some of these problems, another developer and a writer were working to make menu item names consistent and to order menu items names into sensible groups, each of which would appear on a separate card. They also decided that number of cards and number items on a card should be limited to seven, plus or minus two. On individual cards, white space separated conceptually different groups of items.

The redesign of the menus also illustrates the tension between principles of programming, on the one hand, and pragmatic, user-centered concerns on the other. One of the interesting things about the redesign of the menus is that while there had been a great deal of dissatisfaction with the original hierarchical menus, many of the interview subjects admitted that, in principle, the design of the original menus was a good one: "one that a computer scientist would think was just right." That is, the strictly hierarchical, and theoretically infinite, design was one that had certain appeal from a purely programming point of view. However, when this theoretical notion—of infinite hierarchy—was put into practice, it caused problems for users, problems even for expert users. One interview subject recalled that "it was clear we had to think hard about the hierarchical menus" when some developers within the ITC began to "abuse" the menu scheme, adding numerous items and levels so that the menus in some programs took up "huge amounts of space—just went splat all over the screen" when they were invoked. There was also no standardization. This meant that in different programs, the same function (e.g., "quit," might have different names: "close," "kill," "bye"). "We just couldn't get ourselves together to have the same names for the same things," said one developer.

Similarly, some of the reticence about the stack of cards menus came from developers who had relied on a lot of menu commands in their programs and were worried because the number of items that could be put on the menus was greatly diminished. In these cases, developers worried about having to rewrite their applications from the ground up. Other people thought that the white space between items was a "waste of screen real estate," despite articulate arguments from a graphic designer about the aesthetics and usefulness of added white space.

By late 1985, several people from the user interface group had gotten involved in making various kinds of changes to the look and functionality of the stack of cards menus. These included changes to the menu cursor (done primarily by the graphic designer), the addition of a mouse hole (a feature borrowed from the original menus) which quickly allowed a repetition of the previous command, and changes to make the menus paint and repaint more smoothly on the screen. Some of these changes were finally adopted into the default menus for campus release, while others were not, but by the January 1986 release of IBM's RT, the menu scheme was set.

A Second Round of Menu Changes

Not for long, however: In the spring of that year, one member of the UIG began playing around with what came to be called "new menus" or "left-stacking menus." The most obvious feature change in left-stacking menus was that cards stacked to the left, rather than to the right, as in the original implementation. When these left-stacking menus were released within the ITC without warning, they were met with furor. Because the stack of cards allowed an automaticity that had not been possible with the original menus, users tended to use them very quickly and to develop "muscle memory"—invoking menus and issuing commands by feel rather than by actually reading and selecting menu items.

The introduction of the left stacking menus, which laid the cards out in the opposite direction, caused a great deal of confusion. Loud complaining ensued, especially from those who had developed automaticity with the stack of cards menus, which included by this time almost everyone at the ITC. Users who had been able to effortlessly invoke menus and commands were now making glaring and repeated mistakes. "A lot of us felt it was a case of breaking something that didn't need to be fixed," said one member of the ITC. It was precisely because users had become so accustomed to the right-stacking stack of cards menus that their revision caused such an outraged response.

However, according to several developers within the User Interface Group, "once people got past being pissed," there were several advantages to the left-stacking menus which were not obvious at first. Among these were faster invocation of the menus, the differentiation of the axis of card selection (which became left/right) and the axis of item selection (up/down)," and a hysteresis built into the cards so that flipping to the next one inadvertently was less likely.

In discussions in and out of meetings, in offices and halls, and via mail and bulletin boards, members of the ITC debated the relative advantages and disadvantages of the left-stacking versus stack of cards menus. When discussions reached a seeming impasse, several of the senior designers suggested that I design and conduct a study of user tests of the two competing versions of the menus, the right-stacking stack of cards and the left-stacking new menus. At first I was reluctant, since I believed that computer-human interaction studies can never show unequivocally that a particular user interface feature is "best." After I had explained that the results of the study would probably not be definitive, and most of the User Interface Group seemed to accept this, I agreed to conduct a small study which compared time-of-learning and error rates for novice Andrew users (incoming freshman to CMU) and evaluated their affective responses to the two menu schemes. The menus tested combined various features under discussion and compared the two kinds of menus along six dimensions: orientation, cursor location, mouse hole location, mouse hole format, navigation mechanism, and selection mechanism.

The results of this small user study showed a slight advantage for the left-stacking new menus, although because of the small number of study participants, no significance tests were possible. The most striking result of the study, however, was an order effect: Subjects performed better with, and overwhelmingly preferred, the first, menu type which they had learned—regardless of which one it was. As I explained to the User Interface Group, consistency was the most important lesson to be learned from the user testing of menus. The results of the study could also be used to argue that the vocal and adamant preference for the stack of cards menus was primarily because users within the ITC had learned to use that menu scheme first.

Despite the high hopes of some members of the User Interface Group, this study did not solve the problem of which menu scheme was better; a decision was still necessary—and time was getting short. By this time, the User Interface Group was headed up by one developer who had been working on user interface issues for the four years he had been at the ITC. For the first time, there was a User Interface Group leader in place who had ultimate authority over interface decisions. (Of course, when the director of the ITC was heading the group, he had a sort of ultimate authority but he seldom directly used it.) The new manager of the User Interface group was jokingly called the User Interface "Czar" by members of the group, who nonetheless tried to influence him about the menu decision which was before him. The manager eventually decided—at the last minute, just days before the Fall 1986 campus release—that the left-stacking menus (the new menus) would be the default. When asked about this decision, the User Interface Czar recalled that his decision was somewhat influenced by the results of testing which showed a slight advantage for these menus. More important, however, was his own analysis of the two menu schemes in leading him to favor the left-stacking menus. He decided that the left-stacking new menus were primarily a "win" over the right stacking menus because of the distinguished axis of selection: left/right for card selection, up/down for item selection. He jokingly admitted, however, that while his decision on the menus was really one of principled preference, he let others believe that he was "wowed by science;" that is, that it was the menu testing results that had swayed him. "They tended to give me less flack about it once I told them it was the results of the [user] tests that convinced me."

For the most part, this decision closed the books on menu design and redesign, although new multimedia applications in Andrew raised menus as an issue again in 1988. The evolution of the Andrew menus then was somewhat more drawn out and the benefits of the changes less clean cut than was the case with other user interface developments. The revisions to the menus also involved a large number of people, drawing on people outside the User Interface Group and, indirectly through the novice users who participated in testing, outside the ITC computer science community. There was also much less consensus about the end result. As late as 1991, there was a significant minority of people within the ITC who thought that the menus were "basically done wrong."

CONCLUSION

In chapter 2, I discussed two cultural myths about technology, one that it is all-powerful, the other that it is transparent. When considering a question such as "What is the nature of technological development?" each of these myths would suggest a slightly different answer. The myth of a self-determining, all-powerful technology would lead us to believe that technological development is some how "inevitable." The transparent technology myth, on the other hand, assumes that what a certain technology is, is right. In this view, the "best" features of a given technology will somehow win out. The case-study of technology development presented in this chapter shows how both of these myths oversimplify and essentialize technology development, by positing it as a "black box" not open to scrutiny. In this chapter, I have tried to open the black box, and the narratives of the technology development within the Andrew project present a story of technology development that is vastly more complicated than what might be suggested by the cultural myths of transparent and all-powerful technology.

The design of computer features that I have traced here certainly suggests that the shape of computer technology is far from inevitable. Rather, we saw how the design of the scroll bar and the menus in the Andrew computing system was the result of a complex of factors. These factors included issues of power and politics, matters of timing and cost, and rival theories about software design. For example, in the evolution of the scroll bar, politics and social relations came into play in an important way. On their own, the user advocates—who put together the user interface wish list and helped to design the new scroll bar—would have had little power to effect change, given their low status in the ITC. However, when they had the (usually unspoken but still extremely effective) support of the director, their concerns took on more weight. This ambiguous power situation—a relatively low-status group implicitly backed by the director of the center—lead to a situation in which almost everyone tried to have a say in the scroll bar design: hence, the controversy of the scroll bar wars.

Further, we saw in the narratives about the evolution of the scroll bar and the menus that sometimes individual decision-making—human agency— played an important role. Thus, the final decision about the menus design was essentially one of a manager using his authority and making a decision that some may have seen as one of fiat. In addition, the developer who implemented the final scroll bar design "threw all the others away," which meant that all users were forced to use the new design. This had important ramifications, and many users were less than happy about it.

Similarly, the evolution of Andrew user interface features presented here does not support the notion that the "best" features of a given system somehow carry the day. Sometimes the decisions behind the design of the interface could be traced to actual improvements in design, but just as often, the decisions were made by fiat, or because of economics, or because of who was advocating a certain change. Pull-down menus (like those on a Macintosh) may have been "better" in some ways than the pop-up menus that Andrew incorporated, but this option was not even considered once it was clear how labor intensive and time expensive such a change would be. An outsider to the software design process might expect that certain principles or theories of programming would guide designers choices and thereby ensure a user interface design that is "best." However, in these two cases we saw that often two competing sets of principles or theories would come into play in a design decision. For instance, the original hierarchical menus (shown in Figure 3) followed the programming principle of iterative embedding, but violated another: Do not waste screen space. Similarly, the developer who implemented the final scroll bar adhered to one "theory" of design—that is, make decisions and limit options—while violating another: Let expert users customize and maximize their freedom of choice.

Toward the end of the controversy about the menus, the Director of the ITC summed up his recollections about the menus "fiasco" (as one participant termed it) in this way: "Chris, the story of the Andrew menus is either a story of social dynamics, or a story of scientific method, or a story of sheer human cussedness." Like most technology development, it is probably all these stories at once—and more besides. A technology—a computer system, or an application, or even a feature within an application—is not a static, fixed, internally-consistent, unitary object. Rather, a computer system or application is best seen, as are other technologies, as an evolving and fluid but nonetheless powerful cultural system, a system that contains many "voices," some of them contradictory but all of them interested.

FOOTNOTES

[1]At the time, an "ITC T-Shirt Design Contest" was underway, and one imaginative contestant put together several of the competing scroll bars in a t-shirt design commemorating the "scroll bar wars."

7

CONSTRUCTING TECHNOLOGY THROUGH

DISCOURSE

with Ann George

The previous chapter explored some of the complicated and very human ways in which technological tools are developed within particular settings, by particular people, acting with particular beliefs and goals. The story of the Andrew user interface's evolution suggests that, although a well-designed computer system looks "transparent" to users, the actual construction of that system may be fraught with conflicting purposes and motives and influenced by factors such as time, money, and politics. This chapter examines another way in which technologies are constructed: through the language used to characterize technology and to argue about technology's implications.

Contemporary poststructuralists, like Foucault and Derrida, have been influential in revealing and exploiting the constructive nature of all discourse. But as early as 1935, Kenneth Burke was articulating the power of language in maintaining, and undermining, ideology and in shaping individual and collective responses: "Speech," Burke realized, "is not a naming at all, but a system of attitudes, of implicit exhortations. To call a man a friend or an enemy is *per se* to suggest a program of action with regard to him" (1984; p. 177). This chapter similarly argues that all discourse about technology contains implicit theories about what technology is, what it does, and the kinds of relationships that people can have to it. These theories are critical in determining a program of action vis-a-vis technology for literacy studies: They determine what technological problems people identify, the roles they see for themselves in addressing these problems, and the methods they bring to bear upon the problems. If these implicit theories advance the culturally dominant instrumental view of technology (i.e., that technology is either autonomous and all-powerful, or neutral and unproblematic), then little space is left in which to conduct scholarly inquiry about technology because technology is either a force outside human control, or it is a moot point. Similarly, such an instrumental view discourages or even prohibits scholars and teachers of literacy from having a voice in the development or application of literacy tools.

If literacy scholars are to pursue the Technology Question, make decisions about pedagogical uses of technology, and take an active role in technological development, it is essential that we examine the underlying theories of technology that are a powerful (if unarticulated) force shaping attitudes and actions toward technology. This chapter, which takes as an exemplary case the discourse about technology within English Studies, offers such an examination. Here, we seek a more complicated understanding of the ways in which arguments about technology operate by conducting a detailed and systematic rhetorical analysis of the methods of reasoning about technology in recent English Studies publications and the theories implicit in that reasoning. Before the study is presented, however, we first, elaborate the notion that language constructs reality and, offer an overview of how English Studies formulates and addresses the Technology Question.

For Burke—like the contemporary postmodernists who follow him—every account of human meaning in a culture is inextricably bound up with the language available to express it. That is, people's understanding of how the world works, of their place in it, of what is true or beautiful or even what is possible is shaped by the language they use. The available language calls attention to certain objects, ideas, or relationships and allows others to be ignored. Although this concept may be difficult to fathom in the abstract, it is familiar enough in most people's everyday lives. For instance, school children learn about the possibly mythical example of Eskimos having 39 different words for *snow*. Numerous books and articles—Mike Rose's *Lives on the Boundary* (1989) is a particularly compelling example—claim that educational labels such as *gifted, learning disabled,* or *remedial* become self-fulfilling prophecies in the way students perceive themselves and are perceived by others. Feminists and African Americans have argued for years that sexist and racist language perpetuates an oppressive power structure by representing them as invisible or "other." Language enables, encourages, and perhaps even requires certain ways of seeing.

Discourse about technology is equally powerful in shaping cultural views of writing tools and the uses to which they are put. For instance, if popular or scholarly literature about computers and writing assumes that technology is an agent (i.e., if effects result from technology's presence rather than from anything teachers or students do), a teacher might attempt to simply introduce computers into a classroom and expect immediate and positive effects. Similarly, an administrator who believes that computers are mere tools of text production, or a means to present mechanical drill-and-practice, might impose curricula and deploy staff in ways that emphasize those aspects of the technology. Using the technology to stimulate student revision or to enact a collaborative pedagogy through networking might not even be considered if the administrator understands the computer as a machine that efficiently creates an attractive product, or replaces one-on-one teacher instruction in mechanics. In both of these cases, an individual's view of technology has important ramifications for others, especially students. However, these are not simply examples of misguided or uninformed individuals, but rather of pervasive cultural assumptions about technology, assumptions that are exert a powerful influence when they are embedded in discourse.

Discourses of technology, then, determine how the Technology Question is taken up within any particular culture or community. Implicit theories of technology delimit what issues or questions can be raised. For example, if technology is seen as self-determining, questions about human agency can become trivial. Similarly, these theories of technology influence who is authorized to ask questions about the design and effects of technology: computer scientists? cultural critics? writing teachers? Finally, assumptions about technology define the range and sources of possible answers to the Technology Question by eliminating certain disciplines or areas of study from the inquiry (see chapter 2, this volume).

THE TECHNOLOGY QUESTION WITHIN ENGLISH STUDIES

English Studies is a discipline increasingly interested in technology. Growing numbers of writing instructors use of computer-assisted instruction, set up bulletin boards or computer conferences for their classes, and use e-mail to communicate with colleagues and students. In addition, collections of scholarly articles on technology, such as Selfe and Holligoss' *Literacy and Computers*

(1994) appear with increasing frequency, and journals devoted to computers and education, such as *Computers and Composition* and *Computers and the Humanities* have been established. This flourish of discourse about computer technology and literacy is reflected in the theme of the 1995 Conference on College Composition and Communication: "Literacies, Technologies, Responsibilities."

However, the location and tenor of much discourse on technology may, on close examination, be cause for concern for those involved in literacy studies. Although interest in and writing about computers has increased on the whole, the number of articles on technology published in *College English* (*CE*) and *College Composition and Communication* (*CCC*), two of the profession's most important general journals, has decreased significantly, from 22 in 1984-1988 to just 10 in 1989-1993.[1] Taken in conjunction with the increase in specialized publication, this decrease in mainstream articles may suggest that discourse about technology has reached a high enough volume to constitute a subfield of English Studies with its own journals, language, and experts. This adds force to an already established (and, some scholars would say, dangerous) perception among English scholars that the discourse is too specialized for general interest and participation and hence should be left to the computer literacy experts. Jurgen Habermas; (1984-1987) critiques just such a movement in modern society, whereby specialized forms of argumentation become the privileged preserve of experts, and open public discussion is increasingly short-circuited. As discourse about technology moves away from a more public arena, an issue that would seem to have important implications for English Studies at large (i.e., how new technology will be integrated into existing theory and practice) is being debated by a narrowing subset of the profession . In addition, the decrease in *CE* and *CCC* articles might also suggest to readers that the Technology Question is being taken care of by somebody else, or that it, in fact, has already been resolved.

The narrowing sphere of debate about technology within English Studies only serves to compound another troubling characteristic of recent discourse about computers: its lack of critical perspective. Hawisher and Selfe (1991), for instance, note that most discourse about technology is marked by an "uncritical enthusiasm" (p. 56), ignoring some of the negative consequences of classroom implementation. Similarly, Barton (1994) divides discourse on technology into two categories—dominant discourse, which celebrates "improved pedagogy through technology" (p. 71), and the more theoretical antidominant discourse of the cultural Left, which suggests that computers will serve primarily to reinforce existing power relations, and thus have limited benefits for society at large. Barton argues that, in most cases, antidominant discourse occurs only within the framework of dominant discourse, "leaving the field with only one voice, which focuses on the assumed benefits of technology" (p. 56).

Although Barton's (1994) study is interesting for what it suggests about discourse on technology, one central problem with current discourse is a lack of critical awareness of how arguments are constructed and of the implicit theories of technology that underlie them. Indeed, such implicit theories of technology may both feed the lack of caution that Barton notes and explain why it is dominant within this discourse. Barton's strict dichotomization between dominant and antidominant discourse is less than useful because, ultimately, dominant discourse refers to any argument that computers benefit students or education, and antidominant describes any argument in which computers are "bad." Hence, critics like Stanley Aronowitz and Henry Giroux (1985) would be grouped in the same category as Ronald Sudol (1991) in Barton's scheme, even though their skepticism of technology's promise derives from very different sources. Aronowitz and Giroux remain skeptical because they believe computers will reinforce the status quo, particularly existing power relations. Sudol's concerns are the opposite: he worries that computers will subvert the status quo, including adherence to a solid work ethic. More useful distinctions can and need to be made because this lack of reflection on the nature of technology jeopardizes what should be a crucial role for English Studies: providing a critical perspective on how technologies for reading and writing are, and should be, developed, implemented, and used. With this larger purpose in mind, the following study was designed to explore the methods of reasoning and uncover implicit theories about technology within English Studies.

THE STUDY

This study explored two questions: What kinds of claims, evidence, and assumptions do English scholars rely on when they make arguments about technology? What underlying theories of technology shape these scholars' views and uses of technology? The study is a rhetorical analysis of 10 recent publications on technology and writing within English Studies, using a method based on Stephen Toulmin's (1958) model of argument. This method allowed a systematic identification and analysis of the structural components that characterize reasoning about technology. In addition, our adaptation of Toulmin, the identification of "ideological warrants," enabled us to examine some underlying culturally-based theories of technology.

The Sample

Our analysis focused primarily on discourse occurring within the mainstream of composition studies: articles from *College English* and *College Composition and Communication* published in the last five years. These journals are probably the two most widely-read in composition studies, with a circulation of 16,000 and 12,000, respectively. *CE* editors highlight the general nature of the journal, describing it in the *MLA Directory of Periodicals* as a forum "in which scholars working within any of the various sub-specialties of the discipline can address a broad cross-section of the profession." *CCC*, like *CE*, an organ of the National Council of Teachers of English, addresses itself primarily to teachers and scholars of rhetoric, composition, and linguistics.

A survey of these two journals for the years 1989-1993 yielded eight articles on computers and writing—six in *CE* and two in *CCC*. [2] In addition, in order to get a more representative sample of the discourse circulating in the general arena, two widely-read and cited books published recently were included in the analysis: Jay David Bolter's *Writing Space* (1991) and Richard Lanham's *The Electronic Word* (1993), both of which met the requirements of dealing primarily with technology and writing and of being directed to a broad readership. To make sample items similar in length, and to make the intensive Toulmin analysis feasible, selections were limited to one chapter from the books. Introductory chapters were chosen as likely places for the development of key claims and lines of argument. The sample of articles and chapters is shown in Figure 7.1.

Author	**Title**	**Source, Date**
Stephen Bernhardt	The Shape of Text to Come: The Texture of Print on Screen	*CCC*, 1993
Jay David Bolter	Introduction	*Writing Space*, 1991
Frank Boyle	IBM, Talking Heads, and Our Classrooms	*CE*, 1993
Marilyn Cooper and Cynthia Selfe	Computer Conferences and Learning: Authority, Resistance, and Internally Persuasive Discourse	*CE*, 1990
Gail Hawisher and Charles Moran	Electronic Mail and the Writing Instructor	*CE*, 1993
Gail Hawisher and Cynthia Selfe	The Rhetoric of Technology and the Electronic Writing Classroom	*CCC*, 1991
Richard Lanham	The Electronic Word: Literary Study and the Digital Revolution	*Electronic Word*, 1993
Joel Nydahl	Teaching Word Processors to Be CAI Programs	*CE*, 1990
John Slatin	Reading Hypertext: Order and Coherence in a New Medium	*CE*, 1990
Ronald Sudol	The Accumulative Rhetoric of Word Processing	*CE*, 1991

FIG. 7.1. The sample.

Rhetorical Analysis

This section describes: (a) the Toulmin method of analyzing data, claims, and warrants; and (b) the procedures by which these elements were selected for analysis.

Toulmin Method

A method adapted from Stephen Toulmin was used to analyze the arguments in our sample. In *The Uses of Argument*, Toulmin (1958) proposes a study of logic concerned not with the formal relations between propositions but rather with the "practical assessment of arguments" (p. 2) that people necessarily and regularly perform in everyday life. Toulmin argues against a mathematical model of logic in favor of one derived from jurisprudence. Just as jurisprudence seeks to identify the essentials of the legal process, so Toulmin tries to elucidate "the rational process," the procedures by which claims are advanced and supported in more general arguments (p. 7). Argument is seen as a trial played out before the "Court of Reason" (p. 8), with attention focused on both the process of gaining assent and the act of judgment itself.

This legal metaphor brings to the realm of general argument a sense of heightened attention and high stakes, and is especially appropriate for this study because it emphasizes the "critical function of reason" (p. 8). It implies a demand for precise claims, strict standards of relevancy, and a thorough, detailed body of evidence—in short, an argument that will withstand cross-examination. It is exactly this added level of rigor and sense of serious consequences that make Toulmin's model particularly appropriate for studies of discourse about technology by revealing the structure of the arguments and the interaction of various implicit and explicit elements. As argued in chapter 1 (this volume), the stakes in the debate over the Technology Question are high for literacy scholars, but discourse about technology often reduce those involved in the teaching and study of theory to little more than observers or users of technology. The current method, an adaptation of Toulmin's legal model, makes visible the claims, the types and amount of evidence, and the powerful, yet often unacknowledged assumptions operating in these claims. [3] In this way, our method extends beyond a merely "critical" perspective.

For the purpose of examining written arguments, three of the elements Toulmin discusses are central: claims, data, and warrants. A **claim** is an assertion offered for an audience's acceptance. Figure 7.2 provides an example.

> Students using word processors revise
> more than those using pencil and
> paper.

Claim

FIG. 7.2. Example of claim about technology.

Data can be understood broadly as evidence or grounds from a particular situation—"the facts of the case" (1984, p. 38)—presented as the basis for this claim. (See Figure 7.3).

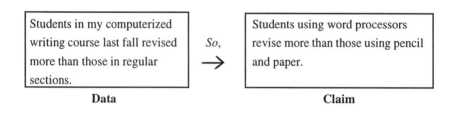

FIG. 7.3. Relationship between data and claim.

A warrant is the authorization, usually implicit, for logically moving from data to claim. Warrants are general statements (e.g., principles or formulas, laws of nature, values, customs, procedures, etc.) which justify, or warrant, making a claim based on certain evidence. Figure 7.4 illustrates the connections between data, claims, and warrants.

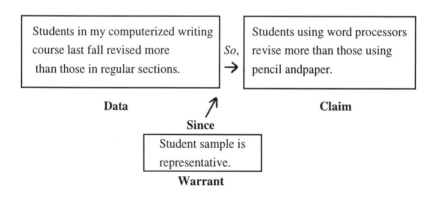

FIG. 7.4. Toulmin diagram of claim about technology.

In *An Introduction to Reasoning*, Toulmin, Rieke, and Janik (1984) catalogue various types of warrants, the most common of which are reasoning from analogy, reasoning from generalization, reasoning from signs, reasoning from cause, and reasoning from authority (p. 216-31). Complex arguments will, of course, consist of many interlocking units of data, warrants, and claims, with the claims of lower-level arguments becoming the data for higher-level claims.

Identifying Claims

Four criteria were used to identify the major claims. First, only those claims that dealt directly with technology (including computers, computer software, e-mail, or hypertext) or with the discipline's discourse about technology were marked. All of the claims identified contained these words or clear referents to these topics. Not included were general claims about pedagogy, texts, writing, or reading. So, claims such as "electronic technology offers us a new kind of book and new ways to read and write" (Bolter, 1991, p. 2) and "electronic mail has received scant attention from the field of composition theory" (Hawisher & Moran, 1993, p. 627) were included. But we did not analyze claims like Cooper and Selfe's (1990) assertion that "we have begun to recognize the need for non-traditional forums for academic exchange, forums that allow interaction patterns disruptive of a teacher-centered hegemony" (p. 847) or Slatin's (1990) that "the assumption that reading is a sequential and continuous process is the foundation on which everything else rests" (p. 871).

Second, we disregarded metadiscourse and forecasting statements, such as "in this paper, we examine the enthusiastic discourse that has accompanied the introduction of computers into writing classes and explore how this language may influence both change and the status quo in electronic classrooms" (Hawisher & Selfe, 1991, p. 56).

Third, in distinguishing "major" from lower-level claims, assertions whose clearest function was serving as data for higher-level claims were not analyized—unless they also were themselves backed by substantial data in the argument. This could often be determined by the placement of a claim in the paragraph or by verbal signals such as "for example." Thus, in the following passage (Nydahl, 1990) the first sentence was marked as the major claim and the second sentence as a supporting claim that grounds the first. Major claims are indicated with boldface.

For many teachers of writing, however, not only is their word processor not familiar territory, it's often more or less unexplored territory. They've been intimidated by writers in the field of computers and composition who either encourage a belief that most word processors are "far more complex and sophisticated than the typical writing student requires" (Collier 154) or who discourage exploration by setting up false dichotomies between CAI programs and word processors (p. 904).

Finally, if a claim was repeated a number of times in a short space, as was often the case, the most developed or detailed instance of the claim was used. In Bernhardt's (1993) article, for example, "we need to first understand the directions that computers are taking written language, and then to consider these changes as we teach our students strategies for reading and writing text in a new age" (p. 152) was chosen over the more abstract statement "we need to anticipate where text is going: the shape of text to come" (p. 151).

Selection of Claims, Data, and Warrants

To limit the data set to a manageable size, the analysis was narrowed to include only the first five major claims about technology in each article or chapter.[4] Because the articles chosen deal directly with technology, we reasoned that key claims about technology would be established early, then developed throughout, giving us a substantial portion of the article to examine. Indeed, the first five claims usually appeared between one-fourth and three-fourths of the way through the piece, and in all but three cases, their supporting data extended through the entire article. To establish the reliability of our claim selection, we began by independently identifying the first five key claims in each piece. The independent agreement on these claims was 78%; in other words, we independently identified the same major claims over three-fourths of the time. The remaining 11 claims were collaboratively determined based on previous independent word- and sentence-level analyses of the argument's structure.

After the claims for the study were identified, each article was analyzed to locate the type and amount of data used to support these claims. Each of us made two passes through this material independently before collaboratively discussing it to confirm the reliability of our analysis. Finally, after identifying the five claims and their data, we established the warrants operating in each argument. Because warrants are almost always implicit assumptions rather than explicit statements found in an argument, determining warrants is a matter of working through the logic of each point, which was done by asking this question: Given these data, what do readers have to believe to accept this claim?[5]

The results of this analysis for each article or chapter were then condensed and transferred to a "claimgrid" (one for each article, as presented in Appendix B). The claimgrids were abstract representations of complex arguments, and they were vital for this type of systematic analysis. Further, the claimgrids clarified both the structure and spirit of the arguments we examined. In short, the claimgrids became an analytic tool by which we could examine views of, and ways of reasoning about, technology.

How Are Claims Grounded?

This section describes the results of our analysis about the data used to support claims in the 10 sample arguments. Included as well is information on how the Toulmin model was adapted for this particular study.

The Nature of Data

We expected that in transferring Toulmin's jurisprudence model to our study of written arguments in English Studies, we would need to modify it to account for this field's standards of evidence and methods of reasoning. Although Toulmin et al. (1984) argued that all rational arguments share certain basic properties (e.g., grounding for claims), they also acknowledge that "different fields employ different procedures of reasoning" (p. 259). In the course of this study, two key adaptations were made. The first adaptation deals with Toulmin's category of *data*. In Toulmin's (1984) model, *data* is a general term applied to any specific supporting evidence, but he does not catalogue or examine the range of evidence that might ground claims (p. 43). In order to increase the detail, and thus the explanatory power of our analysis, we distinguished among the different kinds of data—or what Toulmin later came to call more generally "grounds"—used in these arguments.

In the arguments we examined, we found that Toulmin's large category of data could be usefully divided into the two smaller categories: supporting claims and data. Supporting claims were the lower-level assertions whose primary function is to more specifically develop or explain major claims. For instance, in his discussion of rhetorical theory's traditional indifference to communication technologies, Slatin (1990) presents as a major claim the idea that electronic technology, particularly hypertext, will make such indifference untenable because the "computerization of writing has . . . made the technology itself highly visible" (p. 873). Slatin grounds this main claim with supporting claims that contrast the transparency of print with the visibility of electronic media. Thus, he states that rhetorical theory has been able to ignore technology because "the technology [of print] is so mature that it's simply taken for granted, that it is essentially invisible *as* technology" (p. 873). Slatin notes, however, that "there was a point in history, of course, when writing itself was a radically innovative technology and was regarded as such" (p. 873). The latter two ideas, then, are subclaims that provide elaboration and support for the major claim.

Supporting claims are often, in turn, supported by what in this study we call *data*—the more specific evidence, often empirical, that arguers offer to nail down a case. In the example from Slatin just discussed, he cites Eric Havelock, Walter Ong, and Richard Lanham to substantiate the supporting claim that print was once regarded as a radical technology. Of course, major claims are also often supported by data without the intervening subclaims.

Types and Amounts of Data

In the process of our analysis, we found ten distinct types of data: example, citation, narrative, analogy, analysis, testimony, observations, numerical data, samples, and readers' experience. Specific instances or illustrations of *examples,* like Bolter's (1991) list of print forms transferred to electronic media (e.g., cork bulletin boards with pushpins become electronic bulletin boards, etc.), are plentiful, as are *citations* such as those Slatin (1990) uses to substantiate the revolutionary aspect of print. *Narrative* is the chief means of support at work in Boyle's (1993) article, recounting his experience at an IBM presentation on computers and education. *Analogy* appears in Cooper and Selfe's (1990) suggestion that the electronic medium "is as wild and unsettled as any frontier" (p. 858), *analysis* in Bernhardt's (1993) break down of differences between paper and on-screen texts into nine categories. *Testimony* is identified as statements based on personal authority such as Hawisher and Selfe's (1991) "as editors of *Computers and Composition* , . . . we read primarily of the laudatory influence of computers in promoting a social construction of knowledge" (p. 56). Later in their article, these authors also offer evidence from their *observations* of computer use in writing classrooms nationwide. Hawisher and Moran use *numerical data* to support their claim that composition studies should not ignore e-mail because it is widely used outside academia; they show for instance, that over four million people now have access to the InterNet and that 25 out of 27 college graduates use e-mail at work (p. 28). Cooper and Selfe (1991) support their claims of disruptive behavior and egalitarian exchanges in computer conferences by providing numerous *samples* of their students' writing. Unlike the other types of data identified, *readers' experience* is implicit. Although all data, in order to function as proof, must correspond to readers' experience of the world, we also found direct calls on readers' sense of "how things are" based primarily on assertions made about readers' experience with students or technology. For example, Nydahl's (1990) claim that word processors are "unexplored territory" (p. 904) draws directly on what Nydahl believes his readers' experiences to be.

The results of our Toulmin analysis of types and amount of data are presented in Figure 7.5.

GROUNDING	Number of instances	Number of authors who use this type
Supporting Claim	115	10
Data		
Examples	38	9
Citations	30	9
Analogy	7	6
Analysis	4	3
Readers' experience	3	2
Samples	2	1
Testimony	1	1
Observation	1	1
Narrative	1	1
Numerical support	1	1

FIG. 7.5. How claims are grounded. (n=10).

As might be expected, all the authors use supporting claims to substantiate their major points. Indeed, it would be hard to imagine a scholarly argument that is not constructed upon a hierarchy of claims and subclaims as the author works to explain, develop, and refine ideas in order to persuade readers. What may be more surprising is the extent to which these subclaims take precedence over data as the means of grounding claims. The authors whose arguments we analyzed use 115 supporting claims compared with 88 pieces of all data types combined to support the 50 major claims; supporting claims are used three times more often than examples, the most common type of data.[6]

Of the 10 types of data identified, some are used frequently, and some are not. Our findings indicate the overwhelming perceived superiority of examples and citations; what might be considered more empirical evidence—numerical data, samples, observation—is seldom used. Perelman and Olbrechts-Tyteca (1969) note the power of analogy in persuasion. In our sample, we found that over half of the authors used it, and that they relied upon it more often than every other type of data except example and citation.

The number of data per article ranged from a high of 19 (in Hawisher & Moran, 1993) to a low of 4 (in Slatin, 1990), with a mean of 8.8 pieces of data. An important implication of these figures is that some claims—14%, in fact—are supported by no data whatsoever. A significant number of the claims (42%) are supported by only one piece of data; 44% are supported by two or more.

These findings become significant in light of Toulmin's (1984) discussion of the nature and function of grounds. Grounds, he writes, "are statements specifying particular facts about a situation . . . [that] are already accepted as true, and can therefore by relied on to clarify and make good the previous claim" (p. 37-38). He later qualifies this position, explaining that these "facts" need not be considered unquestionable; they only need to be reasonable enough to provide the necessary common ground on which to build an argument. Nevertheless, the import of Toulmin's statement is clear: A claim is no stronger than the grounds that support it. When those writing about technology rely on further claims rather than on data for support, they are assuming agreement from like-minded readers rather than trying to reach those who are more skeptical. If these arguments are implicitly written for a subgroup within English Studies that is already convinced of technology's import, the effect on the larger discipline may be one of further distancing and isolating issues of technology—even in mainstream publications.

How Are Claims Warranted?

This section describes the results of our analysis of the warrants used to justify claims in the 10 sample arguments. As in the previous section on data, explanations of how the Toulmin model was adapted for this study are included.

The Nature of Warrants

In Toulmin's (1984) model, all claims are warranted by some kind of logical connectives; otherwise, readers would see no necessary relation between claims and data, and the argument would simply unravel. This necessary function is reflected in the question used to determine warrants in each case: What do readers have to believe to accept the claim based on the data presented?

It became clear during the course of the analysis that the sample arguments used two strikingly different types of warrants: warrants that work as direct logical links between data and claims, which we have labeled *logical connections*, and those that work at the level of ideology, the it-goes-without-saying assumptions often embedded within claims. This latter type of warrant, which we call an *ideological warrant*, draws upon values held by the audience.[7] For instance, returning to the earlier example (see Figure 7.4), it can be seen that the warrant is the necessary logical connection validating the move from data to claim. As in this case, logical connections often involve matters of procedure (e.g., the sample is representative, the analysis valid) or matters of authority (e.g., sources cited are reputable). [8]

However, the success of this argument also depends on readers believing at least two other assumptions implied in both the data and claim: that technology can alter discursive behavior and that more student revision is a desired outcome. Thus, Figure 7.6 gives a more complete representation of the workings of this claim—one that acknowledges the presence of multiple warrants of both types.

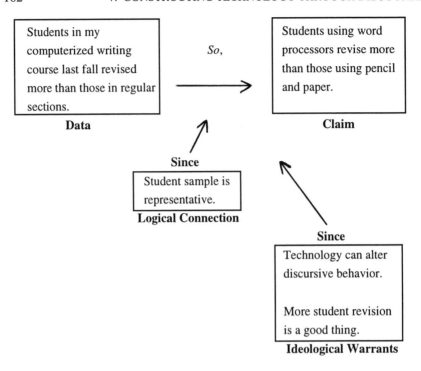

FIG. 7.6. Toulmin diagram of claim about technology.

Ideological warrants are often highly charged value statements that reflect the moral and political judgments that undergird the profession's discourse and practices. Because of this, distinguishing between logical connections and ideological warrants affords a clearer picture of how technology is being taken up and constructed   within English Studies.

Types and Amounts of Warrants

Although we established warrants for all 50 of the sample claims, not all of these warrants were about technology. We found a total of 64 warrants about technology, distributed unequally among the articles. The number of warrants in a single article ranged from a low of 3 in Hawisher and Selfe (1991) to a high of 13 in Lanham (1993), with a mean of 6.4 warrants per argument. Because five claims from each article were examined, these figures indicate that some claims contained no warrants about technology while others relied on multiple warrants. Specifically, 16% had no warrants about technology, 56% had one warrant, 22% had two warrants, and 6% had more than two.

In our analysis, we identified 15 different views of technology operating as warrants in these arguments as illustrated in Figure 7.7 below.

IDEOLOGICAL WARRANTS	Number of authors who use warrant
Technology is an agent.	9 (17)
Technology develops along a revolutionarymodel.	4 (7)
Computer technology is unique.	4 (6)
Communication technologies are historically analogous.	4 (5)
Technology and humanistic studies are distinct enterprises.	3 (4)
Technology is self-determining.	3 (3)
Technology is harmful.	2 (6)
Technology is important.	2 (5)
Technology has positive and negative consequences/uses.	2 (2)
New technology needs a new rhetoric.	2 (2)
Technology is all the same.	1 (2)
New technology is inherently superior.	1 (2)
Technology is unresponsive.	1 (1)
Technology is free-standing.	1 (1)
Technology is culturally-embedded.	1 (1)

FIG. 7.7 Ideological warrants in arguments about technology. Numbers in parentheses indicate how many times each warrant appears in the sample.

As this figure indicates, virtually all the authors we studied drew on the assumption that *technology is an agent*. This warrant is used more often than any other, occurring a total of 17 times in these arguments. A significant number of these authors also evoked the closely-related pair of warrants that *technology develops along a revolutionary model* and that *computer technology is unique*. These three warrants represent technology as all-powerful, as do the warrants that *technology is self-determining* and *technology is harmful*. Nevertheless, just under half of the authors also assumed that *communication technologies are historically analogous*, a representation of technology as transparent. In fact, warrants often function in concert even when they appear to be incompatible (see chapter 3, this volume, for discussion of the myths of all-powerful and transparent technology). The warrant that *technology and humanistic studies are distinct enterprises* was also prevalent, appearing in one-third of these arguments. Other warrants that we identified but that occurred less often included *technology is important, technology has positive and negative consequences/uses, new technology requires a new rhetoric, all technology is the same, new technology is inherently superior, technology is unresponsive, technology is free-standing,* and *technology is culturally-embedded.* A thorough discussion of the most frequently used warrants is found in the final section.

How Are Arguments About Technology Constructed?

This section presents a detailed account of three arguments about technology as represented in the claimgrids found in Appendix B. These three arguments, by Frank Boyle (1993), Gail Hawisher and Charles Moran (1993), and Richard Lanham (1993), provide a cross-section of the diverse arguments in our sample, both in their attitudes toward technology and in their methods of reasoning. Boyle's straightforward argument against the use of technology in higher education provides a clear example of both our analytical method and of how to read a claimgrid. Following are discussions of Hawisher and Moran, and then Lanham both of these articles argue positively for technology, but they ground their arguments in strikingly different ways.

Boyle's (1993) major claim in "IBM, Talking Heads, and Our Classrooms" is "information technology is making us stupid" (p. 19). Boyle supports this thesis by offering an extended narrative of a presentation on computers and education that he attended at IBM (p. 19). The tight, top-down structure of Boyle's argument results from the fact that the other four claims (which, in this case, include all main claims from the article) directly support the thesis.

Boyle (1993) begins his argument with a parallel between the Moderns satirized in Swift's *A Tale of a Tub* and present-day educators, both of whom confuse knowledge, "which is always hard won, with information, which is, and was, easily collected by, if you will, the compact disk full" (p. 18). He uses this parallel to lead into his thesis in the second paragraph. Two logical connections are at work here. First, readers must be willing to believe that real people can be analogous to literary characters. Second, if the claim that technology makes us stupid is to be supported logically by the supporting claim that we confuse knowledge with information, then it follows that readers must equate such confusion with stupidity. In other words, these are the assumptions that Boyle is counting on readers to hold; if readers do not accept them, they will not accept his major claim.

This first step of Boyle's argument is represented in the top portion of the claimgrid, drawn from Appendix B, printed below.

Claim	Grounded by...		Warranted by...	
	Supporting claim	Data	Logical connection	Ideological warrant
1. INFORMATION TECHNOLOGIES ARE MAKING US STUPID.	Like Swift's modems, we confuse knowledge with information.		Real people can be analogous to literary characters	•We don't want to be stupid
		Narrative: "Talking heads" are studpid; i.e., illogical, have faulty theory, are poor teachers etc.	Confusing knowledge with information = stupidity. Narrative is typical and representative.	•Technology is harmful: it can alter intelligence.
	CLAIM 2 CLAIM 3 CLAIM 4 CLAIM 5		We are analogous to talking heads: technology made talking heads stupid and so will make us stupid.	

FIG. 7.8. Claimgrid for Boyle.

Boyle's thesis appears as the first major claim on the claimgrid (on all grids, theses are found in capital letters), indicating that it is the first major claim to appear in the article.[9] Scanning across the grid, readers notice that Boyle includes no data for this particular supporting claim. The fourth column lists the logical connections that links Swift to the large claim that technology makes us stupid.

Having presented his thesis, Boyle begins a narrative that recounts his visit to IBM where corporate representatives, who refer to themselves as "talking heads" because they speak from behind "the metal, glass, and projected light of their wondrous machines" (p. 20), discuss technology and higher education. For Boyle, this image becomes the quintessential symbol of the dehumanization wrought by information technologies, and his narrative emphasizes the talking heads' fuzzy thinking, preference for machines over people, and oversimplification of human nature. Readers are likely to find this narrative compelling if they accept it as typical (i.e., if they believe that most people who deal with computers have these qualities). To the extent that readers do, a second assumption becomes operative: These qualities of fuzzy thinking and oversimplification are somehow carried by the technology itself, so that others who use it (e.g., teachers and students) will adopt such qualities. As Figure 7.8 shows, this narrative works directly in support of the thesis rather than in a more limited role as support for a sub-claim, and it is linked to the thesis by the two logical connections listed directly to its right.

Finally, because Boyle's article is almost wholly comprised of this extended narrative illustrating the stupidity of talking heads and their technology, all succeeding claims directly support his first, and primary, claim. Thus, the last "layer" on the claimgrid under Claim 1 consists of the other major claims in the article. It is important to note that when other numbered claims are listed as support, all their data and warrants are also at work in service of that particular claim. Literally, then, all the data and warrants shown on the claimgrid for Boyle could appear in the columns for Claim 1. However, to increase the grid's clarity, we have listed data and warrants only once.

The final column on the claimgrid in Figure 7.8 lists the ideological warrants—those unarticulated assumptions embedded within claims or data—at work in Boyle's argument. Unlike the logical connections, ideological warrants have not been aligned on the grid with particular supporting claims or data. Rather they can be thought of as "inhabiting" the entire line of reasoning. For instance, anyone reading Boyle's thesis "information technologies are making us stupid" realizes that technology is being condemned because his readers obviously do not want to be stupid. Boyle does not need to explicitly state the final logical leg in his argument because he can count on readers to supply the conclusion on their own: Those who do not want to be stupid must be wary of technology. The second ideological warrant is embedded in the very language of Boyle's thesis: There, technology is represented as a maker. It has the power to create, to shape human lives, but in this case it is a negative power—the power to make its users dumb.

Boyle's second major claim—that information machines mislead educators and students into thinking they can learn and teach without fatigue—arises from a section of his narrative where he gives three examples of talking heads performing a kind of magic: education without work.[10] In the first example, a computer representative demonstrates revision on a word processor, "cleanly" deleting troublesome words and making corrections. "What he had done," Boyle comments, "was reduce an important lesson to a before and after advertisement" (p. 22). Similarly, the other two examples show a talking head teaching algebra, first, by plugging in numbers for the computer to calculate and, second, by showing an "inane" video of two fraternity brothers determining the most efficient spot for the paint can in a room they were painting. In both cases, the focus of the talking head's example is on immediate results and fun.

Again, the power of these examples, as Boyle uses them, depends on the extent to which readers see them as representative of the way computers are used in classrooms; seeing examples as representative is the primary logical connection in this line of argument. Also important, however, is Boyle's use of computers, films, and TV interchangeably: If readers are unwilling to group all of these technologies together, they may balk at accepting his general claim about "information machines" (p. 23), given the specifics of his examples. One of the key ideological warrants of Boyle's article—that *technology is harmful*—returns here: Technology tells "seductive lies" (p. 23), and it impedes true learning, which is, by definition, laborious for both teachers and students. The other ideological warrant—that *technology and humanities are distinct enterprises*—comes into play with the second claim and then becomes a dominant theme of the article. Boyle notes that the presenter is a mathematician, and therefore "might be forgiven for failing to understand that those old-fashioned lines are graphical representations of the editorial thought process" (p. 22). A second presenter is also a "mathematician/talking head" (p. 23). Computer specialists are conflated with mathematicians and presented as the "other," people with methods and values very different from Boyle's and (presumably) from his readers'.

This implicit warrant (that technology and humanities are distinct) becomes an explicit claim in the next section. One talking head tries to illustrate how technology can help students address "the big questions" (p. 23). These take the form of multiple choice questions about *Hamlet* which students can answer on keypads at their desks; their answers will be instantly graphed on a screen only the professor sees. Such a "meddlesome presence," Boyle conjectures, might prompt students to

> slay us with the words Hamlet speaks as he stands over the body of Polonius: "I took thee for thy better?" Our better, here, is not the machine itself but Hamlet's own binary question—to be or not to be—reduced to the binary code—1 or 0—of the machine. (p. 23)

Boyle's claim here—that teachers using computers become dupes for whom "the profound questions of the human condition are reduced to the inane certainties of the mathematical machines" (p. 23)—seems so powerful exactly because the logical connections are so easily accepted. Indeed, readers have hardly begun the example before they are groaning at the inanity of playing Hamlet on the computer—and of finding themselves cast in the role of Polonius. By pitting one of the quintessential humanities texts against a reductionist vision of computer teaching, Boyle again evokes the ideological warrant that *technology and humanistic studies are distinct enterprises.*

By the fourth major claim in Boyle's article, most of the argumentative and ideological work has been done. Continuing his discussion of the fraternity painting video, Boyle claims that canned lessons (i.e., those on film or TV or computers) cheat students out of a real education, which, of course, registers as a negative outcome with most readers. The move from film to computers is, once again, predicated on grouping these technologies together; this move, in turn, connects readers' likely negative associations of television and video with computers. Interestingly, this example also echoes Plato's condemnation of technology: here, computers—like writing itself in the Platonic argument— cannot answer questions (see chapter 1, this volume).

The logical connection that "all technology is the same" becomes a final, explicit claim. The lesson of IBM's talking heads, Boyle asserts, is that "little distinction should be made between television and computer technologies: as television becomes 'interactive' and computers become 'mixed-media,' the messages of these media converge as well" (p. 25). An analogy between students in computer classrooms and children watching "Sesame Street" yokes the negative influence of television to computers.

The next two examples of arguments about technology—by Hawisher and Moran (1993) and by Lanham (1993)—illustrate the range of arguments about technology within English Studies. Boyle argues against technology, whereas Hawisher; and Moran, in their 1993 *College English* article "Electronic Mail and the Writing Instructor," believe that bringing technology into composition studies and the writing classroom is a good thing: it not only makes the discipline more responsive to the "outside" world, but also creates important opportunities for instructors to enact a collaborative, social pedagogy. The authors develop their thesis that e-mail is a "proper subject for study in the field of composition theory" (p. 629) in a carefully substantiated argument. Hawisher and Moran then outline what the inclusion of e-mail would mean for composition, theoretically and pedagogically. First, it would involve developing a new rhetoric of e-mail because this new medium is fundamentally different from paper mail, "as different from the print-letter as the horseless carriage is from the horse-and-buggy" (p. 629). Additionally, they claim that an e-mail pedagogy would be "inevitably collaborative."

Hawisher and Moran's argument is extremely well grounded. The five main claims are grounded with 16 supporting claims. For instance, the claim of e-mail's fundamental distinction from its paper counterpart is supported by six sub-claims of differences in "grammar," form, language, audience accommodation, response time, and social relations. These 16 supporting claims are, in turn, substantiated with 19 pieces of data—the largest amount of any of the ten arguments and double the average—drawn from five different categories (the greatest variety of all the articles): analysis, citations, numerical data, examples, and analogy. Several theories of technology warrant Hawisher and Moran's claims, most notably a cluster invoking the assumption that technology is all-powerful. Their warning that "we cannot afford to ignore this medium" (628) suggests a view of *technology as self-determining*, as a force moving under its own power. Additionally, their strict separation between paper and e-mail presupposes that these two technologies are inherently different and that *technology develops along a revolutionary model*. Finally, their claim that the introduction of e-mail necessarily changes pedagogy depends upon an assumption that *technology is an agent*, that *it*, rather than teachers and students, determines the nature of classroom practice. However, it is important to note that Hawisher and Moran do not draw on ideological warrants often, using only four about technology (the second lowest number in the survey). Their argument is driven primarily by the data presented rather than on the previously-formed ideas readers bring to it.

Lanham (1993) also has a positive attitude toward technology and, in fact, relies on many of the same underlying theories of technology as Hawisher and Moran. In contrast to Hawisher and Moran's cautiously optimistic argument, however, Lanham's book chapter entitled "The Electronic Word: Literary Study and the Digital Revolution" (1993; previously published as Lanham, 1989) represents discourse about technology at its most celebratory. This enthusiasm becomes apparent when Lanham lays out the electronic possibilities for the "verbal creative spirit":

> When inspiration lags...I can reformat a text to make it easier to read, or, using a dozen transformations, make it harder, or just different to read. I can literally color my colors of rhetoric. I can heal the long hiatus of silent reading and make the text read itself aloud... I can embolden my own special key words and places. I can reformat prose into poetry. I can illuminate my manuscript in ways that would make a medieval scribe weep with envy (p. 5).

Lanham's thesis, or major claim, is that "sooner or later, such electronic 'texts' will redefine the writing, reading, and professing of literature" (p. 3). In the remaining major claims, Lanham directly supports this thesis, predicting key areas within English Studies that will be effected by computer technology: (a) the relationship between literature and the others arts; (b) issues of intellectual property, including the publishing industry and the tenure system built upon it; and (c) poetics, particularly the traditional ideal of stylistic transparency.

Readers can sense some of the grandness of Lanham's vision from the relatively abstract level of the argument. The first five major claims are grounded primarily with supporting claims; Lanham uses 28—more than double the average for this group of articles. For instance, in discussing the new rhetoric of the arts necessitated by digitization, Lanham offers five supporting claims. Some of these detail changes that have already occurred as in the digital transformation of musical composition, notation, and performance; some, however, are more speculative such as the assertion that "the norms of electronic art will be so volatile that the volatility of a nonexclusive matrix will be the only norm" (16). In support of his five major claims, Lanham uses only eight pieces of data—or roughly one and a half pieces per major claim. He also uses the second fewest types of data, relying, with the exception of one analogy and one citation, entirely on example.

Lanham's hyperbolic discourse is further evidenced by the high number of ideological warrants about technology operating in his argument—more than in any other article and double the average number. His reliance on the revolutionary model of technology is made explicit in the chapter's title, and the extent to which technology becomes *the* agent in his technological world view is illustrated in his claim that digitization "forces on us" a new rhetoric of the arts (p. 4). Furthermore, in attempting to mobilize his readers, Lanham reproduces a conventional opposition between "the literary world," which has been sheltered from the computer revolution, and the outside, more technologically savvy world (p. 3). This move invokes the ideological warrant that *technology and humanistic studies are distinct enterprises.* To say that Lanham's argument is driven chiefly by thee ideological warrants is *not* to say that it is unconvincing; on the contrary, Lanham's argument may be compelling precisely because these technological myths are so deeply embedded in readers' habitual patterns of thought.

The next section discusses in some detail how the most common ideological warrants operate in this sample of articles. The conclusion then examines how these particular ideological warrants impede the kind of inquiry called for in chapter 2 (this volume).

What Views of Technology Operate in These Arguments?

Here we examine in detail two clusters of ideological warrants that we found in recent discourse about technology within English Studies. The first cluster, *technology as agent,* includes that warrant, as well as the related ones that *technology is self-determining, technology is free-standing,* and *technology is harmful.* The second cluster has to do with technology in history, and includes three ideological warrants: *technology develops along a revolutionary model, computer technology is unique,* and *communication technologies are historically analogous.*

Technology as Agent

This warrant posits that technology itself can create change, transform culture, or shape thinking. As Figure 7.7 indicates, the view of *technology as an agent* is both widespread, used by 9 out of 10 authors we studied, and frequent, occurring over twice as often as any other warrant. Technology is credited, for instance, with transforming discursive behavior, social relations, the function of the discipline of English, or even patterns of human thought. Thus, Cooper and Selfe (1991) argue that computer conferences "encourage participants to treat one another as peers, people whose similar interests outweigh power or status differences" (p. 852). Lanham (1993) writes that "electronic 'texts' will redefine the writing, reading, and professing of literature" (p. 3). And Slatin (1990) argues that "hypertext [is] a new medium for thought and expression" (p. 870). All these authors posit technology as the driving force behind the changes they discuss.

In addition, half of the authors draw on warrants closely related to the view of technology as agent: *technology is self-determining, technology is free-standing*, and *technology is harmful*. The first of these hinges on the idea that technology determines its own uses and effects. This view can be seen at work in Bernhardt's (1993) warning that writing teachers "may not see as desirable all of these developments in the ways text is structured, but they appear to be inevitable. We need first to understand the directions that computers are taking written language" (p. 152). In this account of things, teachers seem almost helpless to influence the course of computer technology. The technology rolls merrily—and inevitably—along under its own power, possibly leaving the English teacher in a pose of stoic resignation.

Cooper and Selfe (1990) use the second of these related warrants, *technology is free-standing*, to argue that "computer networks may provide . . . electronic and cultural 'lacunae' in which both teachers and students can learn to listen to multiple voices, and thus, in Carol Gilligan's words, learn the importance of 'different truths' (p. 858). Cooper and Selfe also suggest that because computers exist on the "intellectual margins" (p. 858), they stand outside existing power relations, unwritten by the practices and values of the culture in which they are developed and used. Inherently revolutionary and liberatory, computers offer a free zone in which people, especially those silenced by traditional discourse forums, can think and write.

Finally, the warrant that *technology is harmful* simply reverses the assumption of technology as an agent, where agency is taken to mean a capability for positive action. It grants technology fully as much power, but power only to do ill; Boyle's (1993) argument that technology can decrease intelligence is an example. Similarly, Sudol (1991) sees word processing "gone amok" (p. 924), weakening students' writing processes by bringing with it the perils of overproduction, flabby style, and "a diminution of meaning and a trivialization of content" (p. 924). In these two arguments, technology is characterized as a malevolent force—tempting but deceitful. Thus, Sudol complains that technology allows us to bypass "the arduous steps of mechanical composing" (920) and "encourages us to postpone hard decisions" (p. 924); Boyle writes of technology's "seductive lies" and "insidious sleight of hand" (p. 23).

Taken together, these four warrants (i.e., *technology as agent, technology is self-determining, technology is free-standing, technology is harmful*) reflect pervasive cultural assumptions that technology is all-powerful. In many cases, people—teachers and students—are absent as agents from these accounts; they become passive consumers of technology or victims of its relentless forward march. And it is not hard to understand where this idea comes from. Given the present division of labor, technology, for many humanists, is something that happens to them. That is, these warrants of technology's unlimited power gain assent because they correspond in some measure to readers' perception of the way the world works. But these warrants only give a partial picture: that is, a realistic acknowledgment that, at present, most humanists do not create technology is very different from the assumption that technology creates itself. As discussed elsewhere (see chapters 2 and 8, this volume), *people* design, develop, and implement technology; the view of technology as all-powerful hides this fact and so prevents users from formulating crucial questions about what technology is created, by whom, and for what purposes. Acknowledging this human agency, then, is a necessary first step for literacy scholars to make if they would claim a role in shaping and critiquing technology.

Paradoxically, this notion of technology as all-powerful is based on a strangely attenuated definition of technology that represents it as nothing more than, say, the terminals that appear in the library, on the desk, or in the classroom. Of the 10 arguments in the sample, only Hawisher and Selfe's recognizes that technology, like all cultural artifacts, is deeply embedded in the specific educational, political, social contexts in which it is developed and used. Thus, Hawisher and Selfe argue that bringing computers into the writing classroom may "simply [reinforce] those traditional notions of education that permeate our culture at its most basic level: Teachers talk, students listen; teachers' contributions are privileged; students respond in predictable, teacher-pleasing ways" (p. 55). Technology both writes and is written by the larger culture surrounding it. This more accurate representation of computer technology as a complex system of people, hardware and software, institutions, and cultural practices makes the view that technological tools are the sole agents of cultural change untenable (see chapter 8, this volume).

Technology in History

Like the message about technology's power as an agent, theories of technology in history presented in these articles are fraught with tension. This tension is, perhaps, not surprising, given the problematic nature of standard analyses of history and technology's role in it (see chapter 8, this volume). Three of the warrants we identified offer accounts of how technology moves in history: *technology develops along a revolutionary model, computer technology is unique*, and *communication technologies are historically analogous*. All three warrants are used in just under half of the articles analyzed, and they appear more often than any others except the assumption that *technology is an agent*.

The first of these theories—*technology develops along a revolutionary model*—posits a relatively sudden and absolute rupture between successive writing technologies, between handwritten manuscripts and print, or, as in the current case, between print and computer technologies. The new technology is seen as something new and different (and usually better) that will replace the old, outdated way of writing as well as change the practices and institutions connected with it.   Lanham, for example, foresees the unification of the academic disciplines of the arts, including English, because the "common digital denominator of the arts and letters" compels a new rhetoric (p. 4). Similarly, he argues that in a world of computerized word and image, copyright law will need to be rewritten *in toto*. He implies that new electronic forms of writing will require a whole new language: computers provide for the "elec-tronic display of what, until a new word is invented, we must call 'text'" (p. 3).

The second historical warrant—*computer technology is unique*—follows directly from this revolutionary model. If technological advances are truly revolutionary, if they wipe away all traces of the existing technology, then it is reasonable to assume that the new technology will be something completely different.   What is at stake for the authors who employ this warrant is the computer's presumed ability to remake the relationships among reader, writer, and text. Thus, both Lanham and Slatin praise electronic text as a medium in which the reader can challenge the author—can, in fact, *become* the author. Similarly, Cooper and Selfe (1990) explicitly draw on this warrant in their claim that the "unique" characteristics of computer conferences allow students to interact in productive ways that are blocked by traditional educational struc-tures.   These authors describe an electronic forum in which students can question and experimentally rewrite the dominant discourses of the university, the teacher, and the assigned texts.

It would be hard to overestimate the power of this revolutionary model in arguments about technology.   The revolutionary model matches, at least partially, readers' sense that the arrival of the computer has brought significant, very visible changes in their own routines of daily life. Although people still pore over manuscripts and books at work, read magazines while waiting in the dentist's office, write letters and grocery lists, they also send email, prepare camera-ready copy of book manuscripts, and watch their kindergartners learn to read on computers. The novelty of the latter activities may overshadow the ubiquity of the former.

The power of these two historical warrants also lies in the promise of progress attached to the idea of revolution and voiced in the enthusiasm, even zeal, with which some of the authors write. This is particularly true in the case of a technological revolution: There is a certain Enlightenment spirit alluded to here, a sense that society is on the brink of a new era of human history. Readers are drawn to the vision of new language, new theory, new "texts," new roles for writer and reader, new disciplinary boundaries—and the implied suggestion that many old problems will go away. The revolution offers, finally, to put power into readers' hands and the hands of their students.

The problems with this widely-accepted historical account of technology as revolutionary (and, thus, of computer technology as unique) are explored in more detail in chapter 8 (this volume). What is particularly interesting here is the tension produced when these assumptions are brought together with a third historical warrant—*communication technologies are historically analogous.* Writers employ this theory of technology to warrant often speculative claims about computers by drawing on readers' experiences with print and their knowledge of its development. For instance, Hawisher and Moran back their claim that compositionists look "through" rather than "at" e-mail by pointing to earlier claims that paper mail was seen as transparent. The pinnacle of historical analogy appears in Bolter's book which opens with a passage from Victor Hugo's novel *Notre-Dame de Paris, 1482.* In this scene, a priest glances from a printed book on his table to a view of Notre Dame cathedral outside his window. "'Alas!' he said, 'This will destroy that'"(p. 1). Bolter comments, "Today we are living in the late age of print. The evidence of senescence, if not senility, is all around us. And as we look up from our computer keyboard to the books on our shelves, we must ask ourselves whether 'this will destroy that'" (p. 2). Strongly implied here is the notion that history is cyclical, that the history of technology repeats itself.

Difficulties arise when these two theories of technology (i.e., as revolutionary and unique and as historically analogous) are used together in a single argument or, even more problematically, to warrant a single claim. The two theories are not inherently contradictory. It seems legitimate logically, if not historically, to hold to a revolutionary model and still claim that each successive writing technology is analogous to its predecessors. The result is a cyclical view of history where each period parallels earlier ones in producing a wholly new technology: Electronic text replaces print just as print replaced handwritten manuscripts and alphabets replaced oral traditions. Although this combination of revolutionary model and historical analogy makes sense at this general level, it becomes logically inconsistent to warrant claims about technological revolution with the kind of elaborate, detailed historical analogies that appear in some of these articles (e.g., Bolter's point by point comparison of print and electronic text).

Bolter grounds his thesis—that computer technology is replacing the printed book—by stressing the parallels between today and Gutenberg's time. In addition to the passage from Hugo discussed earlier, Bolter describes both the introduction of print and the introduction of electronic text as periods in which the potential of the new medium is not fully understood. He notes how early printers attempted to reproduce the "look" of manuscripts through their use of the ligatures and abbreviations, letter strokes, and page layouts of fine manuscripts. "It took a few generations for printers to realize," says Bolter, "that their new technology made possible a different writing space, that the page could be more readable with thinner letters, fewer abbreviations, and less ink" (p. 3). Similarly, Bolter claims, the introduction of electronic writing is characterized primarily by "using word processors and electronic photocomposition to improve the production of printed books and typed documents" (p. 3). This claim is followed by several pages of examples of computer "incunabula" such as electronic bulletin boards, databases, and mail—all "attempts to transfer previous techniques of writing into an electronic idiom" (p. 6). Bolter predicts that full realization of the computer's radical potential may take many years, "as it did with Gutenberg's invention" (p. 3). And in answer to complaints that computers will never replace books because they are physically inconvenient, Bolter notes that "the great advantage of the first printed books was *not* that you could read them in bed. Gutenberg might well have been appalled at the thought of someone taking his beautiful folio-sized Bible to bed" (p. 4).

The notion here is a kind of technological inevitability: If print texts, despite whatever disadvantages they had, replaced handwritten manuscripts, then computers will eventually replace print. Thus, Bolter relies heavily on the historical analogy to support his claim that electronic technology is revolutionary. Indeed, he occasionally seems pressed to make history fit his equation as when he writes that "the earliest incunabula are already examples of a perfected technique; there remains little evidence from the period of experimentation that *must* have preceded the production of these books" (p. 3; italics added). Bolter must posit such a period in order to have his historical analogy hold.

But this historical analogy, which seems so necessary for the revolutionary argument, undercuts that argument at the same time, for it is difficult to reconcile claims that computer technology is something radically new with the insistence that the introduction of electronic text is proceeding exactly like the introduction of print. These difficulties are compounded by Bolter's claim, in this same section of his argument, that "like the specializations on outer branches of an evolutionary tree, the printed book is an extreme form of writing, not the norm" (p. 4). If this is an accurate assessment, if print is indeed an evolutionary anomaly, it is unclear why its development should set the pattern for the more "normal" electronic text. At this point, the historical analogy has broken down. And in the same paragraph, even the assumption that electronic writing is unique starts to break down, in Bolter's claim that it contains elements from earlier writing technologies: "it is mechanical and precise like printing, organic and evolutionary like handwriting, visually eclectic like hieroglyphics and picture writing" (p. 4). (See chapter 8, this volume, for an analysis of technological "predecessors" of computers.)

Like Bolter, Lanham also warrants his thesis that "electronic 'texts' will redefine the writing, reading, and professing of literature" (p. 3) with assumptions that *technology is revolutionary/unique* and that *communication technologies are historically analogous*. Although Lanham relies on historical analogy to a lesser extent   he applies it very specifically, claiming that "electronic 'textbooks' are democratizing education in all the arts in the same way that the invention of printing reinforced the spread of Protestantism" (p. 10). Again, it is hard to reconcile the two views of technology. On the one hand, Lanham presents a technology so revolutionary that it necessitates the restructuring of all the arts and letters; on the other hand, he presents a technology so similar to print that each technology's behavior can be mapped onto the other's.

The tension between these three historical warrants extends deep, for it involves the simultaneous operation of both large categories of cultural myths about technology discussed in detail in chapter 2 (this volume)—the assumptions that technology is transparent and that it is all-powerful. Historical analogies are, at base, a version of technological transparency (writing is writing is writing or, more specifically, handwriting is print is electronic writing), whereas the views of technology as revolutionary or unique are instances of the all-powerful myth. Thus, to use all three historical warrants in support of an argument is to simultaneously claim that technology is nothing and everything—that it does not matter and that it is the only thing that does matter.

CONCLUSION

Interestingly, all four of the authors who invoke the historical analogy (i.e., Bolter, Hawisher and Moran, Lanham, and Slatin) also make the argument that technology is revolutionary or unique. This combination of arguments, problematic as it might be, seems to perform a vital role in building assent for claims about technology within this particular community of English scholars.

Historical analogy is used to legitimize the revolution argument for readers within English Studies. Claims about a computer revolution are, by necessity at this point, largely speculative. With the future unpredictable, the best source of evidence about the nature, scope, and consequences of this revolution would seem to be the past. By creating parallels between the introduction of print and the introduction of electronic text, these authors concretize readers' sense of just how revolutionary—and generally beneficial—computers can be. This is especially true for an audience of humanists who may define themselves via the print book and who, therefore, carry a strong cultural assumption that the switch from handwritten manuscripts to print revolutionized Western culture.

But there is another argument that is supported through the coupling of the revolutionary argument with historical analogies. These authors also want to argue—justifiably, we would suggest—for the legitimate place of technology within the humanities. Most of these authors want to counter the pervasive assumptions of many humanists that technology is inconsequential, and that, in any case, technology is certainly not something humanists "do." As suggested in chapter 2 (this volume), the questions raised by contemporary literacy technologies will—indeed, have—called disciplinary divisions of labor into question. It may be that the overzealousness, or even shrillness, of arguments within English Studies is a natural result of the legitimate attempt to wake readers to the opportunities at hand. This is clearly illustrated in Lanham's concluding remarks:

although [the electronic word] brings compulsions with it, I hope we will think of it less as a technological *vis a tergo* driving us where we don't want to go than as an opportunity to go where we have never been, and do things no one has done before. . . The basic implications of electronic technology may be inevitable but what we make of them certainly is not (p. 26).

Bolter's assertion that we are living in "the late age of print" in which printed materials will soon be replaced, and Slatin's argument that hypertext will remake texts and text processing operate in a similar way. The assumption that technology is revolutionary, then, not only warrants particular claims made by these authors; it warrants the entire enterprise of considering technology within the province of the humanities.

One of the goals, then, of much of the discourse in this sample is to generate enthusiasm for this project of examining technology within the humanities. Paradoxically, however, even as they attempt to so, most of these authors posit only a very limited space for human agency within this enterprise. The space posited is directly tied to the ideological assumptions about technology operating in these pieces. For example, if technology is a self-determining agent, then the only available response is not action as much as reaction. Scholars are free to rebuild English Studies, Lanham seems to say, but only within the framework prescribed by a self-determining technology. If computers constitute a revolution (whose scope and speed are left unspecified), then humanists are invited to "get on board" or stand back while technology roars past them. And if history is a cycle, in which successive technologies take their turn at "remaking" Western culture, then scholarly inquiry about technology becomes rather pointless.

As long as technological theory and practice are guided, even determined, by a discourse in which technology is an agent and history is a cycle of technological revolutions, then the role of scholars and teachers, especially those in the humanities, will be minimal. Granted it may be difficult, given the present division of labor, to envision a world in which humanists take an active role in designing and implementing technology. Those attempting to address questions of technology and literacy within Technology Studies should not underestimate the power of language in shaping visions of what technology is, as well as what our response to it can be. Therefore, a remaking of the language of technology will be a difficult but critical part of the enterprise of Technology Studies.

FOOTNOTES

[1]When the data are broken down by journal, they show that although the number of articles published in *CCC* has declined from 19 to 4, the number in *CE* has risen from 3 to 6. However, given the fact that *CE* publishes 8 issues each year with an average of 4 articles per issue, this increase over 5 years is barely significant — from 1.9 to 3.8% of all articles. Clearly, issues of technology have been—and remain—marginal in these two widely-circulated journals.

[2]We discounted the two "Staffroom Interchanges" located in this search on the basis that they represent a separate genre from the longer, usually more formal and research-based arguments we examined.

[3]Toulmin's method is rather nonideological itself, but we found that our extensions of the notion of *warrant* were useful in uncovering ideological assumptions.

[4]To provide for the possibility that we might not agree on the identification of the first five major claims, we created a large enough pool of independently identified claims — we each began with eight — so that if we did not match the first five, we would have extra claims to work with. However, because our claim identification was so consistent, we rarely had to use this pool, and we never had to go beyond our eight independently identified claims in order to agree.

[5]We need to distinguish between what makes a claim logically valid and what makes it true. In our example from Figure 4, the data "students in my computerized writing course last fall did more revision than those in regular sections" is connected to the claim "students using word processors revise more than those using pencil and paper" by the warrant that the student sample is representative. Our identification of this statement as the warrant signifies only that it serves as the logical link between data and claim, not that the warrant or the claim is true.

[6]To determine these totals, we counted the number of times a type of data appeared on the claimgrid. Particularly in the case of citations, these numbers do not always correspond exactly to the total number of citations in an article. When "citation" appears on the grid, a single reference appears in the article; when the plural "citations" appears, two or more citations were used in support of a single claim.

[7]Ideological warrants can be seen as both prior to and resulting from an argument. That is, they are assumptions that readers bring with them to an argument; however, by evoking these assumptions in the argument, writers help to keep the warrants alive and in play. Writers make use of the warrants, and in the process of using them, reproduce them.

[8]However, it is important to understand that the distinction between logical connections and ideological warrants ultimately rests on their *function* in the argument and not their relative level of abstraction. A logical connection is any assumption that forms the necessary logical link between data and claim. We found a number of cases in which, because of the particular structure of the argument, higher level assumptions function as logical connections. For instance, when Bolter grounds his claim that computer technology is replacing the printed book by presenting evidence that print replaced handwritten manuscripts, readers must assume the logical connection that communication technologies are historically analogous if they are to accept his argument.

[9]We have made every attempt to use the language of the author on the claimgrids; nevertheless, we want to remind readers that in the interests of clarity and conciseness, claims are not quoted exactly from the article but have, instead, been abstracted from it. Information is presented on the grid in the order it appears in the original article or chapter. In addition, we have made a concerted effort, within the confines of the grid space, to align horizontally the supporting claims with their data and connective warrants. Thus, readers can see each logical step in the argument worked out by reading *across* the grid before moving down to the next supporting claim or piece of data. Data that appears next to white space in the "supporting claim" column works directly to ground the major claim rather than an intermediary supporting claim.

[10] Readers will find the rest of Boyle's claimgrid, as well as those for Hawisher and Moran and Lanham, in Appendix B.

PART IV

CONCLUSIONS AND FUTURE INQUIRY

8

HISTORICIZING TECHNOLOGY

It is not an exaggeration to say that technology is the central fact of 20th century literacy. Of course, it is also true that technology has always been the central, defining fact of literacy. It is technology that makes writing possible, as much for the ancient Greek with his stylus or the medieval scribe with his quill and ink as for the contemporary author with her new Powerbook computer. Literacy acts—acts of reading and writing—cannot exist prior to technology but are always and inescapably technological. To say that technology and literacy cannot be separated is not to say, of course, that we yet understand the relationship between them. After all, the questions that Socrates raises in the *Phaedrus* (Plato, 1973) about how the technology of writing will shape the human mind are questions that, after twenty-four centuries, are still open to debate. Indeed, it is the technology of writing itself that allows Derrida and Plato to continue their discussion about the nature of writing—across time, space, and culture. And we listen in on this discussion through the technology of printing, which puts fixed, more-or-less agreed upon authoritative versions of Plato and of Derrida in our hands.

This chapter historicizes current literacy technologies, in particular the computer tools, sometimes called information technologies, that are used for the production and dissemination of written text. By *historicizing* I mean the reciprocal process of placing computer literacy technologies into historical contexts and, in turn, using those historical contexts to more fully understand today's technologies. However, the process of historicizing technology is a complicated, and complicating, process—more complicated than is sometimes assumed. Therefore, this chapter is structured as an extended critique. In particular, I argue against an oversimplification of the history of literacy technologies, using the history of print (and print's relationship to computer technology) as an exemplary case.[1]

However, the goal of this chapter is to go beyond mere critique to make a series of pragmatic arguments about how history might be used in the study of literacy technologies. Specifically, I argue that historicizing technology complicates our understanding of it, and thereby provides a countermove to the cultural dominant of transparent technology (see chapter 2, this volume). Further, although historicizing technology complicates, it also opens up possibilities for a much-needed theoretical grounding for technology studies. To this end, I suggest, following Vygotsky (1966), that to study something historically is to study "phenomena in movement" (quoted in Scribner, 1985, p. 120) and that Vygotsky's historical-genetic method—that is, the historical analysis of movement or change at different systemic levels (Vygotsky, 1978; 1981a)— can be a critical tool in helping us to understand the shape of those technologies that shape our own literate practice.

THE REVOLUTION, AGAIN

It has become commonplace in both popular and scholarly literature to argue that Western culture is experiencing a "computer revolution" analogous to earlier revolutions precipitated by changes in media. Richard Lanham's (1989, 1990) descriptions of what he calls "the digital revolution," and Cooper and Selfe's (1990) call to their colleagues to use "the revolutionary potential" (p. 867) of computers are typical of much writing about computers within the field of English Studies. These revolutionary arguments often characterize changes in media—the move from writing to print, for example, or from print to computers—as having a profound impact on individual thinking as well as far-reaching social and cultural effects. As chapter 7 (this volume) argued, however, some scholars' revolutionary arguments are compromised by their confusion over the relation between old and new technologies.

The following quotes, one from George P. Landow's recent volume; on hypertext and the other from an article by Ronald Sudol in *College English,* are characteristic of historical analogies made between computers and other earlier media, particularly print:

> [Electronic text processing] promises (or threatens) to produce effects on our culture . . .just as radical as those produced by Gutenberg's movable type (Landow, 1992, p. 19).

From orality to manuscripts to print to electronics each transformation has altered the way we manipulate symbols, thus determining our construction of meaning (Sudol, 1991, p. 924).

Sudol's claim is that changes in communication media result in profound psychological changes at the level of meaning construction, whereas Landow's is that radical changes will occur at the cultural level, but both scholars are interested in revolutions precipitated by technologies. Of course, any argument about a revolution is inherently an historical argument: Revolution implies a break with the past, and the beginning of a profoundly different future. Landow and Sudol are presumably seeking to illuminate current technology by situating it historically; but in fact, these statements are less than illuminating because of problems with both historical "facts" and historical method. (Chapter 7, this volume, examines claims about technology and the beliefs that warrant those claims in some detail; this chapter is concerned specifically with arguments about the revolutionary nature of computer technology.) The following sections discuss four potential problems with the historical argument implicit in comparisons of the print revolution and the computer revolution: using historical analogy as a reasoning tool, oversimplifying the history of print, seeing technology as self-determining, and assuming that print and computers are two separate and distinct historical phenomena.

Historical Analogy

The most obvious problem with comparisons between the print revolution and the computer revolution is one of historical method; that is, the faultiness of history by analogy. In their volume *Thinking in Time: The Uses of History for Decision Makers*, Neustadt and May discuss the problem of using historical analogies to understand current situations. Neustadt and May's book was written primarily for policymakers, but their work is useful for anyone interested in how historical analysis can inform contemporary thinking and illuminate current problems. Historical analogies are seldom accurate and usually obscure as much as they clarify; that is, analogous qualities of situations are highlighted, while differences are ignored. Historical analogies can even be dangerous if they focus on salient similarities of situations and obscure critical differences. Further, historical analogies are often made for particular political or rhetorical purposes. Arguments made prior to United State's involvements both in Korea and in Vietnam—that Southeast Asia was analogous to Europe in the early 1930s—were made by those who desired a certain outcome or wanted a certain action to be taken on the part of the U.S. Reasoning about Asia in this way, and formulating policy on the basis of this reasoning, had real and powerful consequences for not only the citizens of Korea, Vietnam, and the United States, but for people around the world, as Neustadt and May illustrate. The circumstances that led to World War II, as well as the historical personage of Hitler, have remained powerful symbols in American thinking, as witnessed by the numerous analogies made between Hitler and Saddam Hussein during the Gulf War of 1991, or between Nazi genocide of the Jews and the situations in Bosnia and Rwanda in 1994.

Of course, it is often useful—in formulating foreign policy or in attempting to understand literacy tools— to look at historical precedents to gauge what might be possible, or what might be reasonable to expect, in a given situation. But drawing broad-stroked historical analogies can obfuscate while appearing to clarify. In contrast to history-by-analogy, Neustadt and May advocate what they call placement; that is, they advocate putting current concerns, decisions, or situations into historical context with the ultimate goal of "seeing time as a stream" (p. 247). Such historical placement would attempt to understand the history of political (or technological) situations not as part of repeating cycles of history, nor as a series of Hegelian historical advances, but rather to view events on their own terms, as far as this is possible, given that historians—like everyone else—view the world with certain biases. "Seeing time as a stream" underscores both the concepts of connectedness in historical developments and of perpetual change and movement in human events. Change, however, is always bounded in at least its general outlines, much as the stream is usually contained within its banks. Interestingly, the notion of time as a stream is similar to Vygotsky's conception of history as phenomena in movement, a conception that I discuss later in this chapter. First, however, the history of print is examined in some detail; the remainder of this chapter is an attempt at placing computer literacy tools into historical context.

The Story of Print

A second problem with trying to understand current literacy technologies through analogies with the print revolution is that, in fact, the advent of print was something less than a revolution. The word *advent*, of course, means arrival or coming, and has religious overtones that are probably not coincidental. The conventional story about print begins with Gutenberg, whose invention allowed texts to be reproduced (relatively cheaply) and distributed to individuals across time, space, and culture, and continued with the spread of literacy across Europe. As a result of print's durability, fixity, and multiplicity, and as a result of widespread exposure to print materials, the story goes, a rupture in both culture and thinking occurred—leading eventually to the growth of bureaucracies, the development of the scientific method, urbanization, the modern mind, and other equally monumentous results (see Kaufer & Carley, 1992, for an extended discussion of the "facts" on print).

The Printing Press

The definitive work on the printing press is, of course, Elizabeth Eisenstein's (1979) massive historical analysis, *The Printing Press as an Agent of Change.* Eisenstein's book, published in two volumes, traces the effects of print culture on the textual habits and views of intellectual communities in early modern Europe. Although it is impossible here to summarize Eisenstein's work in any detail, the book essentially examines historical accounts of the Renaissance, the Reformation, and the Scientific Revolution and argues that in each case, printing has been overlooked as an important contributing agent to these great watershed events in Western history. As an historian, Eisenstein's concern is with the rise of the "modern"; as a technologist, her view is generally a deterministic one.

Eisenstein's work is often invoked by scholars interested in contemporary computer technologies as an example of the transforming power of technology on culture broadly defined, as well as on the lives of individuals. Generally these scholars use Eisenstein as a means to establish print as a causal agent for various kinds of cultural developments, and they then argue that computer technologies constitute an analogous case. J. David Bolter, in *Writing Space* (1991), provides a typical example. Bolter claims that Eisenstein "argued convincingly that printing was a force for cultural unification during the centuries when the modern nation states were being formed" (p. 233) and that computer writing technologies will have just the opposite effect in opposing standardization, unification, and hierarchy. Other scholars, such as Landow (1992; p.19), Slatin (1990; p. 871), and Lanham (1989; p. 280) seem to draw on Eisenstein's work when they construct analogies between print and computer revolutions, although they do not cite her directly. Whether contemporary scholars argue that computer technologies are an extension of print (Bernhardt, 1993; Landow, 1992) or a reversal of it (Bolter, 1991; Lanham, 1989; Slatin, 1990), they read the history of print straightforwardly as establishing the transformative power of technology on human culture.

However, there are problems in this kind of straightforward, nonproblematized reading of what is a very complex and not always consistent historical treatment of the printing press. First, Eisenstein's work is as much about the neglect of print by historians as it is about the printing press *per se*. The book makes fascinating reading—and not only because of the vast and varied sources drawn on and the copious amounts of information about print and print culture presented. The book is also interesting because of its explicit and pointed—sometimes even empassioned—rhetorical purpose: to redress what Eisenstein saw as a critical error in underplaying the power of print. This purpose, and Eisenstein's intended audience (i.e., historians who have made this critical error, or are about to) are invoked, reiterated, and underscored on almost every page. In her desire to awaken an interest among historians in printing, Eisenstein may have deliberately overstated her case (Kaestle, 1985).[2] Eisenstein saw her task as urgent: Ignoring or downplaying print has "led to setting [historical] perspectives [about the early modern period] ever more askew" (p. xvi). And this focus on periodization is critical. As an historian, Eisenstein is committed to identifying and characterizing the uniqueness of the modern period; for her, the printing press provides a transformative event by which she can define the rise of the modern not only in politics and art, but also in science.

Essentially, the problem with invocations of Eisenstein's work in arguments about computer technology is that she is an historican, not a technologist. Consequently, she does not treat the technology of the printing press itself in any detailed way. In the preface, she states her intention of treating the "tool," rather than users of the tool; she also reiterates that, for her, *printing press* is "a shorthand way of referring to a larger cluster" (p. xv) of events and developments. Yet Eisenstein gives little delineation of what elements—social, cultural, political, material, technological—might comprise this cluster. Ostensibly, her focus is on moveable type itself, yet she also focuses on the institution of the print shop, or even the unique character and role of the printer as the site of change. Certainly, a technology—in this case the printing press—is comprised of agents and sites as well as material tools (my own definition of technology includes these; see Preface). The problem is not with Eisenstein's inclusion of these elements, but rather that she fails to define what she means by *technology*, or to delineate the features of print or the printing press. Such delineation and definition seem imperative for the success of a causal argument like the one Eisenstein wants to make. Consequently, considerably more attention is given to critiquing other historians' neglect, downplaying, or misunderstanding of the printing press than is spent establishing how, in what ways, or by what mechanisms print had the effects it did. Ultimately, Eisenstein is a technological determinist. She posits the printing press as a causal agent, then looks through it to the cultural consequences that, for her, are the birth of the modern.

Eisenstein's examination of the Renaissance in Chapter Three, "A Classical Revival Reoriented," illustrates these problems. She argues that the "preservative powers of print" (p. 181) reoriented the quattrocentro revival into a permanent Renaissance. Yet a great deal more of her attention is devoted to countering or chastising other historical sources than is spent developing how permanence of texts made the Italian Renaissance a permanent one. When Eisenstein does turn her attention to printing itself, and its relationship with the Renaissance, many of her claims (e.g., print helped early humanists develop a fixed distance from the past [p. 190] and fostered attention to originality [p. 192]) are in fact claims of psychological effects—effects that are hard to gauge through written records alone. Certainly, she does not specify the mechanisms by which printed texts would or could have such psychological effects. Finally, and most critically, the strong claim she wants to make about the power of print in transforming the 15th-century Renaissance is undermined by her earlier assertions that the first century of print (roughly 1450-1550) was a transition period in which manuscipt and printing culture are all but indistinguishable. Indeed, throughout the volume, Eisenstein insists upon disqualifying the first century of print from her analysis—a move that may be accurate and honest, given that print had few transformative effects in its first century, but one that makes it difficult to sustain the notion that print provided a radical historical rupture.

Finally, Eisenstein repeatedly sets up a dichotomy between revolutionary and evolutionary theories of historical change, and cautions of the dangers of applying an evolutionary model "to a situation that requires a revolutionary one" (p. 45). However, the revolutionary model of cultural change that Eisenstein wants to present is undermined both by some of the data that she presents and by her argumentative strategies. First, print's effects are initially not noticeable at all, and later are only gradual. This is evidenced by the fact that during the first century (1450-1550) manuscript culture remained untouched. Further, although Eisenstein acknowledges that paper, trade patterns, and other factors contributed to cultural changes, she insists that it was the printing press *per se* that was the causal agent (p. 47). After very detailed explication of an evolutionary perspective on the impact of print—a perspective she wants to counter—Eisenstein simply asserts that the alternative perspective, that the changes wrought by print were revolutionary and abrupt, is more compelling and persuasive (p. 33). In terms of detailed support, however, it is the case for evolutionary perspective that emerges as the strongest, or at least the more well-supported.

Certainly it would be hard to imagine modern science, scholarship, law, or even ordinary life in the 20th Century without the indexing, cataloguing, exact duplication of textual materials, and other intellectual and bureaucratic functions made possible by print. But a careful reading of Eisenstein—an understanding of her larger purposes as well as her technological determinism—does not unequivocally support the notion of the rise of printing as historical rupture. Similarly, such a careful reading makes the invocations of Eisenstein's "establishing" the historical rupture of print somewhat suspect. Again, as the argument of an historian to reconfigure the rise of Modernism, Eisenstein's work stands—and has stood—as a tour de force. However, her work is not an analysis of technology itself. For such an analysis of the printing press, the work of David Kaufer and Kathleen Carley (1993) is useful; Kaufer and Carley's book is drawn on heavily in the remainder of this section, as I put forth a counternarrative about print.

So what was the advent of print if not a revolution? First, despite popular folklore, print did not really arrive—it slowly evolved over a long period of time. Kaufer and Carley (1993) document print's evolution and show that although Gutenberg's[3] invention was a first step, the power of print remained in many ways dormant until the industrialization of Europe and the rise of mechanical printing, particularly the steam press. By 1814, the cylinder steam press could produce 1100 copies per hour (up from 300 copies per day with previous methods). But this did not happen until three and a half centuries after Gutenberg.

The Spread of Literacy

In the early centuries after Gutenberg, individuals' encounters with printed materials were limited. In most European countries, literacy instruction and use were initially confined to elite males. It took about 300 years (roughly from 1600 to 1900) for European countries to move from restricted literacy to mass literacy for males, with rates of female literacy increasing rapidly in the late 19th century to close to the male rate (Kaestle, 1985; Resnick & Resnick, 1977). The attainment of mass or even universal literacy in a particular country, however, did not mean that literate individuals were encountering a variety of printed texts and engaging them in sustained and critical ways—the way many would define literacy today. Estimates of literacy were often made on the basis of quite crude measures (e.g., through the ability to sign or read and recite familiar material; Kaestle, 1985).

At a cultural level, the relationship between increasing literacy—which in many cases meant increased exposure to print—and social and economic change is quite complex. Many early efforts at increasing literacy rates were begun by churches, in both North America and Europe. Lockridge (1974) concludes that, at least in Protestant churches in New England, literacy was used to maintain traditional beliefs. Later, popular and civic forces seemed to fuel at least some of the national efforts to increase literacy, leading to what Kaestle (1985) calls "the democratization of reading." But whether literacy (i.e., exposure to print) was a cause or an effect of social and economic change is a open question; possibly it was—and is—both.

Moreover, being exposed to printed materials did not seem to revolutionize individual citizens' lives. The materials that citizens encountered, and the functions that literacy served for individuals, tended to be primarily conserving ones: The mainstays of early encounters with print (in Europe) tended to be religious materials for memorization and patriotic texts, meant to foster a love of country and tradition (Resnick & Resnick, 1977). In a study of mid-19th-century Ontario, Graff (1979) concluded that the literacy may have improved the economic lots of a select few, but in general was much less important than other factors—such as ethnic group—in predicting an individual's economic success.

The Complicated Story of Print

In short, then, the revolution of print was less than revolutionary. It took several centuries for printed material to be widely and cheaply available and for most citizens to attain a minimal competency in reading such materials. Further, the content of early printed materials did not usually promote cultural change, but tended instead to conserve traditional values and habits. Not surprisingly, there is little evidence to suggest that increased literacy trends at a national level, or increased exposure to print at an individual level, led to rapid or transforming revolutionary change in people's lives.

Further, what appears at first glance to be the transforming power of print turns out to be dependent in complex ways on other technological, social, and cultural developments, including things as seemingly mundane as cheap paper and more complex social phenomena such as secularization, the rise of script literacy (Clanchy, 1979), the development of distribution systems (i.e., trans-portation and commodity-moving systems), and a psychological "trust" in written forms (Clanchy, 1979; Kaufer & Carley, 1992). All of these developments predated the advent of print, and in the view of Clanchy and of Kaufer and Carley were necessary preconditions for it.

The term revolution also implies a clean break from the past, the beginning of a new history. When applied to changes in media, revolution suggests that old tools are outmoded, obsolete, and left behind when new tools are developed. However, closer inspection reveals that this is not the case: Lentz (1989) discusses at length how oral habits and traditions existed side by side in ancient Greece with the new technology of writing, and Grafton (1980) argues that the role of the author remained in many ways scribal, after the invention and spread of print and even into modern times. Interestingly, rather than closing down other communication media (such as speech or writing), Kaufer and Carley show that print in fact expanded the contexts of use for these other, older systems—that old and new media were in fact mutually supporting and enriching.

There are four important interrelated points, then, in this revised and complicated story of print that have relevance for understanding today's literacy technologies: (a) the development of literacy technologies is slow, uneven, and seldom unitary; (b) new technologies are dependent in complex ways on other technical and cultural systems; (c) these new technologies are not inherently revolutionary, but may indeed conserve traditional values; and (d) old and new media co-exist and even mutually reinforce one another.

Technology as Self-Determining

Discussions of revolutions in communication are often built on and/or foster a kind of technological determinism. Indeed, terms like *communication revolution* or *rise of technology* suggest a force beyond human control, or even beyond human understanding. But of course technologies do not arise independently. Rather, they are developed—by purposeful human action in complex cultural settings. What is known about the cultural settings in which technologies are developed? Again, we can return to the story of print for at least a partial answer. Clanchy's (1979) work, *From Memory to Written Record: England, 1066-1307*, on the complex shift from oral to written modes in government and business settings, and Kaufer and Carley's (1992) modeling of the impact of print in a variety of cultural systems both suggest how the growth of technologies of literacy, and their impact, is gradual, complicated, and highly dependent on what Kaufer and Carley call "co-evolving elements of society" (p. 295). Some of these co-evolving elements are cultural (e.g., the trust in writing whose slow development Clanchy's traces), whereas others are technological, such as the development of inexpensive paper, the spread of transportation systems, or the refinement of the printing presses themselves (Kaufer & Carley, 1992). In short, conditions must be right, both for technologies to develop and for them to have widespread impact.

Current work on computer technology in its cultural contexts is being conducted by Michael Cole and his colleagues in the Laboratory of Comparative Human Cognition at the University of California at San Diego. Over the course of several years, these researchers introduced computer technologies into vital cultural systems—schools, libraries, day care centers, community centers—and then examined how these cultural systems support, undermine, or change the technologies, and how the technologies grow or atrophy under certain cultural conditions (Cole, in press). Although Cole is primarily interested in cultural change rather than in technology *per se*, his research can tell us a great deal about the relationship between cultural systems and technological systems. The acceptance of particular technologies into cultural systems tended to depend less on the nature of the technology itself, or even the characteristics of the users (some of whom were the same children moving from school to library to community center), than on a complex interplay of cultural norms, existing social structures, and computer features. Further, the survival of a technology seemed to change in surprising ways over time. For instance, while the educational aspects of the system had been heralded and welcomed into the library system at first, it was in the community center setting (where the system had always existed in a somewhat marginal state, used only sporadically by children) that the computer system eventually maintained the strongest and most integrated hold. In short, Cole (like Clanchy and like Kaufer and Carley) found that the relationship between cultural conditions and the development, or even survival, of technologies is not a simple one.

Further, words like *rise* or *advent*, when applied to technological systems, tend to obfuscate the role of human agency in the development of technologies. Technology is not self-determining. Rather, its shape and scope are the result of human-made, purposeful, rhetorical, and political choices, as suggested in the study of technology development in chapter 6 (this volume). The technological determinism inherent in phrases like "the rise of computers" and "the advent of print" has several sources. One is the fact that people in the humanities—not to mention the citizenry at large—are seldom privy to how technology gets developed and thus have limited experience in seeing the human decisions behind the machines they use, current GM automobile ads notwithstanding. Indeed, the specialization of professions purposefully obfiscates the nature of work and decision making of one group by another. This is the very nature of contemporary notions of expertise (Geisler, 1994).

Another source of technological determinism is the leveling of human agency and the disembodying of the material which are strong currents in postmodern thought. Postmodernists tend to be technologically deterministic because human motive—in the form of human agency—is missing (Barthes, 1981). Without a place in history or activity for some human agency, postmodernists have to assume that technology develops and changes of its own volition. Postmodernism is also intrinsically antimaterialisti . For example, for Foucault (1979), the "body" is not a material, physical, biological system, but rather a discursive, linguistic, and cultural construct (see also Baudrillard, 1988). Taken together, postmodernism's antimaterialism and its leveling of agency mean that postmodern analyses of technology tend to look through, rather than at, the technologies under study (Haraway, 1985). Recently, however, postmodern scholars of science like Hayles (1993) and Rotman (1994) have mounted strong correctives to the antimaterialist position.

Another reason why technological determinism is such a temptation is the time-bound nature of historical study itself. Indeed, it is difficult to examine human agency historically. For example, the individuals involved in the development of written language systems in ancient Greece or in China in the Han period are not available for interviews about how this process occurred. Further, post hoc analysis of temporal developments is somewhat suspect precisely because of the tendency to see a consistent, inevitable unfolding of events after the fact. Historian Edward Hallett Carr; discusses at great length the "inevitability" of history, in his book *What is History?* (see especially Chapter 4, "Causation in History") and, interestingly, Freud (1920/24; quoted in Cole, in press) makes a similar point when discussing the retrospective construction of explanations for psychological development. When we look at a phenomenon "with the eyes of the present" (Carr, 1961; p. 28), we tend to see a continuous and consistent story—a story that could have turned out no other way. And of course a story that could have turned out no other way tends to obscure the role of human purpose and choice.

The same is true of tools and artifacts. When you look at your computer (and you probably seldom look at it; you look through it to the task at hand) you see a set of fixed features: a scroll bar with a certain functionality, a set of available fonts, a trash can icon in a certain location. These features, too, tend to have an "inevitability" about them: "the trash can is most convenient in the lower right," "how else *could* a scroll bar work?" The shape of the computer and its features seem inevitable, and, by their inevitability, unconnected to human motive and agency.

However, when we look at developments unfold in real time we can overcome the false sense of inevitability that fosters technological determinism. As Freud (1920/24) said about psychological change, we "notice at once that there might have been another result" (p. 226; quoted in Cole, in press). In other words, when we live through events—rather than looking back at them—the story suddenly seems much less inevitable. This is the draw of historical novels, sweeping epic films based on history, and the notion of time travel. Similarly, when we watch technology-in-development, rather than just looking at completed technological artifacts, we find that the scroll bar could indeed have had another functionality.

Chapter 6 described a systematic study of technology development in the late 1980s at a research site funded jointly by a major research university and a leading computer corporation. This study examined a rather fluid group of software designers and the decisions they made about user interface features in a developing educational computing systems. Such studies can help temper technological determinism; they show that developers' decisions about writing tools are made much like other kinds of human decisions are made: by fiat or by neglect, on a whim or through political power plays, to meet a deadline, to appease the boss, to save money. Unfortunately, such studies of technological phenomena in movement are as yet somewhat rare. On the one hand, there are accounts of "hacker" culture, like Kidder's (1981) *Soul of the New Machine*, that make fascinating reading and offer some insights, but are not detailed enough to offer much definitive about how technologies are developed. Insider accounts like Lundstrom's (1988) *A Few Good Men from Univac* or accounts meant for a popular audience like Levy's (1984) *Hackers: Heroes of the Computer Revolution* tend to be overtly celebratory. On the other hand, most carefully controlled empirical studies of programmers are at too fine a level of detail to tell us much about the messy business of technology development. They examine comprehension or debugging of software programs, rather than the group and individual processes of software design (e.g., see papers collected in Soloway & Iyengar, 1987).

ARE COMPUTERS SOMETHING NEW UNDER THE SUN?

Finally, I want to argue against the assumption that printing and computer literacy technologies are wholly distinct entities. Print culture and computer culture are not separate and analogous situations. Rather, they are part and parcel of the same historical-material process. As an illustration, consider that it seems silly to try and identify when print culture ended and computer culture began. Of course, the beginning of the computer era can be dated with von Neumann's digital computer, or earlier with the publication of Turing's paper "On Computable Numbers" (Bolter, 1984; p. 34, 12), but this is a controversial move and one that might be as suspect as identifying Gutenberg as the "inventor" of print. But how could the end of print culture be dated? Publishing is a live and vital industry, as are a myriad of oral cultures, although it is certainly true that contemporary oral, written, and print cultures have been shaped by the existence of computer cultures.

Second, computer technology has not usurped print, but rather multiplied its contexts for use, in Kaufer and Carley's terms. Consider a couple of mundane examples: Go to a popular or academic bookstore and note the huge volume of printed literature that has grown up around computers, or note that the five volumes of documentation that accompany the HyperCard/HyperTalk authoring system weigh a full seven pounds. Technologies of print and computer technologies mutually complicate and support one another—indeed, computers make print a more vital medium.

Finally, and perhaps most critically, computer literacy technologies are built on top of, and are inherently dependent on, other, earlier technologies, including print. The technologies we write with today are not new: They are built on layers and layers of other technologies—not only solid state physics and digital logic and mass production—but other literacy technologies as well. The older, other technologies on which computer literacy technologies are built include writing itself (which is in turn built upon alphabetic systems) and powerful aspects of print technology, which arose with the printing press but were multiplied by industrialization and later by electronics. A list of some of the features of computer writing tools that have been borrowed from earlier literacy systems include: the Roman alphabet; the difficult-to-learn and error-producing QWERTY keyboard; the notion of scrolling as text movement; the conventions of primary positions as up and left, and forward movement as down and to the right; the notions of tabs and margins; and the placement of movement mechanisms (e.g., scrollbars) on the right of the machine. Further, most computer writing systems (WYSIWYG editors) set margins and line length to the printed page, and standard fonts and practices of adding emphasis with italic, bold, and underlining are imported from the print world (see Figure 8.1). That these examples seem rather mundane in fact proves the point: Alphabets, margins, and directionality are so ensconced into the tools used today that people simply take them for granted—they do not see them and so consequently underestimate the degree to which contemporary tools are built upon them.

Computer Feature	Borrowed from. . Early writing	Manuscript writing	Typewriter	Printing
Idea of written communication	X	X	X	X
Roman alphabet	X	X	X	X
Conventions of position/direction			X	
QWERTY keyboard			X	
Cursor movement (via "return" and "tab")			X	
Spacing conventions			X	X
Placement of text movement mechanisms (arrow keys, scrollbar)			X	
Display size			X	X
Special function fonts (italic, underline, bold)		X	X	X

FIG. 8.1. "Borrowed" features of computer text-production systems.

In short, the literacy technologies used today have not replaced older technologies; in fact, they are dependent on those older technologies. You cannot have a word processor without an alphabet; you cannot have a hypertext without the powerful notions of directionality that were conventionalized, disseminated, and absorbed into print culture.

THE HISTORICAL-GENETIC METHOD APPLIED TO COMPUTER LITERACY TECHNOLOGIES

This chapter has suggested that historical analogies between revolutions of print and of computers may be less than useful, for a number of reasons, in understanding contemporary writing technologies and their complex relationship to thinking and to culture. However, I do not mean to suggest that

Technology Studies is viable without historical analysis. In fact, historical understanding and contextualizing is vital to the enterprise of Technology Studies. Here I return to Vygotsky's notion of studying phenomena in movement by drawing on his historical-genetic method. For Vygotsky, the study of human behavior was the study of the history of that behavior; similarly, the study of human artifacts (including technologies of literacy) is, at least in part, the study of the history of those artifacts. Therefore, *historicizing technology* means examining the "genesis," or historical development broadly conceived, of current technologies. Put another way, historical studies of other technologies are important not so that historical analogies can be made, but because without such historical analyses, we cannot truly understand the nature and shape of current technologies.

When applied to Technology Studies, Vygotsky's genetic method leads to an analysis of movement or change at different systemic levels. One way to historicize technology is at the historical/cultural level, looking to historical precedents to give some idea of the scope and nature of technology's effects on literacy, learning for instance from the history of print that technological change is gradual, less than unitary, and always dependent on other cultural and technological factors. This kind of complicated understanding of the history of technology should ground discussion of technology and its potential uses and caution against hyperbolic claims about immediate or unequivocal effects. Further, an historical grounding for discussions of technology should lead to more realistic expectations about the implementation and use of computer technology in educational, business, or home settings and could provide a counter to promotional and advertising claims about the computer's transformation (note agency) of home, school, or business.

A second systemic level at which the historicizing of technology might take place is at the sociocultural level. Here, technology development in movement, or as it occurs in real time, can be examined. Specifically, a diversity of empirical and textual methods can be used to examine technology-in-the-making (cf. Latour, 1985) in labs, conference rooms, and design studios. Such studies might involve watching how individuals or groups make decisions about computer development, how a particular product or artifact changes over time, or how individuals or groups of users actually employ the tools at their disposal. Such a suggestion may be somewhat disconcerting to humanists raised with the notion that humanistic study is set against science, engineering, and technology studies (cf. Haas & Neuwirth, 1993). However, questions about technology, its nature, and its use are of such import that being bound by outmoded and rigid disciplinary distinctions is not useful. Technology Studies can, and indeed must, be the common enterprise of scholars from language studies, history, philosophy, and culture, as well as computer science and engineering (see chapter 2, this volume).

The historicizing of technology can also happen at the level of individual features. This way of historicizing technology is built upon the understanding that the study of artifacts means the study of the history of artifacts, including the other technologies that are an intrinsic part of new literacy tools. Tracing the genesis of particular features of computer tools (an example is shown in Figure 8.1) gives a more realistic view about the nature of the technologies being used and developed today, and can in turn inform expectations about the impact of these new tools. Such analyses can help temper the technological determinism that would posit technological developments as completely new and infinitely powerful. These analyses can also temper excessively positive expectations about the transformative power of technology—expectations that can be ultimately disappointing, if not dangerous (see Bowers, 1988). Vygotsky's historic-genetic method, then, is vitally important for all of these ways of historicizing technology Such historicizing, in turn, is vital for the conduct of Technology Studies, as defined here.

Ultimately, my goal in advocating that we historicize computer technology more completely and more complexly is to counter the dangerous assumption that technology is transparent—that it is not theoretical and that it is not laden with value. Much recent scholarship on writing and literacy—whether theoretical, empirical, or applied—has tended to bracket questions about technology. As individuals, we may be tempted to think that technologies are given to us (or, more accurately, purchased by us) fully formed, but technologies have complex and vital histories—histories that are part and parcel of the impact that developing technologies will have on our intellectual and material lives.

FOOTNOTES

[1]Another historical case often invoked in discussions of the impact of current computer technologies is what Havelock (1982) calls "the literate revolution." Literacy, and particularly the materiality of the technology of writing, is discussed in chapter 1 (this volume.)

[2] Other reviewers have noted inaccuracies in Eisenstein's work, and a tendency to present sharp, oversimplified distinctions between the scribe and the printer, and their respective contexts and world views. (See Grafton, 1980, for an extended discussion.)

[3]To credit Gutenberg with the "invention" of printing suggests a rather Eurocentric orientation: As Gough notes (1968), printing was widespread in China by 980 A. D.—several centuries before Gutenberg. Handprinting had the qualities of durability and a great deal of the multiplicity (if not the precise fixity) of moveable type, and therefore, Gutenberg's invention is best seen as an *extension* of earlier handprinting, not a radical new formulation of it.

9

THEORIZING TECHNOLOGY

To construct an adequate theoretical account of the materiality of literacy, the studies presented in this volume suggest, two critical questions must be addressed: How is it that material tools can shape mental processes? And what is the relationship of material tools to the culture in which they are embedded? This chapter examines these questions, summarizes how the results of the studies presented here might help answer them, and suggests some further lines of inquiry for the enterprise of Technology Studies. In addition, I will return to two bodies of existing theory: Vygotskian theory and theories of embodied practice. Although these theories do not specifically address the Technology Question, they can be extended in useful ways to construct a theoretical account of literacy's materiality and its relationship to technology.

MATERIALITY AND THINKING

How is it possible that the material technologies, implements, and artifacts of the physical world can alter and shape the mental processes by which writing occurs? Although the relationship between the physical and the mental has been argued in general terms in fields outside literacy studies (e.g., Putnam, 1981; Merleau-Ponty, 1965; Foucault, 1977), few scholars have addressed this question as it bears directly on the technologies of literacy. The cultural bifurcation of the material world from the world of the mind (through dualities such as mind vs. body and matter vs. spirit) make it difficult for many in Western cultures to even conceive of an interface between the mental and the material. This bifurcation is also an impediment to theorizing about how material technologies might impact mental activity. Yet the results of the research presented in chapters 3, 4, and 5 (this volume) suggest that technologies do indeed have an impact on the cognitive processes of writing.

Vygotsky's notion of mediation can be useful in understanding how material technologies can influence mental activity. As discussed in chapter 1 (this volume), Vygotsky's interest in the mediational power of psychological tools allowed him to explore how human development, defined as both individual cognitive growth and cultural change, occurs. I have extended Vygotsky's notion of mediational means to include diverse writing technologies, including computers. As we have seen, computers (like writing generally) are at once material tools and psychological systems: Writing technologies are physical objects, created and existing in space and time, whose materiality structures and constrains the human activities associated with them. At the same time, writing and its technologies are powerful symbolic systems. Vygotsky's theory of mediational means helps to explain the powerful transformative effects of writing, which is at once material and symbolic.

Further, Vygotsky's coupling of individual psychological growth and historical/cultural change through the notion of mediation makes the relationship between the cognitive and the cultural of prime importance. Although cultural change (e.g., new writing technologies) and individual change (e.g., altered cognitive processes) are not reducible to one another, they are related in complex and multifaceted ways. This is because the means of change—in this case, material technologies of writing—are at once culturally based systems (as we saw in chapters 6 and 7) and tools for individual use (as illustrated in chapters 3, 4, and 5).

Vygotsky included artifacts such as maps, diagrams, and works of art as examples of psychological tools. Although the materiality of such artifacts may be implied, or even taken for granted, Vygotsky did not examine in any detail the coupling of material and psychological systems in such artifacts. Further, because he stops short of postulating a mechanism by which the mediation of the material and the mental occurs, Vygotsky's theory only gets us so far in our attempts to address the Technology Question. Here, the theoretical notion of embodied practice becomes useful in more clearly articulating the connection between the material world of technologies and artifacts and the mental world of thought. As discussed in detail in chapter 2 (this volume), the notion of embodied practice has been developed in different ways by Connerton (1989), Johnson (1987), and Lave (1988; Lave & Wenger, 1991).[1] Although these scholars do not treat writing in any great detail, they generally agree that an embodied practice is a culturally sanctioned, culturally learned activity that is accomplished by individual human beings moving through time and space.

Certainly writing can be understood as an embodied practice. Writers use their bodies, and the materials available to their bodies via the material world, to both create and to interact with textual artifacts. Writers' bodily movements and interactions are evident in the conduct of everyday literacy activities: Writers pick up and chew on pencils, they rest their hands on keyboards, they move closer to their texts in some circumstances, push back from them in others; readers hunch over manuscripts with pens, stretch out with books under trees, move through on-line texts by pushing keys or clicking buttons. (Writers' physical interactions with their texts are discussed in more detail in chapter 5, this volume).

Changing the technologies of writing has profound implications, at least in part, because different technologies are materially configured in profoundly different ways. That is, different writing technologies set up radically different spatial, tactile, visual, and even temporal relations between the writer's material body and his or her material text. Writers generally have less of their texts available at once when they read from computer screens, and their bodily orientation toward the text is different, because computer displays are usually vertical rather than horizontal. Computer writers' interactions with their texts are "once-removed," as they do things to texts through the mediation of devices like keyboards and mice, rather than through direct manipulation of the text itself. Further, for most experienced writers, text production is more rapid with computers than with pen and paper, and the time to move from drafting to final copy requires less time-on-task. The spatial and temporal metaphors that writers use to describe their text sense problems (see chapter 5, this volume), then, make a great deal of sense because computers transform writing in the realm of time and space—that is, the realm of the bodily. It is through these worlds of time and space that writers move as they produce written discourse.

Hence, the body (in the sense of an individual, embodied experience, rather than as an abstract cultural construction; see Hayles, 1993) is the mechanism by which the mediation of the mental and the material occurs. Writers' relationships to their texts are embodied in the most intimate of ways, because writers have no other way of either producing text or of interacting with it than through their bodies, particularly their hands and eyes. For the most part, material concerns have remained outside the realm of consideration of writing research, possibly due to the profound distrust of the bodily within scholarly inquiry and within the culture at large. In the past two decades, much of what has been interesting to both theorists and researchers of writing are the psychological processes of writing and the mental constructs or representations that readers and writers build. Indeed, it is possible to argue that these mental processes and constructs are interesting in part because they are tied in complex and ambiguous ways to rather mundane, work-a-day artifacts (e.g., books, pencils, computers). We are fascinated by writing because "the pen" (the world of written discourse) is, sometimes at least and often to our great surprise, mightier than "the sword" (the brutal physical world). It may not be surprising then that considerations of bodily components of writing have been overlooked (but see Emig, 1978). However, in the vastly different technological world of computer writing, ignoring the materiality of literacy, its basis in bodily movements and habits, is no longer possible. Research on writing must begin to acknowledge and examine the material basis of literacy; new technologies provide both the impetus and the means for such an examination.

MATERIALITY AND CULTURE

I now turn to the second theoretical question: What is the relationship of material tools to the culture in which they are embedded? As we saw in chapters 6 and 7 (this volume), the construction and development of technologies are tied to culture in intimate ways: Not only do groups develop technologies with cultural assumptions and power relations in place that guide development efforts, but people also construct certain uses and purposes for technology through discourse that is itself, in turn, shaped in profound ways by cultural beliefs about technology.

Vygotsky's claim that psychological tools and signs are culturally made is useful in further elaborating the relationship between writing technologies and their cultures. Technologies do not make themselves, nor is their development accomplished in a vacuum. Certainly, as seen in chapter 6 (this volume), the notion that current technologies embody the "best" features available is naive, because particular system features can be adopted for a variety of reasons. Once the technology development process is examined in any detail, the notion that technologies are self determining also becomes suspect. In addition, Vygotsky's historical-genetic method authorizes, even demands, an acknowledgment of the historical complexity of any technology: a looking at, rather than through, technology means studying technological systems in use, in development, and across time. It means looking at technological history at a number of levels.

Again, the notion of embodied practice is useful in stipulating how technologies survive as cultural systems. Any embodied practice, including writing, is habitual, in Hayes' (1993) terms (cf., Bordieu). That is, the bodily movements and interactions in which writers engage are repeated by individuals and across individuals over time; a habit is a kind of remembering in and by the body. Further, writing is an incorporating, as well as an inscribing, practice (Connerton, 1989, p. 77). We learn to hold a pencil by watching others do so; we generally place our hands on keyboards in the same way that others in our culture do. This is both due to the nature of learning the physical movements of writing, which are often based on direct instruction and modeling, and because the technologies themselves embody cultural assumptions about what texts are and how writers produce them. Consequently, these technologies enable or even require particular relationships to be set up among writers, tools, and texts. Chapter 8 (this volume) describes how notions of directionality, for instance, are inherent in most computer writing tools, even those that purport to be "nonlinear."

Observing familiar writing technologies in vastly different cultural systems can further illuminate the cultural assumptions that are built into those technologies. Take, for example, a personal computer. Whole sets of Western cultural assumptions about literacy are built into this tool—from a keyboard that allows alphabetic writing but precludes (or makes extremely difficult) other writing systems, to the actual physical setup, with one keyboard connected to one CPU and monitor in front of one chair. How is this personal computer used in a vastly different context, for example a Japanese engineering office where two distinct syllabaries and a complex logographic system replace the alphabet, and where people seldom if ever compose single-authored texts silently and in isolation? In a setting like this, the cultural biases built into machines become more obvious. Indeed, in the Japanese firms that my colleague Jeff Funk and I observed (see Funk & Haas, 1992), engineers often avoided using computers that were configured in these rather Western-based ways. The personal computer is designed and manufactured for an embodied practice that is not universal, but rather specific to Western cultures and literate practices. Moving our familiar literacy technologies to these vastly different cultural systems (different at the level of social interaction as well as at the level of cultural artifacts) might reveal a great deal about what, if anything, is common or essential to the acts of reading and writing. Such questions cannot be answered without making technology the center of inquiry; they cannot even be formulated without looking at, rather than through, familiar technologies.

Finally, embodiment theory underscores the heritage of cultural artifacts: Tools themselves have a history built into them. Cultural artifacts, including writing tools, are the products both of the uses to which they have been put and of the beliefs that guide those uses. Put another way, theories of use are inherent in any tool. This suggests why the effects of computer technologies on writing can be so various and at once powerful and subtle. Today's writing technologies have a heritage that can be traced back to the earliest tools of writing. At each "stage" of a contemporary writing technology's development, theories of use and practice shape how it was, and is, developed. A complex tool like a personal computer, then, has layers on layers of theory and use built into it; the theories we saw operating in the study of technology development in chapter 6 (this volume) only scratch the surface. Similarly, generations and even centuries of embodied use have shaped contemporary technologies. The effects of any given technology—here, computer tools—will multiply in complexity with every level of development and every new use to which the technology is put. Unraveling the threads of technology development and use, through historical as well as empirical studies, will be the kind of interdisciplinary project that Technology Studies can pursue.

THE FUTURE OF TECHNOLOGY STUDIES

The previous sections have sketched some of the kinds of inquiries that might contribute to a theory of the materiality of literacy. The inquiry that should be the basis of Technology Studies extends far beyond studies of computers, or of hypertext, or of the InterNet. Scholars of literacy need to imagine and create a research agenda with questions of technology—as I have defined it as a system of things, processes, people, motives, and uses—placed firmly at the center. Little can be learned about larger questions of knowledge and writing, or thinking and culture, without a research agenda that centers on technological questions.

First, such a research agenda would provide one way to understand the relationship between culture and cognition. Technology is the place where culture and cognition meet—technologies are cultural artifacts imbued with history, as well as tools used by individuals for their own motives and purposes. For better or worse, writers do not reinvent the tools of literacy; they come with a history and a whole set of cultural ways of thinking inherent in them. These tools are at once the products of cultural histories and the shapers of those histories.   At the same time, individuals use technologies, sometimes in loneliness and isolation, to accomplish their own cognitive work and to enrich their own mental lives. Putting technology, in the broadest sense, at the center of a research agenda for literacy studies would allow a "way into" questions of culture and cognition, allowing a more complete understanding of how historically and culturally rich technologies—in Vygotsky's term—mediate the mental lives of individuals.

Second, tackling the Technology Question head on may allow literacy scholars to claim, or reclaim, some power in the shaping of literacy technologies. Many of the humanities and social sciences (including literacy studies, English, and education) have taken a political turn in the past decade, moving toward consideration of power relations and cultural ideologies. But at the same time, much of the work in these same disciplines has seemed to adopt a strangely uncritical and passive stance toward the writing technologies that are so ubiquitous. It may be tempting to think that technologies arise as fully formed and neutral entities, but technologies have both political histories and political implications.

A passive stance toward technology by literacy researchers and theorists may be due to an inability, or an unwillingness, to recognize this very human element in the development of technology. This passive stance means that the enterprise of literacy studies has yet to fully recognize the dialectical relationship between human thinking and culture, on the one hand, and technology on the other. Consequently, the decisions determining the shape of literacy technology are being made mostly outside the discourses of those disciplines concerned with literacy. Until we are willing to recognize the symbiotic and systemic relationship between technology, culture, and individuals, willing to explore the implications of technology on our own literate practice and mental lives, and willing to enter fully into the various discourses of technology, scholars and teachers of literacy—arguably the group that has most at stake as technology remakes writing—are abdicating responsibility and power in helping to determine how technology and literacy are made, through use, in our culture.

FOOTNOTES

[1]Although there is a great deal of connection between embodied practice and Vygotsky's notion of mediation, only Lave explicitly draws on Vygotsky's work.

REFERENCES

Applebee, A. (1984). *Contexts for learning to write: Studies of secondary school instruction.* Norwood, NJ: Ablex.

Aronowitz, S., & Giroux, H. (1985). *Education under seige: The conservative, liberal, and radical debate over schooling.* South Hadley, MA: Bergin.

Augustine. (1977). *Confessions.* New York: Penguin.

Augustine. (1958). *On Christian doctrine.* (D. W. Robertson, Jr., Trans.). New York: Bobbs-Merrill.

Bangert-Drowns, R. L. (1993). The word processor as an instructional tool: A meta-analysis of word processing in writing instruction. *Review of Educational Research, 63* (1), 69-93.

Barthes, R. (1981). The death of the author. In J. Caughie (Ed.), *Theories of authorship* (pp. 208-213). London: Routledge & Kegan Paul.

Barton, E. (1994). Interpreting the discourses of technology. In C. Selfe & S. Hilligoss (Eds.), *Literacy and computers* (pp. 56-75). New York: Modern Language Association.

Baudrillard, J. (1988). *The ecstasy of communication* (B. Schutze & C. Schutze, Trans). New York: Autonomedia.

Bazerman, C. (1988). *Shaping written knowledge: The genre and activity of the experimental article in science.* Madison: University of Wisconsin Press.

Beach, R. (1990). The creative development of meaning. In D. Bogdan & S. B. Straw (Eds.), *Beyond communication: Reading comprehension and criticism* (pp. 211-236). Portsmouth, NH: Boynton/Cook.

Bereiter, C., & Scardamalia, M. (1982). From conversation to composition: The role of instruction in a developmental process. In R. Glaser (Ed.), *Advances in instructional psychology* (Vol. 2; pp 1-64). Hillsdale, NJ: Lawrence Erlbaum.

Bereiter, C., & Scardamalia, M. (1987). *The psychology of written composition.* Hillsdale, NJ: Lawrence Erlbaum Associates.

Berkenkotter, C., Huckin, T., & Ackerman, J. (1988). Conversation, conventions, and the writers. *Research in the Teaching of English, 22,* 9-44.

Bernhardt, S. A. (1993). The shape of text to come: The texture of print on screens. *College Composition and Communication, 44*(2), 151-175.

Bolter, J. D. (1984). *Turing's man.* Chapel Hill: University of North Carolina Press.

Bolter, J. D. (1991). *Writing space: The computer, hypertext, and the history of writing.* Hillsdale, NJ: Lawrence Erlbaum Associates.

Booth, K. S., Bryden, M. P., Cowan, W., Morgan, M., & Plante, B. L. (1987). On the parametes of human visual performance: An investigation of the benefits of anti-aliasing.   In *Proceedings of CHI + GI 1987* (pp. 13-20).   New York: Association of Computing Machinists.

Borenstein, N. S.   (1991).   *Programming as if people mattered: Friendly programs, software engineering, and other noble delusions.*   Princeton, NJ: Princeton University Press.

Borenstein, N., & Thyberg, C.   (1991).   Power, ease of use, and cooperative work in a practical multimedia message system.   *International Journal of Man-Machine Studies ,34*(1), 229-259.

Bourdieu, P. (1977).   *Outline of a theory of practice.*   Cambridge: Cambridge University Press.

Bowers, C. A.   (1988).   *Cultural dimensions of academic computing: Understanding the non-neutrality of technology.*   New York: Teachers College Press.

Boyle, F. T.   (1993).   IBM, talking heads, and our classrooms.   *College English,* 55(6), 618-626.

Brandt, D.   (1990).   *Literacy as involvement: The acts of writers, readers, and texts.*   Carbondale: Southern Illinois University Press.

Brent, D.   (1992).   *Reading as rhetorical invention: Knowledge, persuasion, and the teaching of research-based writing.*   Urbana, IL: National Council of Teachers of English.

Bridwell, L., Sirc, G., & Brooke, R.   (1985).   Revising and computing: Case studies of student writers.   In S. Freedman (Ed.),   *The acquistion of written language: Revision and response* (pp. 172-194).   Norwood, NJ: Ablex.

Bridwell-Bowles, L., Johnson, P., & Brehe, S.   (1987).   Composing and computers: Case studies of experienced writers.   In A. Matsuhashi (Ed.),   *Writing in real time: Modeling production processes* (pp. 81-107).   Norwood, NJ: Ablex.

Brown, P. R. L.   (1988).   *The body and society: Men, women, and sexual renunciation in early Christianity.*   New York: Columbia University Press.

Bruce, B., & Rubin, A.   (1993).   *Electronic quills: A situated evaluation of using computers for writing in classrooms.*   Hillsdale, NJ: Lawrence Erlbaum Associates.

Burke, K.   (1984).   *Permanence and change: An anatomy of purpose.*   Berkeley: University of California Press.

Burtis, P. J., Scardamalia, M., Bereiter, C., & Tetroe, J.   (1983).   The development of planning in writing.   In B. Kroll & G. Wells (Eds.),   *Explorations in the development of writing* (pp. 153-174).   London: John Wiley & Sons.

Card, S., Moran, T., & Newell, A.   (1983).   *The psychology of human-computer interaction.*   Hillsdale, NJ: Lawrence Erlbaum Associates.

Carr, E. H.   (1961).   *What is history?*   New York: Vintage.

Cazden, C.   (1989).   The myth of the autonomous text.   In D. M. Toping, D. Crowell, & V. M. Kobayashi (Eds.), *Thinking across cultures: Third international conference on thinking* (pp. 109-122).   Hillsdale, NJ: Lawrence Erlbaum Associates.

Clanchy, M. T. (1979). *From memory to written record.* Cambridge: Harvard University Press.

Cole, M. (in press). Cultural-historical psychology: A meso-genetic approach. In L. Martin, K. Nelson, & E. Tobach (Eds.), *Socio-cultural psychology Theory and practice of knowing and doing.* New York: Cambridge University Press.

Connerton, P. (1989). *How societies remember.* New York: Cambridge University Press.

Cooper, M. & Selfe, C. (1990). Computer conferences and learning: Authority, resistence, and internally persuasive discourse. *College English ,52*(8), 847-869.

Crowley, S. (1993). Modern rhetoric and memory. In J. F. Reynolds (Ed.), *Rhetorical memory and delivery* (pp. 31-44). Hillsdale, NJ: Lawrence Erlbaum Associates.

Daiute, C. (1985). *Computers and writing.* Reading, MA: Addison-Wesley.

Davydov, V., & Markova, A. (1983). A concept of education activity for school children. *Soviet Psychology ,11*(2), 50-76.

de Beaugrande, R. (1980). *Text, discourse, and process: Toward a multidisciplinary science of texts.* Norwood, NJ: Ablex.

de Beaugrande, R. (1984). *Text production: Toward a science of composition.* Norwood, NJ: Ablex.

de Certeau, M. (1985). *The practice of everyday life* (S. Randall, Trans.). Berkeley: University of California Press.

Derrida, J. (1981). Plato's pharmacy. In B. Johnson (Ed. and Trans.),*Dissemination .* Chicago: University of Chicago Press.

Doyle, W. (1983). Academic work. *Review of Educational Reseach, 53*(2), 159-199.

Durst, R. (1989). Monitoring processes in analytic and summary writing. *Written Communication, 6* 3), 340-363.

Dyson, A. H. (1988). Unintentional helping in the primary grades. In B. Rafoth & D. Rubin (Eds.), *The social construction of written language* (pp. 218-248). Norwood, NJ: Ablex.

Eisenstein, E. L. (1979). *The printing press as an agent of change* (Vols. I and II). Cambridge: Cambridge University Press.

Eklundh, K. S. (1991). *Problems in achieving a global perspective in computer-based writing* (IPLab Report No. 38). Royal Institute of Technology, Stockholm, Sweden.

Eklundh, K. S., Faton, A., & S. Romberger (in press). The paper model for computer-based writing. In H. van Oostendorp (Ed.), *Cognitive aspects of electronic text processing.* Norwood, NJ: Ablex.

Eklundh, K. S., & Sjoholm, C. (1991). Writing with a computer: A longitudinal study of writers of technical documents. *International Journal of Man-Machine Studies, 35,* 723-749.

Emig, J. (1978). Hand, eye, brain. In C. Cooper & L. Odell (eds.),*Research on composing: Points of departure* (pp. 59-72). Urbana, IL: NCTE Press.

Engels, F. (1948). *Dialectics of nature.* New York: International.

Faigley, L. (1992). *Fragments of rationality: Postmodernity and the subject of composition.* Pittsburgh, PA: University of Pittsburgh Press.

Farr, M. (1993). Essayist literacy and other verbal performances. *Written Communication, 8,* 4-38.

Fish, S. (1980). *Is there a text in this class? The authority of interpretive communities.* Cambridge, MA: Harvard University Press.

Flesch, R. (1974). *The art of readable writing* (25th ed.). New York: Harper & Row.

Flower, L. (1988). The construction of purpose in reading and writing. *College English ,50,* 528-550.

Flower, L., & Hayes, J. R. (1980). The cognition of discovery: Defining a rhetorical problem. *College Composition and Communication, 31,* 21-32.

Flower, L., & Hayes, J. R. (1981a). A cognitive process theory of writing. *College Compositon and Communication, 32,* 365-387.

Flower, L., & Hayes, J. R. (1981b). Plans that guide the composing process. In C. H. Frederickson & J. F. Dominic (Eds.). *Writing: The nature, development, and teaching of written communication* (Vol 2., pp. 39-58). Hillsdale, NJ: Lawrence Erlbaum Associates.

Flower, L., & Hayes, J. R. (1981c). The pregnant pause: An inquiry into the nature of planning. *Research in the teaching of English, 15* (3), 229-243.

Flower, L., & Hayes, J. R. (1984). Images, plans, and prose: The representation of meaning in writing. *Written Communication, 1,* 120-160.

Flower, L., Stein, V., Ackerman, J., Kantz, M. J., McCormick, K., & Peck, W. (1990). *Reading-to-write: Exploring a cognitive and social process.* New York: Oxford University Press.

Foucault, M. (1979). *Discipline and punish: The birth of a prison* A. Sheridan, Trans. New York: Vintage.

Funk, J. L., & Haas, C. (1992). The elements of Japan's corporate culture that support teamwork. In J. L. Funk, *Teamwork Japanese style: An inside look at Japanese product and technology development* (pp. 121-188). Cambridge, MA: Productivity Press.

Geisler, C. (1994). *Academic literacy and the nature of expertise.* Hillsdale, NJ: Lawrence Erlbaum Associates.

George, A. (in progress). *Using rhetorical analysis to uncover ideology: A method based on the work of Stephen Toulmin.* Working paper in progress.

Goody, J., & Watt, I. (1968). The consequences of literacy. In J. Goody (Ed.), *Literacy in traditional societies* (pp. 27-68). Cambridge: Cambridge University Press.

Gough, K. (1968). Implications of literacy in traditional China and India. In J. Goody (Ed.), *Literacy in traditional societies* (pp. 69-84). New York: Cambridge University Press.

Gould, J. D., Alfaro, L., Finn, R., Haupt, B., Minuto, A., & Salaum, J. (1987). Why reading was slower from CRT displays than from paper. In *Proceedings of CHI + GI 1987* (pp. 7-12). New York: Association of Computing Machinists.

Gould, J. D., & Grischkowsky, M. (1984). Doing the same work with hard-copy and with CRT terminals. *Human Factors ,26*(3), 323-337.

Grafton, A. T. (1980). The importance of being printed. *Journal of Interdisciplinary History, 11*(2), 265-286.

Gronbeck, B. E. (1993). The spoken and the seen: The phonocentric and ocularcentric dimensions of rhetorical discourse. In J. F. Reynolds (Ed.), *Rhetorical memory and delivery* (pp. 139-156). Hillsdale, NJ: Lawrence Erlbaum Associates.

Haas, C. (1989a). Does the medium make a difference? Two studies of writing with pen and paper and with computers. *Human-Computer Interaction, 4*(2), 149-169.

Haas, C. (1989b). How the writing medium shapes the writing process: Effects of word processing on planning. *Research in the Teaching of English, 23* (2), 181-206.

Haas, C. (1989c). Seeing it on the screen isn't really seeing it: Computer writers' reading problems. In G. Hawisher & C. Selfe (Eds.), *Critical perspectives on computers and composition instruction* (pp. 16-29). New York: Teachers College Press.

Haas, C. (1990). Composing in technological contexts: A study of note-making. *Written Communication ,7*(4), 512-547.

Haas, C. (1994). Learning to read biology: One student's rhetorical development in college. *Written Communication, 11,* 43-84.

Haas, C., & Flower, L. (1988). Rhetorical reading and the construction of meaning. *College Composition and Communication,39*(2), 167-184.

Haas, C., & George, A. (in progress.) *The dangers of expert discourse in technology studies.* Working paper in progress.

Haas, C., & Hayes, J. R. (1986). What did I just say? Reading problems in writing with the machine. *Research in the Teaching of English, 20* (1), 22-35.

Haas, C., & Neuwirth, C. M. (1994). Writing the technology that writes us. In S. Hilligoss & C. Selfe (Eds.), *Literacy and computers* (pp. 319-335). New York: Modern Language Association Press.

Habermas, J. (1984-1987). *The theory of communicative action.* Vols. I and II. (T. McCarthy, Trans.). Boston: Beacon Press.

Hansen, W. J., Doring, R., & Whitlock, L. (1978). Why an examination was slower on screen than on paper. *International Journal of Man-Machine Studies, 10*, 507-519.

Hansen, W. J. & Haas, C. (1988). Reading and writing with computers: A framework for explaining differences in performance. *Communications of the ACM, 31*, 1080-1089.

Haraway, D. (1985). A manifesto for cyborgs: Science, technology, and socialist feminism in the 1980's. *Socialist Review, 80*, 65-107.

Haraway, D. (1988). Situated knowledges: The science question in feminism as a site of discourse of the privilege of partial perspective. *Feminist Studies, 14*(3), 575-99.

Havelock, E. A. (1976/1977). The preliteracy of the Greeks. *New Literary History, 8*, 369-391.

Havelock, E. A. (1982). *The literate revolution in Greece and its cultural consequences.* Princeton: Princeton University Press.

Havelock, E. A. (1986). *The muse learns to write.* New Haven: Yale University Press.

Hawisher, G. E. (1989). Research and recommendations for computers and composition. In G. Hawisher & C. Selfe (Eds.), *Critical perspectives on computers and composition instruction* (pp. 44-69). New York: Teachers College Press.

Hawisher, G. E., & Moran, C. (1993). Electronic mail and the writing instructor. *College English, 55*(6), 627-643.

Hawisher, G. E., & Selfe, C. L. (1991). The rhetoric of technology and the electronic writing classroom. *College Composition and Communication,42* , 55-65.

Hayes, J. R. (1987, June). *On the nature of planning in writing.* Paper presented at the 1987 Office of Naval Research Project Director's Meeting, Ann Arbor, MI.

Hayes, J. R., Flower, L., Schriver, K., Stratman, J., & Carey, L. (1987). Cognitive processes in revision. In S. Rosenberg (Ed.), *Advances in applied psycholinguistics, Volume II: Reading, writing, and language processing* (pp. 176-240). New York: Cambridge University Press.

Hayes-Roth, B., & Hayes-Roth, F. (1979). A cognitive model of planning. *Cognitive Science 3*, 275-310.

Hayles, N. K. (1993). The materiality of informatics. *Configurations, 1*(1), 147-170.

Heath, S. B. (1983). *Ways with words: Language, life, and work in communities and classrooms.* New York: Cambridge University Press.

Heidegger, M. (1977). *The question concerning technology and other essays.* New York: Harper.

Heim, M. (1987). *Electric language: A philosophical study of word processing.* New Haven: Yale University Press.

Hoetker, J., & Brossell, G. (1986). A procedure for writing content-fair essay examination topics for large scale assessment. *College Composition and Communication, 37*(3), 328-335.

Horowitz, R. (1987). Rhetorical structure in discourse processing. In R. Horowitz & S. J. Samuels (Eds.), *Comprehending oral and written discourse* (pp. 117-160). New York: Academic Press.

Howard, J. H. (1988). An overview of the Andrew File System. *Proceedings of the USENIX Technical Conference.*

Hunt, R. A. (1990). The parallel socialization of reading research and literary theory. In D. Bogdan & S. B. Straw (Eds.), *Beyond communication: Reading comprehension and criticism* (pp. 91-108). Portsmouth, NH: Boynton/Cook.

Johnson, B. (1981). Introduction. In J. Derrida, *Dissemination* (pp. vii-xxxiii). Chicago: University of Chicago Press.

Johnson, M. (1987). *The body in the mind.* Chicago: University of Chicago Press.

Kaestle, C. F. (1985). The history of literacy and the history of readers. *Review of Research in Education, 12,* 11-53.

Kaestle, C. F., Damon-Moore, H., Stedman, L. C., Tinsley, K., & Trollinger, W. V. (1991). *Literacy in the United States: Readers and reading since 1880.* New Haven: Yale University Press.

Kaufer, D., & Carley, K. (1992). *Communication at a distance: The influence of print on sociocultural organization and change.* Hillsdale, NJ: Lawrence Erlbaum Associates.

Kaufer, D. S., Hayes, J. R., & Flower, L. (1986). Composing written sentences. *Research in the Teaching of English, 20*(2), 121-140.

Kennedy, G. A. (1980). *Classical rhetoric and its Christian and secular tradition from ancient to modern times.* Chapel Hill: University of North Carolina Press.

Kidder, T. (1981). *The soul of the new machine.* New York: Little Brown.

Kintsch, W., & van Dijk, T. (1987). Toward a model of text comprehension and production. *Psychological Review, 85*(5), 363-94.

Kozulin, A. (1990). *Vygotsky's psychology: A biography of ideas.* Cambridge, MA: Harvard University Press.

Landow, G. P. (1992). *Hypertext: The convergence of contemporary critical theory and technology.* Baltimore: Johns Hopkins University Press.

Lanham, R. A. (1989). The electronic word: Literary study and the digital revolution. *New Literary History, 20* (2), 265-290.

Lanham, R. A. (1990). The extraordinary confergence: Democracy, techology, theory, and the university curriculum. *The South Atlantic Quarterly, 89*(1), 29-49.

Lanham, R. A. (1993). *The electronic word: Democracy, technology, and the arts.* Chicago: University of Chicago Press.

Langer, J. A. (1986). *Children reading and writing: Structures and strategies.* Norwood, NJ: Ablex.

Langer, J. A., & Applebee, A. N. (1987). *How writing shapes thinking: A study of teaching and learning.* Urbana, IL: National Council of Teachers of English Press.

Latour, B. (1985). *Science in action.* Cambridge, MA: Harvard University Press.

Lave, J. (1988). *Cognition in practice: Mind, mathematics, and culture in everyday life.* Cambridge: Cambridge University Press.

Lave, J. (1993). The practice of learning. In S. Chaiklin & J. Lave (Eds.), *Understanding practice: Perspectives on activity and context* (pp. 3-32). Cambridge: Cambridge University Press.

Lave, J. & Wenger, E. (1991). *Situated learning: Legitimate peripheral participation.* Cambridge: Cambridge University Press.

Lentz, T. M. (1989). *Orality and literacy in Hellenic Greece.* Carbondale: Southern Illinois University Press.

Leont'ev, A. N. (1978). *Activity, consciousness, and personality.* (M. J. Hall, Trans.). Englewood Cliffs, NJ: Prentice-Hall.

Levy, S. (1984). *Hackers: Heroes of the computer revolution.* Garden City, NY: Anchor/ Doubleday.

Lockridge, K. A. (1974). *Literacy in Colonial New England.* New York: Norton.

Lundstrom, D. (1988). *A few good men from Univac.* Cambridge, MA: MIT Press.

Marx, K. (1959). Theses on Feuerbach. In L. S. Feuer (Ed.), *Marx and Engels: Basic writings.* Garden City, NY: Doubleday.

Marx, K., & Engels, F. (1846). *The German ideology.* New York: International Publishers.

Matsuhashi, A. (1981). Pausing and planning: The tempo of written discourse production. *Research in the Teaching of English, 15,* 113-134.

Matsuhashi, A. (1987). Revising the plan and altering the text. In A. Matsuhashi (Ed.), *Writing in real time: Modeling production processes* (pp. 197-223). Norwood, NJ: Ablex.

Merleau-Ponty, M. (1965). *The structure of behavior.* London: Metheun.

Morris, J., Satyanarayanan, M., Conner, M., Howard, J., Rosenthal, D., & Smith, D. (1986). Andrew: A distributed personal computing environment. *Communications of the ACM, 29* (3), 184-201.

Murray, D. (1984). *A writer teaches writing.* Boston: Houghton Mifflin.

Neel, J. (1988). *Plato, Derrida, and writing.* Carbondale: Southern Illinois University Press.

Nelson, J. (1990). This was an easy assignment: Examing how students interpret academic writing tasks. *Research in the Teaching of English, 24*(4), 362-396.

Neuwirth, C. M., & Kaufer, D. S. (1989). The role of external representation in the writing process: Implications for the design of hypertext-based writing tools. *Hypertext '89 Proceedings* (pp. 319-341). Baltimore, MD: Association for Computing Machinists.

Neuwirth, C. M., Kaufer, D. S., Chandhok, R., & Morris, J. H. (1994). Computer support for distributed collaborative writing: Defining parameters of interaction. In *Proceedings of the Fifth Conference on Computer-Supported Cooperative Work* (CSCW '94), pp. 145-152. Chapel Hill, NC: Assocation of Computing Machinists.

Neuwirth, C. M., Palmquist, M., Cochran, C., Gillespie, T., Hartman, K., & Hajduk, T. (1993). Why write—together—on a computer network? In B. Bruce, J. Peyton, and T. Batson (Eds.), *Network-based classrooms* (pp. 181-209). Cambridge: Cambridge University Press.

Newell, G. E. & Winograd, P. (1989). The effects of writing on learning from expository text. *Written Communication, 6* (2), 196-217.

Nydahl, J. (1990). Teaching word processors to be CAI programs. *College English, 52* (8), 904-915.

Nystrand, M. (1987). The role of context in written communication. In R. Horowitz & J. Samuals (Eds.), *Comprehending oral and written language* (pp. 197-212). New York: Academic Press.

Olson, C. P. (1987). Who computes? In D. W. Livingstone (Ed.), *Critical pedagogy and cultural power*, pp. 179-204. South Hadley: Bergin.

Ong, W. J. (1982). *Orality and literacy: The technologizing of the word.* London, Methuen.

Palay, A. J., Hansen, W., Kazar, M., Sherman, M., Wadlow, M., Neuendorffer, T., Stern, Z., Bader, M., & Peters, T. (1988). The Andrew Toolkit—An overview. In *Proceedings of the 1988 USENIX Technical Conference* (pp. 9-21). Berkeley, CA: USENIX Association.

Perelman, C., & Olbrechts-Tyteca, L. (1969). *The new rhetoric: A treatise on argumentation* (J. Wilkinson & P. Weaver, Trans.). London: University of Notre Dame Press.

Plato. (1973). *Phaedrus.* W. Hamilton (Ed.). London: Penguin.

Poster, M. (1990). *The mode of information.* Chicago: University of Chicago Press.

Putnam, H. (1982). *Reason, truth, and history.* New York: Cambridge University Press.

Radway, J. A. (1984). *Reading the romance: Women, patriarchy, and popular literature.* Chapel Hill: University of North Carolina Press.

Resnick, D., & Resnick, L. B. (1977). The nature of literacy: A historical exploration. *Harvard Educational Review, 47*, 370-385.

Reynolds, J. F. (1993). Memory issues in composition studies. In J. F. Reynolds (Ed.), *Rhetorical memory and delivery* (pp. 1-16). Hillsdale, NJ: Lawrence Erlbaum Associates.

Rhetorica Ad Herennium (1937). Trans. H. Caplan. Loeb edition. Cambridge: Harvard University Press.

Rogers, E., Geisler, C., Glinett, E., Ingalls, R., & Musser, D. (1994). *Improving software design and development education through technological innovation.* NSF Computer and Information Sciences and Engineering Directorate, Education Infrastructure Grant, CDA-9214892.

Rorty, R. (1981). *The consequences of pragmatism.* Minneapolis: University of Minnesota Press.

Rose, M. (1989). *Lives on the boundary: A moving account of the struggles and achievements of America's educational underclass.* New York: Penguin.

Rothkopf, E. Z. (1971). Incidental memeory for location of information in text. *Journal of Verbal Learning and Verbal Behavior, 10*(6), 608-613.

Rotman, B. (1994). Exuberant materiality: De-minding the store. *Configurations, 2*(2), 257-274.

Rumelhart, D. E., & Ortony, A. (1977). The representation of knowledge in memory. In R. C. Anderson, R. J. Spiro, & W. Montague (Eds.), *Schooling and the acquisition of knowledge.* Hillsdale, NJ: Lawrence Erlbaum Associates.

Scardamalia, M., Bereiter, C., & Goelman, H. (1982). The role of production factors in writing ability. In M. Nystrand (Ed.), *What writers know: The language, process, and structure of written discourse* (pp. 173-210). New York: Academic Press.

Schneiderman, B. (1992). *Designing the user interface.* Reading, MA: Addison-Wesley.

Scribner, S. (1984). Studying working intelligence. In B. Rogoff & J. Lave (Eds.), *Everyday cognition: Its development in social context* (pp. 9-40). Cambridge, MA: Harvard University Press.

Scribner, S. (1985). Vygotsky's uses of history. In J. V. Wertsch (Ed.), *Culture, communication, and cognition: Vygotskian perspectives* (pp. 119-145). New York: Cambridge University Press.

Scribner, C., & Cole, M. (1981). *The psychology of literacy.* Cambridge: Harvard University Press.

Selfe, C. & Hilligoss, S. (1994). *Literacy and computers* . New York: Modern Language Association Press.

Slatin, J. M. (1990). Reading hypertext: Order and coherence in a new medium. *College English,* 52(8), 870-883.

Soloway, E., & Iyengar, S. (1987). *Empirical studies of programmers.* Norwood, NJ: Ablex.

Spivey, N. N. (1987). Construing constructivism: Reading research in the United States. *Poetics,* 16(2), 169-193.

Sudol, R. A. (1991). The accumuative rhetoric of word processing. *College English, 53*(8), 920-932.

Toulmin, S. (1958). *The uses of argument.* Cambridge: Cambridge University Press.

Toulmin, S., Rieke, R., & Janik, A. (1984). *An introduction to reasoning* (2nd ed.). New York: Macmillan.

van Dijk, T. (1987). Episodic models in discourse processing. In R. Horowitz & S. J. Samuels (Eds.), *Comprehending oral and written discourse* (pp. 161-196). New York: Academic Press.

Vipond, D., Hunt, R. A., Jewett, J., & Reither, J. (1990). Making sense of reading. In R. Beach & S. Hynds (Eds.), *Developing discourse practices in adolescence and adulthood* (pp. 110-135). Norwood, NJ: Ablex.

Vygotsky, L. S. (1966). Development of the higher mental functions (abridged). In *Psychological research in the U.S.S.R.* (Vol. 1). Moscow: Progress Publishers.

Vygotsky, L. S. (1971). *The psychology of art.* Cambridge: MIT Press.

Vygotsky, L. S. (1978). *Mind in society.* Cambridge: Harvard University Press.

Vygotsky, L. S. (1981a). The genesis of higher mental functions. In J. V. Wertsch (Ed.), *The concept of activity in Soviet psychology* (pp. 144-188). Armonk, NY: M. E. Sharpe.

Vygotsky, L. S. (1981b). The instrumental method in psychology. In J. V. Wertsch (Ed.), *The concept of activity in Soviet psychology* (pp. 134-143). Armonk, NY: M. E. Sharpe.

Vygotsky, L. S. (1986). *Thought and language* (A. Kozulin, Trans. and Ed.). Cambridge, MA: MIT Press.

Vygotsky, L. S. (1993). *Studies on the history of behavior: Ape, primitive, child* (V. Golod & J. Knox, Trans.). Hillsdale, NJ: Lawrence Erlbaum Associates.

Wertsch, J. V. (1981). *The concept of activity in Soviet psychology.* Armonk, NY: M. E. Sharpe.

Wertsch, J. V. (1985). *Vygotsky and the social formation of mind.* Cambridge: Harvard University Press.

Witte, S. P. (1992). Context, text, intertext: Toward a constructivist semiotic of writing. *Written Communication 9* (2), 237-308.

Witte, S. P. (1985). Revising, composing theory, and research design. In S. Freedman (Ed.), *The acquisition of written language: Revision and response* (pp. 250-284). Norwood, NJ: Ablex.

Wright, P., & Lickorish, A. (1983). Proof-reading texts on screen and paper. *Behavior and Information Technology, 2*(3), 227-235.

Yates, F. A. (1966). *The art of memory.* Chicago: University of Chicago Press.

Appendix A

Comparison of Planning Proportions and Text Sense Scores

Subject	Proportion of Planning*		Text Sense Score ("C")		Negative Text Sense Sense Score ("X")	
	Pen	WP	Pen	WP	Pen	WP
S1	19	16	64	29	16	29
S2	46	39	43	38	29	0
S3	28	12	67	50	33	50
S4	58	43	55	29	33	57
S5	36	21	83	14	16	43
S6	51	41	58	0	25	57
S7	33	23	67	43	0	57
S8	26	16	50	100	17	0
S9	35	30	63	50	12	38
Higher scores	9	0	8	1	2	7

*From Haas, 1989a.

Appendix B
Claimgrids

Bernhardt, S.A. (1993). The shape of text to come: The texture of print on screens. *College Composition and Communication* 44 (2), 151-175.

Claim	Grounded by... Supporting claim	Data	Warranted by... Logical connection	Ideological Warrant
1. CHANGE IN TECHNOLOGY LEADS TO CHANGE IN STRUCTURE OF TEXT.	CLAIM 4 CLAIM 5	<u>Analysis</u>: Nine dimensions of variation between paper and on-screen texts.	The nine dimensions are exhaustive and inclusive. No other causal factors are apparent. The analysis "makes sense."	•**Technology is an agent.** •**Technology is important.** •Structure and format are critical aspects of texts.
2. A new rhetoric of electronic texts will depend on existing rhetoric of print.	In current state of "rapid evolution" we are borrowing strategies from print experiences.		In transitional period, people rely on already well-developed practices and skills.	•We are moving into a new period in reading/writing. •**New technology requires a new rhetoric.**
3. Teachers need to understand how computers are changing written language so they can teach students strategies for "text in a new age."				•**Technology is self-determining.** •Our job is to prepare students for the future. •Knowledge and understanding of the world makes our pedagogy better.

	Citations		
4. One important difference between screen and paper texts is how they are used.		Sources are reputable and relevant.	
CLAIM 5			
5. Screen-based text is more situationally-embedded than is print text. (First of nine dimensions.)	Example: People read novels, newspapers, etc. alone and regardless of physical circumstance. Example: Help systems are for use, not for reading.	Examples are representative.	•Solitary reading of novels and newspapers is prototypical print reading. •Reading of Help texts is prototypical on-line reading.
Students use screeen text to support social interaction.	Citations	Sources are reputable and relevant.	

Bolter, J.D. (1991). *Writing space: The computer, hypertext, and the history of writing.* Hillsdale, NJ: Lawrence Erlbaum.

Claim	Grounded by... Supporting claim	Data	Warranted by... Logical connection	Ideological warrant
1. COMPUTER TECHNOLOGY IS BEGINNING TO REPLACE THE PRINTED BOOK.	The printed book displaced handwriting. Printing press displaced manuscripts.	Citation	**Communication technologies are historically analogous.** Source is reputable and relevant.	• **Technology develops along a revolutionary model.**
	Soon, book publishers will distribute texts electronically.		When new technology used for text production, old technology will have only marginal use.	
	CLAIM 2 CLAIM 3			
2. Electronic technology offers new ways to read and write.	Print text is unchanging; electronic writing emphasizes changeability.	Examples: CAI programs, bulletin boards.	Changeability, distance, fluidity, etc., are all dimensions along which texts can differ.	• Print texts are straightforward, nonproblematic.
	Print distances reader and writer; electronic text turns reader into author.		If texts differ along these dimensions, they allow different ways to read and write.	• Reading and writing print texts are straightforward and stable processes.
	Print is static; electronic text, fluid. Print text addresses homogeneous audience; electronic text speaks to varied readers. Electronic text is customizable.	Example: Electronic encyclopedia Example: *New York Times* Information Service	Examples are representative. **Computer technology is unique:** characteristics of electronic text are new.	• **Technology develops along a revolutionary model.**

			Communication technologies are historically analogous.	**•Computer technologies are unique**: they combine radical and traditional elements.
3. Today we are in a Gutenberg-like interim in which potential of new media is not fully understood.	Early printers make books look like manuscripts. Publishers use computers to print books more efficiently. Word processor makes printed matter easier to produce. Discovering true shape of electronic text may take decades.	Examples: textual database represented as file cabinet; CAI modeled on exercise book; electronic bulletin boards mimick non-electronic counterpart.	Examples are representative.	
4. Electronic writing is both radical and traditional.		Analysis: Electronic writing is precise like printing; organic like handwriting; eclectic like hieroglyphics. But also more fluid and dynamic than previous technologies.	The analysis "makes sense." A blending of old and new elements means that a technology is both radical and traditional.	
5. Electronic writing shows that print is an extreme form of writing, not the norm.	Print requirement of unity and homogeneity is relatively recent.	Example: Medieval and early print volumes often bound unrelated texts. Analogy: Print is like specialization on outer branches of evolutionary tree.	If medium's requirements are recent, they are not the norm. Example is representative. Analogy is valid and appropriate.	**•Technology is an agent**: computers "correct" extremes of print. •Extremes are bad/not to be trusted.

Boyle, F.T. IBM, talking heads, and our classrooms. *College English* 55 (6), 618-626.

Claim	Grounded by... Supporting claim	Data	Warranted by... Logical connection	Ideological warrant
1. INFORMATION TECHNOLOGIES ARE MAKING US STUPID.	Like Swift's moderns, we confuse knowledge with information.		Real people can be analogous to literary characters. Confusing knowledge with information is stupid.	•We don't want to be stupid. •**Technology is harmful:** it can alter intelligence.
	CLAIM 2 CLAIM 3 CLAIM 4 CLAIM 5	<u>Narrative:</u> Talking heads are stupid; i.e., illogical, have faulty theory, are poor teachers, etc.	Narrative is typical and representative. We are analogous to Talking heads: technology will make us stupid too.	
2. Information machines seduce us into thinking we can learn/teach without fatigue.		<u>Example:</u> Talking head demonstrates how word processor makes revision "cleaner." <u>Example:</u> Computer-based instruction replaces knowledge of concepts with knowledge of software. <u>Example:</u> Television teaching suggests work can be made simple, amusing, and quick.	"Clean" and easy revision is misleading and/or wrong. Knowledge of software yields quick and easy answers. Examples are representative. **Technology is all the same:** television and computers are analogous.	•**Technology is harmful:** it can mislead us; it impedes learning. •Procedural knowledge is inferior to concept knowledge. •**Technology and humanities are distinct enterprises:** technologists avoid complexity. •True learning is slow and difficult.

3. Teachers using computers become "accessories" in the crime of reducing "profound questions" to "inane certainties."	Example: Talking head demonstrates computerized multiple-choice response to Hamlet. Analogy: Teachers using computers are like "foolish prating knave[s]."	Example is representative. Testing Hamlet by multiple choice is inane. Analogy is valid and appropriate.	•Technology and humanities are distinct enterprises: humanists do not reduce the complex to the inane.
4. "Canned" lessons cheat students.	Example: Filmed lessons are worse than teachers who teach from notes and refuse questions.	Technology is all the same: films and computers are analogous. Films are a negative influence on education. Example is representative.	•Technology is unresponsive: face-to-face interaction is preferable. •Cheating students is wrong.
5. Television and computer technologies are converging.	Analogy: Students in computer classrooms are like children watching Sesame Street. Example: Computer graphics are like "special effects."	Television is passive learning. Analogy is valid and appropriate. Special effects are superficial. Example is representative.	•Television is a negative influence on education. •Technology is harmful: it impedes true learning.

Cooper, M. & Selfe, C. (1993). Computer conferences and learning: Authority, resistance, and internally persuasive discourse. *College English* 52 (8), 847-869.

Claim	Grounded by... Supporting claim	Data	Warranted by... Logical connection	Ideological warrant
1. COMPUTER TECHNOLGY IS REVOLUTIONARY AND THUS CAN FOSTER STUDENT RESISTANCE TO ACADEMIC AND AUTHORITARIAN DISCOURSE.	Computers exist in the intellectual margins of most academic discourse. Computers can provide boundary spaces in which previously "silenced" voices can be heard.	<u>Citations</u> *Analogy:* Computers are "wild as any frontier." <u>Citations</u>	Intellectually marginal media are revolutionary. Geographical space is analogous to intellectual space. The analogy is valid. Sources are reputable and relevant. Giving voice to silent voices is revolutionary.	•**Technology is free-standing**: it has inherent values apart from those of the culture in which it is developed and used. •**Technology is an agent**: it can effect revolutionary change. •Disruptive effects in classrooms are good.
2. The unique characteristics of computer-mediated conferences enable discourse that is frustrated by institutional structures.	Hegemony, evaluative structures, and ideology cause students to respond in ways that are culturally "appropriate." CLAIM 3 CLAIM 4 CLAIM 5	<u>Citations</u>	Students' accommodation is a sign that they are not learning what we would like them to about discourse. Sources are reputable and relevant.	•Resistant behavior is good: accommodating behavior is bad. •**Computer technology is unique**: it enables unique pedagogy. •**Technology is an agent**: it can alter discursive behavior.

3. Computers are capable of making classroom exchanges more egalitarian.	In computer conferences, participants treat one another like peers. Computer conferences encourage those who might be shut out of classroom discussion	Example: Social cues are often missing. Example: Pseudonyms can be used. Example: Classroom in which students ignored teacher's comments. Samples: Showing students determining tone, pace, topics, etc.	Missing social cues and anonymity can contribute to egalitarian classroom atmosphere. Examples and samples are representative. Some students don't contribute in class because they feel "silenced" rather than through "choice." Student-controlled discussion is egalitarian.	•Making classroom exchanges egalitarian is a worthy goal. •**Technology is an agent**: it changes social interaction.
4. Computer conferences can be set up to encourage competition of ideas rather than personality.	Computer conferences create anonymity.	Citation	Anonymous discussions will focus on ideas. Source is reputable and relevant.	•Competition on the level of ideas is better than competition on the level of personality.
5. Computer conferences encourage disruptive behavior.		Samples: Showing students questioning authority, examining values of their profession, questioning university education, being "irreverent."	Questioning, examining values, being irreverent constitute disruptive behavior. Samples are representative.	•Disruptive behavior is good. •**Technology is an agent**: it can alter discursive behavior.

Hawisher, G.E. & Moran, C. (1993). Electronic mail and the writing instructor. *College English* 55 (6), 627-643.

Claim	Grounded by... Supporting claim	Data	Warranted by... Logical connection	Ideological warrant
1. Composition scholars have devoted too little attention to email.	Compositionists overlook email because we have only partial access to it and because of antitechnology bias in English Departments.	Analysis: Articles in composition journals ignore email.	Compositionist ignore things against which the field has a bias. If we noticed email, we would write about it. The analysis "makes sense."	•Paying insufficient attention to something important in wrong. •Cultural factors influence our scholarship.
	Compositionists look "through" email.	Citation: Boorstin shows we look "through" postal systems.	**Communication technologies are historically analogous.** Source is reputable and relevant.	
2. We should not continue to ignore email.		Analysis: Other related fields study email. Numerical Data: Email is important in world outside academia. Citations	Compositionists should pay attention to all communication forms. The analysis makes sense. Numerical Data collection procedure is valid. Sources are reputable and relevant. Contemporary theory/ pedagogy is "correct."	•**Technology is self-determining:** email exists independent of its users.
	Email is consistent contemporary composition theory/pedagogy. In the future, email will become more widespread.			

			be historically consistent.	**•Technology develops along a revolutionary model.**
			Examples are representative.	
			Our teaching should prepare students for their futures.	
	Compositionists should teach students about academic and disciplinary forms.	the past included pandisciplinary genres in our study.		
PROPER OBJECT OF STUDY IN COMPOSITION.				
4. EMAIL IS FUNDAMENTALLY DIFFERENT FROM PAPER MAIL.		Analogy: Email is to letter as the car is to horse-and-buggy.	The analogy is valid and appropriate.	
	Email and paper mail have different "grammars."	Example: E-readers have difficulty determining salient. Citations	Differences in grammar, structure, language, constraints, and social relations constitute a new medium.	
	Email writers have to pay extra attention to structure, form, etc.	Citations		
	Email language between spoken and written.	Citations Examples: greetings, "emoticons," other conventions.	Examples are representative.	
	Writers less constrained with email.	Citations Example: flaming	Sources are reputable and relevant.	
	Email demands and provides for quick response.	Citation Example: new messages supercede old.		
	Email changes social relations.	Example: hypothesis that women, minorities respond differently.		

		Citations		•**Technology is an agent**: it can determine nature of classroom pedagogy.
5. Pedagogy that includes email will be "inevitably" collaborative.	Email dissolves temporal and spatial boundaries of classroom.		Temporal and spatial boundaries inhibit collaboration.	
	Teachers will set agenda via email.		Sources are reputable and relevant.	
	Students will communicate with one another via email.	**Examples**: Bulletin boards at Skidmore and Babson.	Student-to-student communication is collaborative.	•Collaborative pedagogy is good pedagogy.
			Examples are representative.	
	Teacher will not be able to "control" email and will move out of position of authority.		Teacher authority inhibits collaboration.	

Hawisher, G.E. & Selfe, C.L. (1991). The rhetoric of technology and the electronic writing classroom. *College Composition and Communication* 42 (1), 55-65.

Claim	Grounded by...: Supporting claim	Data	Warranted by... Logical connection	Ideological warrant
1. Technological change has influenced how writing is taught.		<u>Examples</u>: Teachers depend on computers in classrooms; teachers use networks as teaching environments.	Examples are representative.	•**Technology is an agent**: using new technological tools can result in new pedagogy.
2. Teachers often incorporate computers without necessary scrutiny.	Scrutiny necessary because of large investment technology requires. CLAIM 3			•**Technology has positive, negative uses and consequences.** •Scrutiny and the insights it brings are positive.

3. COMPOSITIONISTS DO NOT REALIZE THAT TECHNOLOGY CAN SUPPORT NEGATIVE CULTURAL VALUES AND PEDAGOGICAL APPROACHES.	Computers often reinforce traditional cultural values. Computers do not automatically create ideal learning situations. CLAIM 4 CLAIM 5	Examples: Drill-and-practice grammar software and teacher monitoring of students' screens. Testimony: As journal editors, we see scant attention paid to negative uses of technology. Citations Examples: On-line conferences create opportunity for disciplining students.	Drill-and-practice and monitoring students are poor pedagogies. Examples are representative. Technologies which reproduce cultural values or support poor pedagogy should be considered. Manuscripts submitted constitute a cross-section. Sources are reputable and relevant.	•Reinforcing traditional cultural and educational values is not a worthy goal. •**Technology is culturally-embedded.**
4. Rhetoric about technology is mostly positive.		Examples: Published articles and surveys.	Examples are representative.	
5. OVERLY POSITIVE RHETORIC INFLUENCES COMPUTER USE AND PERCEPTION.		Obervations: Classrooms in which negative aspects are glossed over.	Observed classrooms are representative. Observations are a sign that rhetoric influences perception and practice.	•Teachers should be guided by actual effects, not by rhetoric.

Lanham, R.A. (1993). *The electronic word: Democracy, technology, and the arts.* Chicago: University of Chicago Press.

Claim	Grounded by... Supporting claim	Data	Warranted by... Logical connection	Ideological warrant
1. ELECTRONIC TEXTS ARE GOING TO CHANGE READING, WRITING, AND THE PROFESSING OF LITERATURE.	Computer forces English studies to consider technology.	<u>Examples</u>: interactive fiction.	Responsive readers, vanishing boundaries, new literary history, new texts, unifying arts, and rise of rhetoric will remake English studies.	•**Technology develops along a revolutionary model.**
	Boundary between creator and critic "vanishes."	<u>Citation</u>	Source is reputable and relevant.	•**Technology is self-determining.**
	Electronic text reveals assumptions of the book: text is authoritative, static, etc.		Assumptions of electronic text are vastly different from those of print.	•**Technological and humanistic studies are distinct enterprises**: technology is something "outside" English studies.
	Electronic text changes literary history.	<u>Example</u>: re-evaluation of Greek, Latin classics as oral not print texts.	**Communication technologies are historically analogous.**	•**Computer technology is unique**: it creates interactive system.
	Electronic text reveals limitations of print textbooks.	<u>Analogy</u>: Electronic texts democratize education like printing reinforced Portestantism.		
	Students will enter a work world of electronic texts.	<u>Example</u>: Lexis and Westlaw legal database.	Analogy is valid and appropriate.	•**Technology is an agent**: it is able to drive other, diverse kinds of change.
	Rhetoric will become central theory for arts.			
	Technological change forces literary study to look outward.		Examples are representative.	**Computer technology is unique**: it democratizes the world of arts and letters.
	CLAIM 2, 3, 4			

2. Digitization of arts and letters "forces on us" a new rhetoric.	Digitization forces realignment of alphabet and graphics. Music has been transformed by digitization. Digitization gives arts quasi-mathematical equivalency. Digitization desubstantiates arts, creates metamorphosis. Rhetoric of digitization will beinclusive. Digital arts are volatile.	<u>Examples</u>: real light holography; Music Mouse; FM synthesizers and digital sampling techniques; image processing.	New characteristics of art call for new rhetoric. Music, visual and literary arts are analogous. Realignment of components, equivalency, inclusiveness, metamorphosis, and volatility are elements of new art. Examples are representative.	•**Technology is an agent**: it forces change--even in the arts. •Arts and rhetorics develop--following technology--along an revolutionary model. •**New technology requires new rhetoric.** •An inclusive rhetoric is good--it democratizes the arts.
3. Most immediately felt change of electronic text is in area of intellectual property.	Copyright developed for print; in electronic world, copyright must be reformulated. With electronic texts, definitive version is not possible. Intellectual property will become intellectual "potentiality." Definition of scholarly publication changes.	<u>Examples</u>:who owns electronic textbook, interactive novel, or scholarly hypertext edition of a novel? <u>Example</u>: hypothetical on-line scholarly journal.	Systems of existing technology will not work fornew one. Non-definitive versions and intellectual "potentiality" unclear authorship make existing copyright obsolete. Examples are representative.	•**Technology develops along a revolutionary model.**

		Example		•Technology is an agent.
4. Electronic texts will even change our fundamental poetics.	CLAIM 5 Electronic texts will have irresolution. Digitization questions the status of art.		Stylistics, structure, and status of art are fundamental poetics. Print text is stable.	
5. Digitization calls stylistic transparency into question.	Transparency has been a textual and social ideal. The electronic textual surface is bi-stable and this creates oscillation. It is easier to make radical oscillations in electronic text. Computers reveal print as "racial artifice."	Example: desktop publishing.	Print text is straightforward, nonproblematic. Example is representative. If the "verbal creative spirit" can "play," it will.	•Transparency is misleading; oscillation is closer to reality. •Technology is an agent: computer technology "corrects" extremes of print. •Technology is an agent: it determines decorum. •Decorum determines social ideals.

Nydahl, J. (1990). Teaching word processors to be CAI programs. *College English* 52 (8), 904-915.

Claim	Grounded by... Supporting claim	Data	Warranted by... Logical connection	Ideological warrant
1. Writing teachers do not understand their word processors.	Teachers have been intimidated by computers.	Citations	People do not understand things they are intimidated by.	•We should understand the technology we use.
	Teachers have accepted distinctions between CAI and word processing.	Readers' own experiences [implicit]	Sources are reputable and relevant. Readers' experiences are representative.	•Teachers can have some control over of the software their students use.
2. CURRENT SOPHISTICATED WORD PROCESSING CAN MIMIC ELABORATE CAI SOFTWARE.		Examples Microsoft Word keystroke-playback and formatting. Example: hypothetical student uses word processing to reorganize paper.	Features identified are common to CAI programs. Examples are representative.	**•Technology is important:** features of CAI programs are good pedagogical tools.
3. Writing software should extend writers' power, not make them dependent on it.	Understanding principles behind software helps extend writers' power. For writing instruction to "stay with" students, it needs to provide training in "self-management."	Analogy: Software should be like a Nautilus machine. Citations	Analogy is valid and appropriate. Sources are reputable and relevant.	•Learning depends on awareness. **•Technology has positive, negative uses and consequences:** word processing easier to understand than CAI. **•Technology is important:** different software has different consequences.

4. CAI potential of word processing can help teachers retain control of their teaching tools.	Utilizing CAI potential minimizes risks of bad software. Some software designers more concerned with profit than pedagogy. Teachers can more readily customize word processors.	<u>Citations</u>	Designing for profit may interfere with effective pedagogy. Sources are reputable and relevant. Customization leads to greater control.	•Teachers should control teaching. •**Technology is important:** different software has different consequenses. •**Technological and humanistic studies are distinct enterprises:** teachers design better software.
5. CAI potential of word processing can help students take control of their own instruction.	Word processors require more active problem solving by students.	<u>Example</u>: hypothetical student revises paper independently. <u>Citations</u>	Example is representative. Active learning leads to student control. Sources are reputable and relevant.	•Student control of learning is good. •**Technology is important:** different software has different consequenses.

Slatin, J.M. (1990). Reading hypertext: Order and coherence in a new medium. *College English* 52 (8), 870-883.

Claim	Grounded by... Supporting claim	Data	Warranted by... Logical connection	Ideological warrant
1. HYPERTEXTS ARE DIFFERENT FROM TRADI-TIONAL FORMS OF TEXT.	"Everything" rests on viewing reading as a sequential process.	<u>Citation</u>	Source is reputable and relevant.	•**Technology develops along a revolutionary model.**
	Fixity of print makes it mentally stable as well.		Physical world "maps onto" mental one.	•Reading and writing with print are straightforward processes.
	Reading and writing hypertext are "radical departure."		Co-authorship and interactive reading are infrequent in print world.	
	Book is closed system; hypertext is open.			•Dynamic, interac-tive systems are good.
	Coherence of tradi-tional documents at text level; coherence of hyperdocument at metatext level.		Differences described here are significant.	•**Computer technology is unique**: it creates interactive system.
	CLAIM 5			•**New technologies are inherently superior.**

	CLAIM 1			
2. HYPERTEXT IS A NEW MEDIUM OF THOUGHT.	Organization of memory determines thinking. Machine memory has no print analogue. Discontinuity is basis of digital information.	<u>Citation</u> <u>Citation</u>	Large number of differences between old and new forms of text suggests "new medium" Structure of information determines patterns of thinking. Sources are reputable and relevant.	•**Technology is an agent:** changes in text form can cause changes in thinking.
3. A new medium requires a new praxis and a new theory.				•**Technology develops along a revolutionary model.**
4. Computerization of writing makes technology visible.	Print technology is mature and therefore invisible. Writing was once innovative and visible. Hypertext and hypermedia still emergent.	<u>Citations</u>	Mature technologies are invisible; new technologies are visible. Sources are reputable and relevant. **Communication technologies are historically analo-**	•**New technologies are inherently superior:** "visible" technologies are superior for developing theory.
5. Difference between text and hypertext is technology that supports it.	Hypertext exists only in on-line environment.			•**Technology is an agent:** it determines form of text.

269

Sudol, R.A. (1991). The accumulative rhetoric of word processing. *College English* 53 (8), 920-932.

Claim	Grounded by... Supporting claim	Data	Warranted by... Logical connection	Ideological warrant
1. Experienced writers laud word processing.		<u>Citations</u> Readers' experience [implied]	Testimonials and readers' experiences are representative.	•**Technology is an agent**: it can constrain/liberate writers.
2. WORD PROCESSING PROVIDES MEANS OF EXECUTING HARD DECISIONS ABOUT PROSE; BUT WRITING TEACHES DIFFICULT HABITS OF REVISING.	Students (not trained by inscription) do not have skill and determination to revise. CLAIM 1 Clarity and brevity are result of difficult process of revision.		Only writers trained by inscription have ability and desire to revise. Because true revision must be slow and hard, only writers practiced in inscription revise well.	•**Technology is an agent**: it determines writing ability and desire. •Difficult things are better than easy things.
3. Students like word processing primarily because generating prose is easy.	Students struggle to create prose. Our pedagogy has recognized this, stressing invention, process. Word processing encourages adding not revising.	<u>Readers' experience</u> [implied] <u>Citation</u> <u>Example</u>: "Dear Abby" writer.	Writers who struggle to produce will appreciate word processing. Readers' experiences are representative. **Technology is harmful**: it derails writing process. Source is reputable and relevant. Example is representative. CLAIM 2	•Difficult things are better than easy things.

		Citations		
4. Differences in experienced and student writers' experiences of word processing should help guide pedagogy.	Word processing's effects include: overproduction, verbose style, trivialization. Students need compensatory strategies.		Teachers should integrate word processing in ways that make it more like mechanical inscription. Sources are reputable and relevant.	•**Technology is harmful**: it can impede writing. •Inscription is superior to word processing.
5. Writers using word processing feel unimpeded by rhetorical constraints.		<u>Examples</u>: Baker's persona; "Dear Abby" column. <u>Citation</u>	Examples are representative. Source is reputable and relevant.	•Rhetorical constraints impede writing. •Constraints lead to better writing.

271

Author Index

Subject Index